W9-AFQ-248

Road to Valour

PRESSE

Road to Valour

A True Story of World War II Italy, the Nazis, and the Cyclist Who Inspired a Nation

Aili and
Andres McConnon

Doubleday Canada

Library and Archives Canada Cataloguing in Publication

McConnon, Aili, 1980-
The road to valour : a true story of a Tuscan cyclist and secret World War II hero / Aili and Andres McConnon.

Also issued in electronic format.
ISBN 978-0-385-66948-1

1. Bartali, Gino, 1914-2000. 2. Cyclists--Italy--Biography. 3. World War, 1939-1945--Underground movements--Italy-- Biography. 4. Tuscany (Italy)--Biography. I. McConnon, Andres II. Title.

GV1051.B37M33 2012 796.6092 C2011-908506-2

Book design by Donna Sinisgalli
Maps by David Lindroth
Jacket photographs: Publifoto/Olycom (cover image and lower spine image),
The Horton Collection (top spine image)
Authors photograph: Helen Tansey
Printed and bound in the USA

Published in Canada by Doubleday Canada,
a division of Random House of Canada Limited

Visit Random House of Canada Limited's website: www.randomhouse.ca

10 9 8 7 6 5 4 3 2 1

For our mother and late father

Contents

Authors' Note ix

Prologue 1

PART I

Map of Tuscany and Umbria

1. Across the Arno 7
2. In the Saddle 22
3. The First Test 31
4. "Italy's Number One Sportsman" 47
5. Storm at the Summit 68

PART II

Map of World War II in Italy

6. From the Stars to the Stables 91
7. An Impossible Choice 111
8. The Counterfeiters' Ring 123
9. Free Fall 144

PART III

Map of France

10. Ginettaccio 165

11. Les Macaroni 181

12. Four Bullets 193

13. A Frozen Hell 211

14. The Road Home 228

Epilogue 241

Where They Are Now 259

Notes 261

Acknowledgments 313

Photo and Illustration Credits 317

Authors' Note

THIS BOOK IS A work of nonfiction. All characters, events, and dialogue that we include come from a wide variety of historical sources, including Gino Bartali's three autobiographies, declassified secret Fascist police reports, dozens of French and Italian newspapers and books, filmed interviews with Gino and his teammates, an extensive body of photographic and newsreel footage of cycling races, and more than two hundred hours of interviews with Gino's widow, Adriana; son, Andrea; former teammates; friends; former Italian politicians; historians; Italian Jews; and others. We have also visited the locations of Gino's key races and other life events in Italy and France, and conducted interviews in Israel with some of the people with whom he interacted during World War II.

Where accounts conflicted, we tried wherever possible to consult multiple sources to arrive at the most likely version of an event. Whenever we indicate a character thought or felt something, that information comes directly from our interviews with the character depicted or material left in a published interview or memoir. We have not invented any dialogue. Conversations are drawn from records left by at least one of the direct participants. In the rare occasions where we describe an event from Gino's life that he never wrote or spoke publicly about, we have relied on the memories of those events that he shared with family and friends, and their characterizations of his behavior in a variety of situations. In most cases the primary source material we consulted was in Italian or French.

We have translated as accurately as possible to maintain the spirit and letter of the original.

Gino Bartali moved through many different worlds throughout his life and consequently this book shines a light on different aspects of professional cycling, Fascist and Nazi-occupied Italy, the experience of Jews in Italy during World War II, and postwar Italian politics. While much more could be said about all of these subjects, we have limited the scope of our discussion to what fit into the context of the narrative.

Let your virtues expand to fill this sad situation:
Glory ascends the heights by a precipitous path.
Who would have known of Hector, if Troy had been happy?
The road to valor is built by adversity.

—OVID, *TRISTIA*

Prologue

AT THE STEEP FOOT of the Vars, on a windswept slope high in the French Alps, Gino Bartali lost his temper. The two cyclists following him were drafting, riding so close to his back wheel that he was forced to be their shield against the icy wind and drag them along. They refused to take their turn at the front of the group, and this galled him to no end. Ahead of the trio, a lone figure was getting smaller as he cycled away along the muddy road, a coagulated laceration zigzagging its way up the barren escarpment, winding around craggy pinnacles, stunted fir trees, and piles of rock debris until it vanished into the cold mountain mist. Gino had to make his move *now* if he would have any chance of catching the leader disappearing into the fog before him.

It was July 15, 1948, and *L'Étape Reine*—The Queen Stage—the most important day of the Tour de France. A rough swipe at his dirt-caked goggles revealed a sobering scene, even for a man who had won the Tour on the exact same terrain ten years earlier. In 1938, Gino had soared up the imperial snow-crowned Alps toward azure heavens above. Now he could barely see where mountain met sky as heavy clouds rolled in around him and the mud beneath his wheels became thick as glue.

The dismal surroundings echoed the pain screaming inside his body. After pedaling more than seventeen hundred miles over the most challenging topography cycling had to offer, his throat and lungs were burning, his thighs felt heavy as bronze. Unable to see far beyond his handlebars, he had to depend on his other senses to fill in the details. He could feel the pitch under his wheels as the grade of the road steepened.

He could taste the icy rain turning into jagged snowflakes as he gulped the thinning mountain air. And all he could hear, beyond his own body heaving atop the bike, was an eerie, forlorn silence.

Gino marshaled every last muscle and ounce of mental focus to silence the critics with this next climb. *Il Vecchio* they were calling him in the press, "The Old Man" at thirty-three years of age! He was fed up with being dismissed as an embarrassing has-been, defiant despite his humiliating twenty-one-minute disadvantage behind the Tour leader. He had even lashed out at the Italian journalists, yelling at them for doubting him. No matter—the reporters had already nicknamed him *Ginettaccio*, "Gino the Terrible," and the newspapers would just chalk it up to another one of his outbursts. But what the press didn't know was that Gino Bartali had a secret. He had much more bottled up inside him, beyond his frustration with being so far behind, and he had not sat idle during the war. Unlike some of the competitors he now raced against, his toughest moments came not on the steepest pitches of the Tour de France, but during the darkest hour of the Nazi occupation of Italy, risking his life for strangers.

The memories of that chaotic era were still raw, and they were the reason the surprising phone call last night had unhinged him. Reports of large-scale protests and fighting in the streets back home had filled Gino's mind, and his breath shortened as he thought of his wife and young sons. He had listened aghast as the prime minister of Italy, on the other end of the telephone, explained how important a Tour victory would be to their homeland.

As he rode toward the mountaintop town of Briançon, instinct told Gino to turn his head around. Looking back over his shoulder, he saw his competitors behind him cracking, their pale faces contorted, their drenched bodies swaying precariously atop their bikes. He had let them draft long enough. With a surge of raw power, he stood up out of his saddle and sped forward. Soon the French cyclist in the lead came back into sight.

Sensing his foe, the French cyclist cast a worried look back. He was right to be alarmed; Gino cut an intimidating figure. His eyes invisible under his muddy goggles, he appeared almost supernaturally welded to his bike; his lithe racer's body flexed forcefully, maneuvering his bicycle up the switchbacks.

Closing in on his rival, Gino sat back down, letting the French cyclist regain some ground and some hope. When he found his rhythm again, Gino stood to attack once more. Again and again, they played this grueling game, all the way to the peak. By the time the French cyclist crossed the top of the mountain pass, he was utterly exhausted. Gino, in contrast, trembled with excitement as he neared the summit less than a minute behind. *I am at one with the mountain,* he thought as he flew over the top.

As he faced the harrowing descent, Gino's lips curled into a knowing smile beneath his grime-spattered face. It was time for the cat to catch his mouse. It was time to show the world that the war had not broken him. And his return to the Tour, he was beginning to understand, was about more than just a bike race in France.

It was the final leg of a journey for a man and his country that had begun more than twenty years earlier on a dusty back road in Tuscany.

Part I

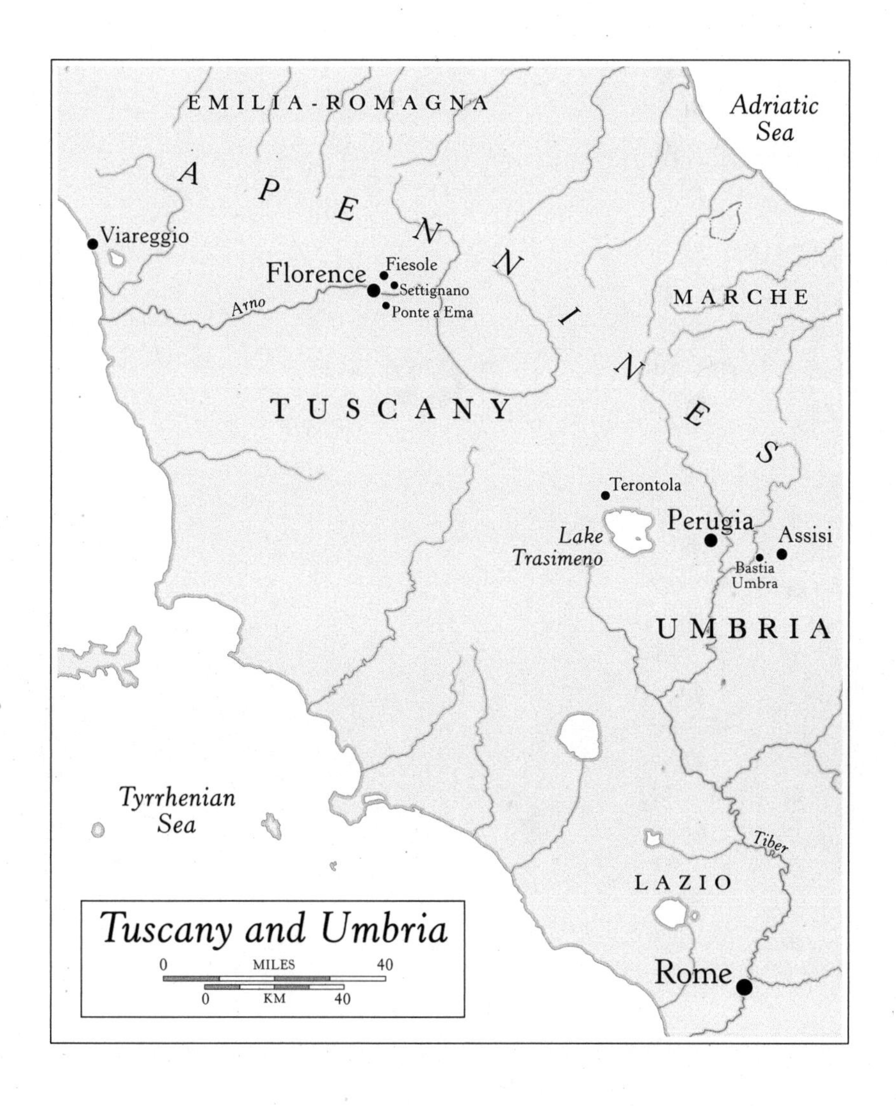
EMILIA-ROMAGNA
Adriatic Sea
APENNINES
Viareggio
Florence
Fiesole
Settignano
Ponte a Ema
Arno
MARCHE
TUSCANY
Terontola
Lake Trasimeno
Perugia
Assisi
Bastia Umbra
UMBRIA
Tyrrhenian Sea
Tiber
LAZIO
Rome
Tuscany and Umbria
0 MILES 40
0 KM 40

1

Across the Arno

The view of Florence and the Arno from near one of Gino Bartali's favorite boyhood cycling routes.

"WHEN WE RACE TOGETHER, let's each win a little! This time you, and the next time me," Gino shouted ahead to his younger brother, Giulio, as they pedaled up the steep, sun-drenched hills surrounding Ponte a Ema. Their tires kicked up clouds of grit, and it was all Gino could do to avoid swallowing a mouthful. He rubbed a sweaty palm against his shorts, trying to brush off the stubborn rust flakes from his bike frame, and tucked his elbows in alongside his body, the way his idols did as they sprinted to victory, clutching their sleek curved handlebars. Gino leaned into the pedals and sped past Giulio. He turned and grinned at his younger brother as they started their descent toward home. They would race again tomorrow, and on that forgotten stretch of Tuscan road their tomorrows seemed endless.

Cycling had become the Bartali boys' passion, a flash of excitement and adventure in their tiny, workaday hometown. For Ponte a Ema in the 1920s was a sleepy place, just beyond the sophisticated world of Florence. Resting on the banks of the Ema, a tributary of the Arno River, Ponte a Ema brimmed with the vineyards, rolling hills, and waves of sweet lavender undulating out to the horizon, which have since made Tuscany world-renowned. Still, the village itself, located across a small bridge on the road from Florence to Bagno a Ripoli, looked like little more than an afterthought. One would be hard-pressed to find it on a map, hidden as it was some four miles southeast of Florence's central square. And though it included a short litany of establishments common to any small Italian town of the time—a church; a bank; a bike mechanic's shop; a simple barbershop; a grain mill; a small wine store; a five-room school set up in a farmer's house—it lacked a town hall and a proper piazza, the pulsing heart of Italian life where *nonni,* or grandparents, gather to play cards and stray cats dart out of the way of running children and bouncing soccer balls. Without a nucleus, Ponte a Ema conveyed the impression of an accidentally inhabited byway between more important places. That more important places existed would not occur to Gino until much later. Back then, Ponte a Ema was all the world a boy could want.

Born July 18, 1914, Gino Giovanni Bartali was a wispy, blue-eyed boy with a moppish head of curly dark hair. He lived with his parents, Torello and Giulia, his older sisters, Anita and Natalina, and his brother, Giulio, in one of the cream-colored, three-story tenement buildings that lined Via Chiantigiana, Ponte a Ema's main street, where all the hubbub of daily life played out. Like most of the apartments along Chiantigiana, the Bartalis' consisted of one room and a small kitchen. Home reminded Gino of Carlo Collodi's *Pinocchio* and the humble abode of Geppetto, the hot-headed Tuscan carpenter who was known for getting into scuffles with anyone who insulted him. "The furniture could not have been much simpler: a very old chair, a rickety old bed, and a tumble-down table," wrote Collodi. "Little as Geppetto's house was, it was neat and comfortable."

The Bartalis' home possessed a similar modest charm. The children helped Giulia cart jugs of water from nearby springs. Together with several families, the Bartalis shared a privy at the end of the hall on their floor, which consisted of a hole in a bench through which refuse dropped into a small container on the ground floor. Running water, like electricity, would only come several decades later, after the end of the Second World War.

These were cramped quarters to be sure, but Gino didn't know any different. Besides, outdoors was where the action was. Along the road, the boys from town would huddle for hours around a game of marbles, keeping a stern eye on the rainbow array of tiny glass globes that already belonged to them, and hawkishly watching the ones that would soon join their collection if luck and skill were on their side that day. The game was serious business for Gino and his friends, and almost always ended in a violent brawl, broken up only by the clatter of a pair of dark green window shutters being flung open above to make way for somebody's mother leaning out to deliver a strident scolding. Gino always got a particularly severe tongue-lashing when he came home for dinner covered in bruises. Thin and undersized, a cuff from another child was enough to topple him to the ground, but that did little to deter him from bounding up and swinging right back. Gino knew he was the weakest, but he hated being teased. "I would have liked to have friends who didn't take advantage of being stronger than me so that they could beat me up after every game of marbles," he said later. Already headstrong as a youngster, however, he was willing to stand up for himself, even if the outcome was rarely favorable. "I was an unlucky marbles player, and an even unluckier boxer."

When he and his friends would scatter into the surrounding fields for games of tag or cops and robbers, winning and losing was a more straightforward affair and fisticuffs could be kept to a minimum. The orchards outside town were ideal for any pastime that involved hiding and chasing, draped as they were with row upon row of rippling white washing hung out to dry. For Ponte a Ema was a laundry town; many of its villagers labored for small businesses charged with cleaning the linens and finery of Florence's gentlemanly class. Men organized the transportation for this industry, picking up and delivering laundry with a mule pulling a dray. Women, predictably, bore the brunt of the dirty work. With brushes and lye ash soap, they scrubbed soft mountains until they were spotless. They cleaned shirts in large cement basins called *viaios*; they rinsed large bedsheets on the banks of the Ema River, by the *ponte* or bridge for which the town was named. Once each stain had been painstakingly removed, everything was carried out to the orchards and hung to dry in endless bay-scented fabric corridors, perfect for dodging potential jailers or for lying in wait to snatch a slippery thief and triumphantly march him back to town, where his punishment would be determined and duly meted out.

"As children we had fun with little, in fact nothing," Gino said. They played *murielle*, a game that involved tiles and smoothed stones, in the small rectangular schoolyard, and *diecone* in the Ponte a Ema cemetery; whoever knocked down the most graveside candles by rolling coins at them won the ten-cent piece. They would sneak off to the Arno for a forbidden swim—the river was known for claiming lives with its currents and sudden whirlpools, and Gino's mother once had to resort to stealing her son's clothes from its banks, forcing him to scurry home naked, to teach him a lesson. Most days, though, Gino and his friends would scamper out of the water, get dressed, and, when somebody had a spare coin or two, run over to a riverside cookie factory that sold broken pieces of biscotti, with flavors like fig and sambuca, at an end-of-day discount.

Gino's favorite pastime was one he had to keep completely secret or risk an encounter with his father's leather belt. Torello's bicycle had always fascinated Gino and one day he hatched a plan to learn to ride atop it. It was far too big for a boy his size, but he was determined to master it. Like a bullfighter closing in on a bull in an arena, he approached it. Standing one foot on the left pedal, he slid his right leg under the crossbar to reach the right pedal. Balancing precariously, and much too short to sit on the bike seat, he stretched up to grip the handlebars from below. Crooked and wobbling, he learned painstakingly to maneuver the unwieldy contraption and barely noticed the smirks and giggles his clumsy expeditions elicited. He was too busy keeping his balance as he pedaled along Ponte a Ema's side streets.

Gino would have spent all of his waking hours outdoors at play if he could. Unfortunately, school was a constant interference. "I had little will to study," he said.

Gino's lack of discipline aggravated his father; his mother was irritated that her son had worn out more pairs of pants on the playground pavement than on the school benches where he was meant to be learning. Yet their lectures fell on deaf ears, and so a familiar scene began to play out regularly in the Bartali household.

"I don't like school, period," Gino would say.

"You are going and that's that," Torello would respond.

But Torello's persistence did not produce a scholar. Gino failed the first grade, and in the years that followed, the only charitable remark his teachers could muster about him as a student was that he had good personal hygiene. Still his father insisted he complete *la sesta*, the equivalent of sixth grade. Ponte a Ema's schoolhouse, however, only taught up to fifth grade—so Gino would have to travel to Florence to attend his final year. "To go to Florence you need a bicycle, and a bicycle costs money," Torello told his son. "You will have to earn it."

✦

Like so many men of his era, Torello Bartali was the primary breadwinner of his family. Although his name meant "young bull" in Italian, Torello moved with the quiet ease of an old workhorse. The features of his face betrayed little about him. He always wore a beret, and a thick mustache covered the edges of his mouth, from which normally dangled a cigar. His physique was more revealing. Short and sinewy, he had a body of considerable strength.

Torello was used to hard work, but his job stability as a day laborer did little to inspire confidence. He worked principally in the fields, and when that type of job wasn't available, he worked in a local quarry, which mined the bluish shale used to pave the neighboring streets of Florence. When quarry work couldn't be found, Torello worked as a bricklayer, laying the foundation for countless Florentine homes. When both of those jobs were in short supply, he went down to the Arno River to collect sand that in turn was used for making cement. And as a last resort, he picked up work extinguishing the oil-fueled street lamps at dawn. For all his efforts, a laborer like Torello earned little more than the modern equivalent of about a dollar an hour.

Necessity forced Giulia to work as well, even if a woman's hourly wage in that era was often less than half a man's. In fact, money was so scarce in the Bartali household that Giulia barely made it home in time to give birth to Gino because she had hiked to a hillside convent that same morning to inquire about a maid's position. Like Torello, she toiled for long days in the fields, tending to the crops and the vines. Though she was small and sturdy, this heavy manual labor took its toll, and she was often plagued with severe leg pains. But Giulia was as ingenious as she was resilient. After particularly punishing days, she would soak a cloth in vinegar and salt, wring it out, and hold it against her legs for five minutes. For more severe pain, she rubbed a compress of wet cigar stubs over the sore areas until the pain subsided.

Primitive as they were, such remedies allowed Giulia to endure a workday that continued well after the sun set. After the long hours in the fields, Giulia spent her evenings earning extra money by embroidering, creating the kind of fine lacework found in the bridal trousseau of any Florentine woman of means. The work of running her household and feeding her husband and four children was balanced precariously atop her other labors. All of this added up to a hardscrabble life that paused only on Sundays, but it was hardly a unique one in Ponte a Ema or even the rest of Tuscany. In the early part of the twentieth century, Tuscan peasants worked an average of fourteen hours per day and a third more of the calendar year than Italians today.

✦

Torello had already given Gino more than one dressing-down about the value of a lira. When Gino would meekly take his seat at the dinner table, hair tousled from his schoolyard scuffles, he knew he could expect the usual admonishment: "Money is necessary for food and certainly not for buying books for a boy who uses them to hit his friends over the head with." *La sesta* was fast approaching, and with it the need for transportation. Twelve-year-old Gino had to find a job. Though he and Giulio had helped their mother and sisters make embroidery for as long as they could remember (Gino was particularly skilled at making lace), his father believed it was time his elder boy found work of his own. Gino was too weak to begin apprenticing as a day laborer or bricklayer with his father, so Giulia decided to ask around for a simple and minimally strenuous position for her son. After some time, she found some farmers in a nearby town looking for a boy to help unravel piles of raffia, the long fibers from the leaves of certain palm trees, whose threads could be used to make ties for grapevines and delicate nursery plants. The work was easy enough, but for an energetic boy who longed to be outside with his friends, it was also an exercise in excruciating boredom. Only the promise of his very own bicycle kept Gino focused on the task at hand.

Consumed by his new goal, Gino was mesmerized by bikes wherever he saw them. But Ponte a Ema was not a worldly place. No races ever passed through town. The only groups of men cycling together that Gino saw were bricklayers on their way to work in Florence. They would ride by on their bicycles, many of them without pedals, which were too expensive to replace once broken. "A lot of time was still to pass before I set eyes on a sports paper and before I knew about the existence of a world in which you could go racing in a pair of black shorts and a colored jersey." Still, he kept working to earn money for his own bicycle, and in the meantime he snuck in rides on his father's, slowly acquainting himself with the vehicle that would change his life.

✦

The bicycle had been born more than a century before Gino, but the earliest versions were little more than wooden horses mounted on wheels. In 1790 in Paris, a Frenchman rode one of these devices in a rudimentary race around the Champs-Élysées. In the late 1830s, a Scottish blacksmith named Kirkpatrick Macmillan experimented with building a hobbyhorse with pedals so that a rider did not need to push off the ground to propel the machine forward. This pricey new amusement quickly became popular in North America. Oliver Wendell Holmes describes the years before the Civil War in the United States when "some of the Harvard College students who boarded in my neighborhood had these machines they called velocipedes, on which they used to waddle along like so many ducks."

The next innovation came from France with the invention of a crank to power the front wheel. But this edition didn't last long, and its nickname "the boneshaker" explains why: it was excruciating to ride for any great distance. The British followed the French with their own design, characterized by its ludicrously oversized front wheel and tiny back wheel. As one writer described the high-wheeler, "The rider was a stratospheric eight feet off the ground, making a first encounter distressingly akin to sitting atop a moving lamppost." By the late 1800s, with the invention of the inflatable tire and its inner tube, which provided more cushioning and safety for the rider, the modern bicycle emerged. In 1885 the first Italian bicycle manufacturer, Bianchi, was founded in Milan, following the creation of the Touring Club Ciclistico Italiano a year earlier in the same city. Improved manufacturing methods and higher wages for factory workers in Italy and abroad would allow bicycles to become more widely accessible to the average laborer. In 1893 a French worker had to toil for the equivalent of about twenty-three weeks to earn enough to buy a new bike. By 1911, thanks to rising wages and falling prices, that number dropped to just five weeks of work. In Italy, Catholic and Socialist organizations made it even easier for people to start riding by founding cycling clubs and renting out bicycles to their working-class members.

In next to no time, Europe's busiest boulevards and avenues were invaded by bicycles. At a moment when most average workers had few options for efficient personal transit in cities, the bicycle opened up a new world of opportunity—and speed. H. G. Wells captured the simultaneous exhilaration and terror of riding a bike in his book *The Wheels of Chance*: "A memory of motion lingers in the muscles of your legs, and round and round they seem to go. You ride through Dreamland on wonderful dream bicycles that change and grow; you ride down steeples and staircases and over precipices; you hover in horrible suspense over inhabited towns, vainly seeking for a brake your hand cannot find, to save you from a headlong fall; you plunge into weltering rivers, and rush helplessly at monstrous obstacles."

Not everyone was as enthusiastic as Wells, and several experts lambasted this new form of transit. A prominent French doctor and scientist claimed the bicycle posed serious health risks, especially if ridden after sexual intercourse. He was particularly concerned about women riding bikes because cycling could "procure genital satisfactions, voluptuous sensations" or even "sportive masturbations." Other leading authorities, including a famous criminologist, fretted that the physical exertion required to propel a bike could "stimulate criminal and aggressive tendencies."

Ultimately, few paid any heed to such alarming health warnings. People of all walks of life became cyclists, and as they did, the bicycle itself rose to a golden age of cultural prominence that would last for nearly half a century. In doing so, it became such a part of everyday life that it was impossible to miss. Cyclists enjoyed jaunts around town and complained about the traffic and accidents. Expensive advertisements filled newspapers with pictures of the latest cycling accessories, and politicians instituted bicycle taxes to raise revenues. There were even reports of desperate sons who stole their mothers' bicycles, and of notable figures assassinated while cycling. A once-newfangled apparatus had become a familiar staple, a convenient and economical mode of transport for adults the world over. And for young boys, a shiny new bike reigned supreme at the top of every wish list.

✦

Gino spent the summer before the sixth grade with his eye firmly on the prize. "From that pile of raffia that covered me up to my knees—my good father Torello would tell me—should come a solid bicycle with which to reach Florence every day as soon as autumn came." And so it did. At the end of the summer, Torello added some of his own money to Gino's earnings, and Anita and Natalina contributed from the nest eggs for their dowries. "I certainly wouldn't have been able to buy a new bicycle, much less a racing bicycle," Gino said, but he had scrounged up enough to get a rusty fourth-hand bicycle he could finally call his own. And once he did, it was all he could think about. "You can imagine my joy. The first nights I kept tossing and turning in my bed from the desire for it to be day so that I could ride it."

Day broke, and with it emerged a whole new world beyond the haphazard borders of Ponte a Ema. "The roads that led to us were all up-and-down, inviting routes for those who could pedal. My passion for the bike led me to use it to go to school every day with my friends from town and from other neighboring areas," Gino explained. They would always choose the longest and most difficult roads, showing up for class with mottled faces "like a bunch of ripe apples." In the evenings, Gino would occasionally lead his friends on adventures. As they watched him from afar, he would pedal quietly and sneak up on a member of the *carabinieri* or police. When he got close enough, Gino would startle the officer with a shout—and then race away laughing into the darkness before he could be caught.

Gino's favorite ride included a particularly steep hill nicknamed the Moccoli, Tuscan slang for "curses," because most people couldn't help but swear in anguish as they climbed up it. The route took Gino some six hundred yards above the south bank of the Arno River to the Piazzale Michelangelo, referred to by locals as the "balcony" of Florence. Completed in 1876, the Piazzale offered a breathtaking view of the city in all of its glory. There were the obvious landmarks like Ponte Vecchio, Florence's most famous bridge, and the Duomo, the imposing cathedral that rises from the city's red-roofed central area. There were also the lesser known treasures like the Jewish synagogue, built from ocher- and cream-colored stone and topped with a striking trio of cupolas, covered in copper that had turned sage green with age. All of these came together at Piazzale Michelangelo to form a panorama worthy of any museum.

Once he arrived at the Piazzale, sweaty and with his heart heaving, Gino would savor the view as he caught his breath. Then he would hurl himself into the exhilarating ride downhill toward Florence. "When I descended into Florence the air was clear, one could smell the fresh perfume of the green from the trees and from the meadows. The water from the Arno was limpid, like the pure water of the creek in my native village, the Ema," Gino said. After so many childhood days spent in quiet Ponte a Ema, Florence was a tantalizing hive of activity, buzzing with strange new sounds, colors, and tastes. To start, there were the men plying trades that Gino had never seen before: rag men who sold used strips of cloth for cleaning, men who mended broken umbrellas, rod men who offered to fix broken terra-cotta bowls with iron thread. In the late spring there were even men selling crickets to anyone planning to attend the popular Cricket Festival in Le Cascine park.

On Florence's busy streets, Gino found the city's legendary food vendors. Pumpkin-seed sellers offered up their ever-popular treat near public gardens; other men cooked *pattone*, sweet loaves made from chestnut flour, and asked passersby to feel how hot their bread was. Butchers sold *roventini*, a mixture of fried pig's blood and Parmesan cheese, and advertised it with an image of a pig exclaiming, "I was killed for you." Elsewhere, farmers rode around the city on bicycles, selling lettuce and radishes, while tripe vendors built small stations on streetcorners, only to find themselves surrounded by legions of mewing cats. And perhaps most alluring for an inveterate sweet tooth like Gino's were the *perecottari*, who set up stands near many of the city's schools and sold cooked pears and apples flavored with syrup.

For all the excitement of the city streets, nothing beckoned more than the Florentine bike mechanic's shop where Gino's older cousin Armando Sizzi worked. With bike frames hanging on hooks across the ceiling in various states of disrepair, it looked like a butcher's store. But the ambience, a heady mix of bike grease, cigarette smoke, and men's laughter, suggested something more akin to a barbershop. Although it was difficult to tell from its unassuming storefront, the shop was a veritable neighborhood institution. On a busy afternoon, it hummed with life. Serious racers, both amateurs and aspiring professionals, came in to purchase new tires and swap stories about training rides and local races. They mingled with more everyday riders, waiting for repairs, and interested locals who just stopped by to chat. With a wrench in hand, Sizzi tended to them all, exchanging jokes as he repaired broken chains and replaced damaged wheels.

A warm-hearted and voluble man, Sizzi frequently introduced his clients and friends to his shy cousin. None of these individuals appears to have had a lasting impact on Gino—except one, a man named Giacomo Goldenberg. Goldenberg had come to Florence from Eastern Europe and he had brought with him a life story dramatically different from any Gino had encountered before.

✦

Giacomo Goldenberg was a hazel-eyed, bespectacled young man with hair the color of charcoal. He was born near the city of Kishinev, then a part of the Russian empire, and today a part of Moldova. Goldenberg's family came to Italy around 1912, part of a wave of immigrants who left Eastern Europe in the wake of several attacks that scourged the Jewish communities. Although Italy was a place where Jews were fully integrated into daily life, the change in lifestyle that came with the relocation was considerable. After years of being immersed in Yiddish and Russian, they had to learn Italian from scratch and then navigate the tricky world of *dialetto*, or regional Italian dialects. Older immigrants had to find new jobs; children had to enroll in Italian schools and make new friends. Even food and music, the creature comforts of everyday life, changed in the land of pasta and Puccini. It all added up to a dramatic shift that left many feeling disoriented as they tried to find a place in their new country.

Few young men rose to the challenge of building a new life in Italy as well as Goldenberg. By all accounts he embraced his adopted homeland with zeal. Within a short time after his arrival, he was fluent in Italian. He then enrolled in a course of study at an Italian university, an accomplishment out of reach even for many native Italians. When he graduated, he started working in a shop in Florence that sold textiles. Along the way, he befriended many Italian Gentiles like Armando Sizzi, who had little experience with or patience for the kind of anti-Semitism Goldenberg had witnessed in Kishinev.

When Sizzi introduced Gino to Goldenberg around 1925, something clicked. At a time when Gino was just starting to uncover a powerful feeling of wanderlust within himself, Goldenberg was sixteen years older and perhaps the worldliest young man Gino had ever met. He was educated, spoke multiple languages, and had traveled across the European continent in an era when most Italians of Gino's class lived their whole lives within the city or town where they were born. Goldenberg in turn saw something appealing about Sizzi and Gino—they were the kind of welcoming spirits that turn a foreign place into a friendly one. Over an occasional chat in the shop or perhaps a bowl of pappardelle or risotto, this shared curiosity was forged into a common bond of friendship and mutual esteem.

After a couple of years, Goldenberg would leave Florence and move to Fiume, a port town in northeastern Italy, where he would marry a baker's daughter and start a prosperous trade importing lumber. Still it was undeniable that a solid foundation of friendship had been formed.

Neither Goldenberg nor Sizzi nor Gino knew it yet, but time would reveal it as one of the most important relationships of their lives.

✦

Beneath the enticing, cosmopolitan bustle of this adult world that Gino was just beginning to discover, ominous forces lurked. On an autumn night in 1925, Gino listened carefully as his father, Torello, handed him various Socialist papers and books and gave him a stern warning: "Politics is a trap. Remember that. Keep your distance."

Torello Bartali urged the boy to go and hide the pile of materials in the attic. "Put it in a corner where no one will find it," his father commanded. From the somber expression in Torello's eyes and the strain in his voice, Gino knew he was being entrusted with an important task.

Torello had reason enough to feel anxious. Though he was a day laborer and hardly prominent in political circles, he had been involved with the Italian Socialist Party and campaigned locally for laborers' rights at a time when Mussolini's Italy was becoming a frightening place for anyone who dared to speak out against him. Soon after he came to power in 1922, *Il Duce,* as Mussolini was known, moved quickly to shut down the opposition, particularly those who were vocal about their dissent in the press. In short order, he issued various decrees that made it dangerous for journalists to write freely, and created a daunting atmosphere for any who questioned Fascism more broadly. Midway through 1924, a prominent Socialist named Giacomo Matteotti suggested in Parliament that the Fascists had rigged a recent election. Days later, Matteotti was kidnapped and killed. His death shocked Italians throughout the country.

In Florence, a group of activists known as the Italia Libera circle had been mobilizing anti-Fascist sentiment for some time. Formed by World War I veterans, this group of Florentines, ranging from lawyers to railroad workers, felt Fascism was an affront to democracy. To fight back, they published an underground newspaper called *Non Mollare!*—"Don't give in!"

Gaetano Pilati, a retired Socialist deputy who owned a firm where

Torello Bartali sometimes worked as a laborer, actively supported Italia Libera. At eleven thirty one night, late in October 1925, Pilati was fast asleep in bed with his wife. A couple of Fascist bandits leaned a ladder against his bedroom balcony and forced the window open. The first one, a small man with a hat pulled over his eyes, brandished two revolvers. The second commanded Pilati to follow them to the Fascist headquarters. Pilati obeyed and started to dress, sitting on the edge of his bed to pull the trousers over his one leg, the other having been lost during World War I. As he readied himself, one of the bandits asked him a question.

"Are you really Pilati?"

"Yes," Pilati replied.

Seconds later, both bandits shot him. Pilati rolled off the bed, injured but still alive. His wife screamed in horror as the intruders left the same way they had come. Pilati lived for three days, until he finally succumbed to the bullet wounds.

The murder of his employer devastated Torello. "You see?" he told his young son as he handed him his incriminating Socialist papers. "I defended an ideal because I wanted a more just world for myself and for others. And this is the result: they have killed my companions in faith and I have to hide my books and my opinions."

Like few other men, Gino would come to understand politics as the elemental force that it is—singular in its ability to build up a man or tear him down, unify a country's citizens around a common goal or turn them against one another in bloody persecution. Torello's warning would stay with him for the rest of his life. At eleven years old, however, these concepts must have felt a world away. Gino could understand the seriousness of his father's tone. But ultimately politics was just an abstraction, a distant notion to a boy whose heart was consumed by something altogether different.

2

In the Saddle

Gino Bartali points playfully at his younger brother, Giulio.

THE BARTALI BROTHERS WERE destined to become a cycling dynasty, Gino was sure of it. Two years apart in age, he and Giulio rode together on their bikes all over the countryside near Florence with a band of their classmates, like a herd of Tuscan horses that galloped in the grasslands nearby. "I felt like one of those foals," Gino said, "the young horses who ran with their manes in the wind without the slightest restraint." The boys tackled the dusty Tuscan hills for the thrill of sprinting until their lungs burned, and they challenged each other to races. "Let's see who can reach the top of that hill up there first!" someone would shout, and they would be off. Gino would always arrive ahead of everyone else, followed closely by Giulio, and they would get off their bikes and wait for the others. "Heavens, how they struggled!" Gino said. "I sweated less and I didn't huff and puff as much."

It quickly became obvious that Gino was the strongest racer of the group. But it wasn't until he tested his mettle against real racers, every once in a lucky while, that he began to realize that he was different, special even. Sometimes when messing about on their bicycles, Gino, Giulio, and their friends would run into amateur racers training along the steep Tuscan roads. "Annoyed by our presence on their wheels, they would do battle with us. Despite their perfect bicycles, they didn't always beat us, even though the bikes we pedaled were like lumbering horse buggies. In fact, on many climbs with me, they would lose," Gino said. "At first, even I was astounded and embarrassed by this discovery."

Gino wasn't the only one who was becoming aware of his talent. He had taken a part-time job three days a week during the sixth grade in the shop of a Ponte a Ema bicycle mechanic named Oscar Casamonti. Casamonti was an amateur racer himself and had been hearing the talk around town about his young apprentice. Wanting to see with his own eyes if the rumors were true, he brought Gino along one day for a ride with him and his training partners. Gino stayed well behind, trudging along with his heavy touring bike. "Everyone had a racing one, and I had my work cut out for me to seem equally confident," he said. It was decided that they would cover about fifty-five miles, and from time to time Casamonti would dart forward. When they reached the midway point, Gino's boss raced ahead and left everyone else in his wake. Some of the others began to drop away, but Gino did everything he could to keep up. To a point. Not daring to pass Casamonti, he didn't push quite as hard as he could have, explaining, "I didn't want to disrespect him, he was my boss!" When Casamonti was sure that he was alone in the lead, he turned back and saw young Gino right behind him. His eyes became as big as saucers. Upon returning home he went directly to speak with Torello and Giulia.

They had a boy on their hands who was born to race.

✦

In 1920s Italy, few things were remotely as appealing as cycling for boys like Gino. Soccer found its faithful in cities from the fall through the spring, but cycling was the symbol of summer. Like no other sport, it succeeded in captivating the attention of people living in the countryside as well. From villages high in the Italian Alps all the way down the peninsula to Sicily, cycling drew crowds of onlookers, journalists, and newsreel directors. One well-known Italian journalist described the transformative effect of the Giro d'Italia, the multistage competition that was the most important cycling race in Italy. "For many houses lost in the mountains, for much of the countryside drowned in sun, for many people from villages perched at the tops of hills, the Giro is life's only spectacle, the fleeting vision of a faraway world that races from one big city to another, and ties all of Italy into a single ring." Nor did cycling's popularity stop at Italy's borders. The rest of continental Europe embraced it, and the international fan base in North and South America was growing swiftly.

It was hardly a tough sell. Competitive cycling took the age-old excitement of horse racing and unleashed it from the confines of the racetrack onto the familiar roads of everyday life. Audiences flocked to competitions, mesmerized by the sight of men jockeying against each other atop their iron horses. Race organizers cashed in on it all and competed among themselves, each trying to make their race the longest, their route the most challenging, and their prize the largest. Manufacturers of bicycles sponsored whole teams and helped establish a season of races. A freewheeling sport was transformed into a major industry; an international obsession became a fixture of modern life.

By the time Gino was a young boy, a class of cyclists had emerged who could make their living by competing for large prizes. Three days before Gino turned thirteen, the Italian cyclist Alfredo Binda won a striking victory at the first professional World Cycling Championship in Germany, and Gino began to dream of a world he had never imagined before. With colorful personalities and even more colorful entourages, racers like Binda had quickly become as famous as the races themselves. They hailed from different parts of Europe, but came almost universally from the working classes. Many were from long lines of families who worked in the mines; others were lumberjacks, cheese merchants, and millers. Young Gino and his contemporaries could not resist the allure of these pedaling cowboys; astride the latest bicycles with exotic curled racing handlebars, they wore spare tires draped over their shoulders and donned racing glasses that resembled modern-day swim goggles. "Back then, racers were personalities," recalled one Italian rider. Gino fell in love with these larger-than-life characters.

So did the press. They described the racers in Homeric prose:

> These racers were once similar to you, and many, in fact, are still the same as you: farmers, day laborers, builders, gardeners. They took a bicycle and they conquered the world on the back of that fragile steel seahorse. Now cities wait for them and acclaim them, because they are strong, because they have challenged the dust and the rain, because they have fallen and, though injured, they have gotten up again, because they have conquered the mountains, because they have raced, always, nonstop and breathless. They are the heroes of a humble and exciting tournament who have made themselves knights of hard work.

With such praise, the sport quickly became a fertile ground for a class of famous stars.

The most prominent of these won prizes at the big races and then cashed in on their success by collecting fees for appearing at smaller events afterward across the continent. Reporters followed them devotedly, hungry to depict characters who traveled greater distances in one race than many people would travel in their lifetimes. Popular art filled any gaps that the newspapers neglected. The fictive exploits and intrigues of cyclists quickly became the fodder for countless novels and films.

Charles Terront, who raced wearing blue stockings, white flannel knee breeches, and a silk ascot, was the first major cycling icon to ride to the top of the cultural zeitgeist. After he won a 743-mile round-trip race between Paris and Brest in 1891, he was met at the finish line by thousands of spectators. He proceeded to devour four meals and then reportedly slept for twenty-six hours. As he slumbered he became a national sensation. After he awoke, he attended eighteen consecutive banquets organized to celebrate his success. The rewards didn't stop there. Terront received a seat of honor and a free box in the Paris Opera, and the writer Paul D'Ivoi turned him into a fictional hero in his novel *Les cinq sous de Lavarède*.

In the United States, "wheeling" peaked in 1896 when the *New York Times* declared, "The wheel is triumphant." Tiffany issued a silver-plated bicycle frame, Thomas Edison experimented with an electric tricycle, and the League of American Wheelmen blossomed to 75,000 dues-paying members including John D. Rockefeller. Thousands of Americans flocked to Madison Square Garden, originally built by Cornelius Vanderbilt for cycling races, to watch the grueling "Six Days." Cyclists from around the world raced for six days and six nights, and the racer who covered the most total distance won.

America had its moment, but European cyclists stole the show in the first decades of the twentieth century. The aspiring racer became a cultural fixture in Europe, like the Jazz Age flapper in America, a defining image of an era and its ambitions. Countless young Italian men earnestly believed this fantasy could be their reality.

Young women proved no less willing to be swept up in the hoopla. Scores of them flocked to see famous cyclists at the finish lines, and the most daring delivered lipstick kisses to the victors along with their contact details. (One racer was reported to have gathered the personal information for some five hundred women during one multistage race.)

Such was the prevalence of women that some men even considered them a moral hazard. In his book on cycling, Henri Desgrange, the founder of the Tour de France, warned cyclists about these "pretty little lecherous souls who would be charmed to experiment with you . . . to determine whether your qualities as a man in bed are as remarkable as your qualities as a racer on the track."

It was no great surprise that few riders paid Desgrange any heed. Most were all too happy to repay this romantic interest in kind, using their time off their bikes to take their admirers out to lunch, to dance, or even back to their hotel rooms. Other riders were less interested in the chase and chose instead to spend their rest days in bordellos. One Italian rider became such fast friends with the women who plied their trade in Rome's red-light district that he knew nearly every one of them by name and routinely stopped by their salons just to say farewell whenever he left the city for an extended period. The teams' sports managers were happy to turn a blind eye to such pursuits as long as racing results didn't suffer.

Henri Pélissier, a legendary French rider with a soft smile that made women's hearts flutter, was so popular that he had to develop an unconventional strategy for rebuffing his many female fans: he solicited his wife's help. Pélissier won the Tour de France in 1923, and during every Tour he raced he received dozens of marriage proposals that he passed on to his wife to answer. Eventually she tired of this arrangement. Ten years later, out of desperation, she took her own life. Pélissier took up with a new lover, but tragedy continued to haunt him. In the midst of an argument, she shot and killed him, using the same gun his first wife had used to end her life.

Pélissier's murder was the sensational stuff of headlines, but it was far from typical. Most cyclists were treated with admiration by their supporters. Ardent fans were ecstatic if they could simply get the autographs of their favorite cyclists at the finish line. Everyone else was just happy to bask in their presence. "We were all gods," remembered one racer with amusement. "We had no idea what was happening to us."

✦

This was the exhilarating vapor that swirled around young Gino, beckoning from newspapers, radio, and the wistful chatter of cyclists at Casamonti's. He drank it all in. "There I was, enchanted, hearing about those adventures that seemed marvelous to me," said Gino about the shop, his "second home." "I would leave a bit of my heart and my dreams there." The transformation was astounding. The boy who had struggled to pay attention in school could sit for hours focused on the most minute adjustments for a customer's bicycle. And any waking moments when he wasn't working a shift in Casamonti's, he would be happily riding his own bicycle, that ponderous one-speed iron contraption that hardly seemed worthy of the name.

The only thing that would have made Gino happier was his father's permission to race in official competitions. Despite Casamonti's urging, Torello refused to allow his son to get involved in what he considered to be a wild and hazardous world. Gino's father knew full well that a cyclist, let alone a child, was no match for a car if they collided on the road. "*Babbo* didn't want me to bicycle race with my friends," Gino explained, "because he was always afraid I'd get into trouble." Nor was Giulia Bartali favorably disposed to the sport. Any mother would have been terrified by the loud groups of youth that ripped around dangerously in Florence's streets with reckless abandon, leaving frazzled onlookers in their wake. Newspapers in that era regularly reported the violence wreaked by bicyclists as they crashed into pedestrians, fracturing their bones and even killing them on occasion.

Torello made his feelings abundantly clear one day after a friend of Gino's borrowed his bike. The friend had attached his own pair of curved racing handlebars, replacing Gino's regular touring set. When he returned the bike, he left the new equipment affixed. In this way, Gino got his first taste of riding a racing bicycle. Intoxicated by the thrill of training on the vehicle of his heroes, he forgot to remove the handlebars at the end of the day. He paid a steep price when Torello discovered his bike later. "When Torello returned home from work and saw the bicycle bastardized in that way, he told me simply that if I didn't remove it immediately from his sight, he would have it reduced to scrap metal in five minutes." Gino fought back his tears, stung by his father's disapproval.

Torello couldn't stomach the idea of his son as a racer because Gino's health seemed borderline at best. On one cold day in the winter of 1929, when Gino was fifteen years old, he settled into one of the usual neighborhood games of cops and robbers. Snow was falling, a rare occurrence in Ponte a Ema. Drawing the short stick saved for the robber, Gino hid himself for the better part of a day while his companions searched for him. As the sun dropped below the horizon, he started walking home, assuming that the game was finished. One of his friends, however, caught sight of him and insisted that Gino had been captured. The others soon gathered around and agreed with this verdict. Gino was indignant but outnumbered, and so he unhappily accepted his punishment. They forced him to the ground and covered him from head to toe in snow. His friends left him, and his mother discovered him some time later, wet and shivering. A high fever took hold, and Gino's parents grew petrified that he would come down with pneumonia. In an era before penicillin, pneumonia, along with any number of other infections, could be a death sentence.

Somehow Gino survived. In time he strengthened enough to move around, though it would be six months before he could speak normally. He wanted to move past this harrowing experience, but his peers made that virtually impossible. They began calling him *Careggi,* the name of Florence's most famous hospital. It was his first nickname and one he would remember forever, a reminder of the ordeal he had suffered.

Gino responded by devoting himself to training. Perhaps he was trying to convince his friends and family that he had recuperated completely. Or perhaps he was just trying to persuade himself. Whatever it was, he began to obsess about stripping away his weaknesses and building a stronger version of himself. He wanted to train and he wanted to race.

Unfortunately, his fervor did not elicit a change in his parents' attitudes about cycling. Now more than ever, their elder son's ambitions filled them with dread. They had almost lost him to a menacing illness, and it was no secret that cycling was a dangerous sport. Even seasoned professionals occasionally died in accidents during competitions. Torello put his foot down. There would be no racers in his family. Casamonti continued relentlessly to champion Gino's cause. He told Torello it would be a crime not to let the boy race, but Torello was deaf to his pleas. "One day you will bring him back in pieces," Torello said. He had no idea how his words would come back to haunt him.

On the day of Gino's seventeenth birthday, July 18, 1931, something unexpected happened. As the family ate dinner that night, Gino asked whether his brother could take part the following day in a competition that several of Giulio's classmates had entered in a nearby town. Torello quickly replied that Giulio was too young to race. "If need be, you do it," he said to Gino. "With this mania in your blood, you won't even let me sleep." Maybe his attitude had softened on his son's birthday, or maybe he was just tired of fighting the inevitable for so long. Worn out by years of pleading from his son, countless townsfolk, and even the Ponte a Ema parish priest, Torello finally relented. "My heart leapt," Gino wrote afterward. "I took off before the sound of his words, so sweet to my ears, disappeared. It was one of the best presents I had ever gotten in my life."

Gino won the race the following day and savored his first taste of victory. It didn't last long. He was immediately disqualified because the race was for fourteen- to sixteen-year-olds, and having just turned seventeen, he was no longer eligible. Yet this unfortunate outcome could do nothing to overshadow the larger victory Gino had won.

He had become a racer.

3

The First Test

Gino Bartali, circa 1936.

TORELLO'S BLESSING WAS HARD won, and Gino didn't want to let his father down. His first goal was to ease his parents' financial woes or, at the very least, avoid adding to them. He developed some particularly creative strategies to do so. He started waking up at 4:30 a.m. to fit in his training rides ahead of his day's work in Casamonti's shop. Still, his paltry income as a bicycle mechanic barely covered the new expenses of training and racing. During most races, for instance, his bicycle pedals tore up the soles of his shoes. But it quickly became expensive to pay five lire—half his day's wages—to replace them. So Gino came up with a more economical fix: he had the rubber from old bicycle tires sewn onto the soles.

Gino's early triumphs earned him a spot in a local amateur sports club called L'Aquila, or "The Eagle." He continued to struggle, however, to become financially independent. One of his fellow racers hatched a solution:

"Listen, Gino, if we arrive together at the finish line, will you let me go first? I have a girlfriend waiting for me and I'll give you the first prize. What do you say?" he asked.

"All right," Gino responded, knowing he could then bring home the first- and second-prize purses. He knew he was bending the rules, but he was getting desperate. "Up until this point I hadn't brought home a single lira and my father was about to blow," he said. In the end, the ruse did not last long. The directors of L'Aquila soon caught on that he was ceding wins here and there. When he explained why, they offered to give him a stipend of fifty lire per race, a typical award for a first-place finish.

Slightly relieved of his financial torments, seventeen-year-old Gino turned his energies elsewhere. Determined to rid himself of all frailty, he adopted a rigorous series of exercises that developed muscular strength. He had always resented being picked on for being small. "Often my classmates jeered at me and teased me because I was the weakest," he said. "I was scrawny, I didn't have the physique suited to my age. I prayed to the Lord that he would make me grow strong. But meanwhile I suffered. I suffered in silence, I held everything closed inside of me, for fear that my pain would be the motive for more jokes."

Now he had found a method for channeling his pent-up frustration. His training bible was a booklet by a Dutch professor that detailed twenty-four exercises for cyclists that moved through the arms, neck, legs, and the rest of the body's muscles. He did these calisthenics so religiously that his mother, Giulia, grew to expect the familiar sight of her son exercising at daybreak each morning, soon after the neighbor's rooster crowed, in front of an open window, even in the dead of winter. Within a year he had increased his chest size by more than three inches.

His bike offered other opportunities for training. On steep climbs, he worked on slowing down his breathing. He taught himself to make do with less water, tempering his ability to withstand the thirst that would grow over hundreds of miles of riding with just a few drops. He built his endurance on hills around Tuscany, and his speed on any flats he could find. Like an inventor tinkering with a new design, he fastidiously recorded all of his observations and experiments in logbooks, a practice that earned him the nickname "the Accountant" for being so meticulous. In everything, he focused on a cyclist's most important strength—his tolerance for pain, or what Gino called his "capacity for suffering."

Nutrition also became an obsession. Gino experimented with different combinations of foods. Plain pasta and bananas became favorites; tomatoes, a staple of most Italian diets, were abandoned because of their acidity. Aware of the Bartalis' circumstances, his neighbors pitched in to help fuel their budding champion. One butcher provided him with free steaks before key races, and other villagers shared extra bread when they had it.

On race days, breakfast began with an espresso or a caffe latte and some bread with jam or Gino's favorite: honey. Next he ate pasta or rice with a cheese or butter sauce, ideally accompanied by eggs, veal, or steak. For a midday snack, he liked a couple of panini with cheese, marmalade, or salami, sometimes all three at once. During a multiday race, the portions became much larger to account for the increased caloric output. In one such race, Gino was eating almost a dozen raw eggs a day while cycling, breaking their shells on his handlebars before swallowing the yolks. In another, he confessed to eating a whole rabbit and a chicken in one sitting.

Sports nutritionists now know that eating so much meat, particularly steak, hours ahead of rigorous physical activity is a terrible strategy. So much blood is diverted away from the muscles to the stomach to digest a large quantity of meat that a rider is likely to feel nauseated. Yet in the early years of cycling, eating huge amounts of meat had been part of the accepted nutritional wisdom. In fact, a French physician in 1869 (in what was likely one of the first newspaper columns about nutrition and cycling) advised cyclists competing in a road race to pause every twelve to fifteen miles of the race to consume food and drink, preferably a steak and a couple of glasses of Madeira or sweet white wine. Then, after fifteen minutes' rest, he suggested the riders walk alongside their bicycles for a few minutes before getting back on. By the 1920s and 1930s, the thinking had evolved and simplified. The goal became to fuel up with enough calories to endure lengthy races, since many cyclists came from families like the Bartalis, where food could be scarce at times. Meat was considered very high-quality food for the task because it contained a lot of protein and calories.

✦

In all of his training, the only area that seemed impervious to tinkering was Gino's riding style. Perhaps it couldn't change because there was no discernible method behind it. Most other racers took whole climbs either standing or sitting, depending on the grade of the hill. If the slope was mild, they would stand on their pedals to get extra power. If the hill was more extreme, they would get off their bike and flip their rear wheel to move their chain onto a lower gear on the other side of the wheel, which made it easier to take more of the climb sitting. They would only need to stand for the steepest moments. Gino, in contrast, bounced up and down out of his seat haphazardly. "Bartali did a climb in bursts, he was jumpy," said one teammate. His strength meant he could climb both standing *and* sitting, and could wait longer than most of his rivals before having to flip his wheel. Newspaper reporters chalked it up to an unusual personal style. A rival racer, however, was more candid: "He looked like he was being electrocuted."

Defensive cycling had its place, but it was the adrenaline rush of a charge that electrified Gino. Risky, all-or-nothing offensives earned him considerable success as an amateur. As word spread, more and more riders learned to recognize his signature attack. Late in a race, usually during a climb when the peloton was pushing at full tilt, Gino would ride up behind the leader. When he thought the moment was right, he would charge forward, tempting the leader to follow him. If he did, Gino would soon slow down again and let him catch up. When it looked like the other rider had found his cadence once more, Gino would start his quick charge all over again. "He would burst forward," explained one teammate. "Then two hundred yards after he had done his burst he'd stop for a moment, for twenty to thirty yards, and then burst forward again." After four or five of these bursts, he launched a longer attack, well aware that his opponent was now utterly exhausted. By varying his speed so dramatically, Gino broke his adversary's rhythm and wore him down. "To respond to his attacks was to race to suicide," explained one of his competitors.

In a sport where fluid pedaling is vital, Gino's unorthodox way of riding a bike did offer one unexpected benefit. Other racers were so transfixed by watching him that they didn't realize he was watching them even more closely. Like a veteran card shark, Gino carefully eyed his competitors, looking for any "tell" or sign that indicated that they were weakening. It could be something as obvious as a quick grimace, or something as insignificant as a minute muscular twitch. When faced with one particularly strong rider, Gino scrutinized him for days, riding so close to him he could have reached out and held on to his rear wheel. On the final day, after seven hours of monitoring this cyclist's body for change, Gino noticed something unusual. A small vein behind the rider's knee was swelling up. Soon after, he started slightly faltering in his pedaling. Gino was ecstatic. To celebrate this discovery he launched a blistering attack and left his opponent in his dust. From that time onward, he knew that a crisis was likely to assail his rival when he noted a vein "dancing behind the knee."

Later in his career, Gino became even more devious in his attempts to sniff out and study the strategies of rivals. He thought nothing of breaking into his opponents' rooms after they had left for a race, or when they were out for dinner, to inspect their bathrooms. In an era before drug testing, most riders had a mix of vials and flasks of various liquids, pills, and powders their trainers recommended they use. Many were herbal concoctions, placebos that actually did nothing but provide a psychological boost. Others were more powerful, like the white amphetamines known only as "dynamite" that sped up the heart for a short period. During one such illegal reconnaissance mission, Gino broke into a competitor's room "like Sherlock Holmes" and used a teammate as a guinea pig, having him imbibe a mysterious green liquid he found there. Little came of it, but his obsessive quest to follow his opponents' every move continued unabated.

✦

Relentlessly pushing his opponents in every way he knew how, Gino rose through cycling's different competitive categories with ease. Only four years after his first race, he turned professional in 1935. He was right where he had dreamed of being, but cycling at this new level took some getting used to. As an amateur, he had been an independent racer and had been responsible to no one but himself. "No one could tell me anything," he said. "I took off, went forward, stayed back, as many times as I liked. I was free to make my own way. No one helped me in races. Except in rare situations, everyone was on his own. And to get to the end, you really had to give it your all." To be sure, this also meant that there was no one to come to his rescue in times of need. In one amateur race, he lost a shoe a few miles before the end. "I finished with a bare foot and there was snow on the ground!" he remembered. In another, he did the final sprint with two flat tires, having pierced both of them just before the finish line. "Among the many little misadventures in those days, though," he said, "there was at least the satisfaction of being free, of not owing anything to anyone." Now he belonged to a team, and as its newest member, he had to pay his dues as a *gregario,* a supporting rider whose own race is devoted to ensuring victory for the captain. "I felt degraded. Being the water carrier and the pacesetter for others is not satisfying!" Gino's older cousin, Armando Sizzi, urged him to be patient. "You could be like Binda, the master of the mountains," he said, referring to Gino's childhood idol. Still, Gino was solemnly reprimanded more than once in his first few team competitions for taking off on his own and winning without the captain's permission, and at his expense.

Gino chafed in the role of a supporting rider, but the reality was that in the professional world he was little more than another fresh-faced young racer. Such was the extent of his anonymity that when he did start winning those races where he wasn't obliged to follow someone else's orders, he caught more than a few journalists off guard. After he took first place in a major race in Spain in 1935, for example, the writers of one of the most prominent Spanish sports journals heralded him in a flashy cover story. He was so unknown, however, that they misidentified him, and mistakenly referred to him throughout the article as "Lino." In the months that followed, no magazine would forget Gino's name as he became the most-talked about rookie that season.

Success upended Gino's life. He soon became the captain of a professional team and quickly became the wealthiest member of his family. His team contract saw him earn 22,000 lire annually, about five times as much as the average factory worker in Italy, and nearly fifteen times as much as he himself had been earning as a mechanic only a few years earlier. Large as it was, this was just his base salary. The real money was in race purses, which Gino started racking up with wins across the country and around the continent. He was soon able to afford to build a new house for his parents, a two-story home much closer to Florence than the building they shared with various families in Ponte a Ema. It had a *dinello,* or dining room, a living room, several bedrooms, and even a small garden so his parents, still country people at heart, could keep chickens and grow Tuscan staples such as green beans.

The greatest reward, however, was not financial. Despite their father's fretful apprehensions, Gino's younger brother, Giulio, had followed him into cycling. Gino couldn't help but be impressed by his riding. Even though he was two years younger, Giulio could keep up with his brother better than could most of Gino's peers. As young boys they had dreamed of dominating the cycling world. Now the Bartali brothers started envisioning their future life together as professional racers. While Gino was a rookie sensation, Giulio was beginning to emerge as an important racer in his own right. By the first half of the 1936 season he had already won six races, including one that he captured with a jaw-dropping ten-minute lead. As the pair trained side by side, they plotted their rise to the top. "I tried to give him advice," Gino said. "I talked to him about my experiences and he would listen and then he would tell me how he had won this race or lost that one. . . . How I liked to hear him talk. Not that he was a chatterbox; he was a closed type, like me. But when we were together we confided everything." They made a pact to help each other in races and agreed that once they were competing in the same category, they would team up to trounce their rivals. They were young, but their early victories suggested they had every right to dream big.

All this success, both for himself and then for his brother, introduced its own set of complications into Gino's life. "I was barely of age and in a couple of years I had become popular like I would never have imagined," he said. His string of triumphs quickly drew considerable attention from journalists. In a time before the exploits of Hollywood stars had fully captivated Europe, cyclists were the celebrities that everyone spoke about. And so Gino soon found himself eddying in the froth generated by the press. His face became so famous he was obliged to employ a press secretary to handle his correspondence and requests for photographs. Public errands could be handled at what was at best a stuttering pace, as more and more people would interrupt whatever he was doing to ask him for autographs. Even his relations with women had changed. Girls he had only just met gushed over him, and others sent long, impassioned letters. One of these fans' obsessive love for Gino seemed to speak for them all: "You're the salt of my life," she wrote. "Food doesn't have any taste, bouquets smell, fabrics softness since you installed yourself in my heart."

Female fans made him bashful, but the most startling aspect of fame for Gino was how intensely his rivals' supporters lashed out at him, providing an early taste of the conflicts he would face later in his career. They filled his mailbox with mocking letters, going so far as to send him suggestions for an epitaph to put on his grave. "Here in the dust lies the champion of Ponte a Ema," wrote one spectator who encouraged fans *not* to put flowers on Bartali's grave, but rather to use them to decorate his rival. Gino was crestfallen. His mother saw how the letters saddened him. "It's better that you don't read them Gino," Giulia urged. "They do nothing but rot your blood. I will tell the postman to give them to me so that I can use them to get the fire started."

In the end, these were all just comparatively small inconveniences. Gino understood how good he had it. The bike mechanic who had once struggled to get work now walked around Florence in well-cut suits. He had tamed his body, his mind, and even his fate, turning a bleak future into one of limitless possibility. "I was in seventh heaven. I was not yet twenty-two years old and I had arrived."

✦

On Sunday, June 14, 1936, Gino was in Turin in the Italian Alps waiting for the rain to ease up enough so that his race could begin. Some three hundred miles south, his younger brother was also competing, in an amateur cycling championship. Nineteen years old, Giulio was racing against impossibly high expectations. Just a week earlier his older brother had won the Giro d'Italia. Despite this, Giulio was faring rather well, and Gino was convinced he was developing into the most talented Bartali on the bike. "Giulio was physically more gifted than me. He was regular in his pace, he beat me on the final sprints, and on ascents he was the one who held my wheel better than a lot of professionals who raced with me at the time. He was the best amateur in Tuscany," he explained.

Unlike their counterparts in Turin, the organizers of the amateur championship chose to start their race. The rain did not let up. On a particularly muddy stretch, Giulio fell behind and then launched an impressive uphill attack to catch the two leaders. On the descent, the three drafted closely together. Behind them a car that had either missed or ignored signs about the race veered dangerously toward them. The first two cyclists swerved to avoid it. Giulio didn't stand a chance. He hit the vehicle with full force, his clavicle slamming against the door handle as his body crumpled to the ground. He was rushed to the hospital.

Gino took the train home after his own race was canceled, completely unaware of what had happened to his brother. In Florence, a close friend waited for him in the station. Before the friend even had a chance to say anything, his face betrayed him. Gino sputtered instinctively, "Has something happened to Giulio?" At the hospital, the brothers were able to talk briefly. "These things happen," Giulio told him weakly, braving a smile. He had already received several blood transfusions, but Gino donated his own blood, too. Giulio underwent an operation the following day, and Gino passed the hours praying in a nearby chapel. The procedure did not go well; Giulio emerged too weak even to speak. Suffering from massive internal bleeding, his condition deteriorated quickly. He died squeezing his older brother's hand.

"The deepest sadness fell on us like lead," said Gino. "We went from the greatest joy to the most terrible pain."

Torello, who had never wanted his children to race in the first place, got angry with Gino. "You see now that my fears were justified?"

All Gino could muster in reply was, "It's destiny, *Babbo*."

His mother forbade any discussion about cycling, and begged Gino to reconsider his career. Wrestling with his own sense of guilt, he needed no further encouragement. He quit racing and exiled himself to a small cabin by the sea.

As he wandered restlessly along the water's edge, Gino's way of seeing himself and the world transformed dramatically. He began to think of his brother's death as not just an accident but also as a divine warning against the excesses of his earlier life. He had let himself be intoxicated by success; the road to sobriety required that he anchor his life to something larger than himself. Already a practicing Catholic, he devoted himself further to the Church, and turned to his faith to ground him in the world. The lay group Catholic Action, of which Gino had been a member since he was ten, became even more important to him. Formed in 1867, this group organized a wide range of religious and social activities for young boys and men, ranging from prayer meetings and Bible classes to summer camps and athletic associations. By 1928 the group claimed to have 600,000 young members throughout Italy. After Giulio's death, Gino assumed a more visible role, speaking frequently to young boys at Catholic Action meetings, explaining the role of his faith in his success.

In their family home, Gino built a small chapel and dedicated it to Giulio. It stood barely eight feet wide but it was large enough for an altar with a statue of the Madonna holding the cross, several candles, and a kneeler for quiet prayer. Gino had become painfully aware of the attention he drew at the local church, where his presence distracted other parishioners from the service. In the family chapel, the Bartalis would have a private place to offer daily prayers for the repose of Giulio's soul. Soon after its construction, the space would be blessed by the archbishop of Florence, Cardinal Elia Dalla Costa, a figure who was emerging as an important friend to Gino. Bishop Placido Nicolini of Assisi, another friend, would provide a chalice to be used by visiting priests who said mass.

In time, the darkness of Gino's grief lifted slightly. Giulio, his brother and best friend, was gone, but Gino knew he had to move forward somehow. The problem was determining what he might do outside of cycling. His options, he realized, remained as limited as they had been before. He was twenty-two years old, but he had barely managed to get a sixth-grade education. Factory work was a possibility in Milan or Turin, but that would mean leaving behind friends and family and abandoning Tuscany altogether. He could return to being a bike mechanic, but the pay that had seemed pitiful to him as a thirteen-year-old would have appeared minuscule at twenty-two. The only other alternative, working around Florence as a day laborer, would mean a descent into his father's grinding poverty.

As Gino weighed his options, his isolation from the outside world came to an end. Friends from home began visiting again. Teammates implored him to return to lead them. Former stars gently explained that accidents were as much a part of the sport as they were of life itself. Hundreds of fan letters began pouring in. His press secretary who had earlier handled all his fan mail wrote him a moving letter of his own. His sister Anita brought him his bike.

No amount of pleading, however, could lessen Gino's feelings of guilt. "Giulio is gone. My Giulio, my brother. Do you understand?" he told his friends in moments of despair. Giulio's death was a wound that cut him to the core, leaving him with deep misgivings about his life's passion. Cycling had given him everything, but it had also stolen the one person who was dearest to him. Ultimately he would carry his grief over his brother's death to the grave. Until the moment he was too frail to travel at all, Gino rarely missed a chance to stop by his brother's tomb in Ponte a Ema whenever he left or returned to Florence.

In that summer of 1936, however, Gino was intent on figuring out how he would spend his remaining days. It would take the advice of a bewitching newcomer to help him make the choice. She told Gino not to let Giulio's tragic death become his final memory of cycling. He had to race to honor his brother's memory. Gino listened and made the difficult decision to get back in the saddle.

✦

Her name was Adriana Bani, and Gino had spent the better part of 1935 trying to muster the courage to speak to her. She was just shy of sixteen years old, slim-figured, with mahogany curls. From the moment he saw her, Gino was smitten. Adriana came from a conservative family who lived on the northeast edge of Florence. Her father had served in the artillery in World War I and now worked as a railway administrator. Her mother was a housewife. When Gino first set eyes on Adriana, she was working in downtown Florence near Palazzo Vecchio in a shop called 48, a type of early department store that sold all kinds of fabric for forty-eight centesimi. Her sister had worked there, and when she married, her job opened up. The timing suited Adriana, who had just finished up school and wanted to help her parents by getting a job.

At first Gino simply watched Adriana while she worked. A friend of his ran a *pasticceria,* a pastry and chocolate shop, across the cobbled street from 48. Already a lover of chocolate and sweets, Gino needed no further excuse to visit his friend. A colleague of Adriana's soon noticed Gino lurking across the road. Adriana, however, didn't follow sports and had never heard of the famous cyclist.

After several days of fretting, Gino finally gathered his nerve to speak to Adriana. He ventured into the store, hoping to engage her casually in conversation. But his confidence failed him. He quickly retreated after fumbling haplessly about as only a man in a women's fabric store can. After that, he returned to watch her from his post in the pastry shop. Adriana pretended not to notice. Most of the time. Sometimes she did steal glances at her mysterious mute suitor. "With these looks we came to understand each other a bit," she explained. As she left the shop one day, Gino finally decided to make his move. Swallowing his trepidation as best he could, he walked over to her and awkwardly asked whether he could accompany her to the tram she took home at night. She told him she already had an escort, her brother-in-law, but agreed to let Gino tag along. He did—with his eyes fixed on the pavement and in total silence all the way to the stop. Amused and touched by his shyness, Adriana finally asked him, "Shouldn't you say something?"

The cyclist's anxieties slowly disappeared as he began walking her home once in a while, with Adriana's brother-in-law always hovering behind them. Adriana was certainly attractive, but it was her intelligence and modesty that captivated Gino. Though he was famous across the country, she was unfazed by his celebrity status. Adriana in turn was attracted to Gino's sincerity. "He was so embarrassed and funny in his shyness that it was sweet. And I fell in love with that, his purity of soul and his ingenuousness in everyday life," she explained. The two were lovestruck. They shared their first kiss in a piazza in Florence on a day when Adriana's brother-in-law escort was bedridden with a fever.

In time Adriana told her mother a young man had caught her eye. Her mother was skeptical.

"A racer? But what does he do? What does he earn?" she said.

"He rides a bicycle," Adriana replied.

"But how is he able to make a living on a bicycle?" her mother countered.

"He's good. He's starting to be a champion," said Adriana.

"Well, then, introduce him to me," her mother replied, unconvinced.

Adriana suggested to Gino that he meet her parents.

"Let's wait a little. I think it's a bit soon," he said. Given all the media attention he was garnering, Gino was worried about the scrutiny a new girlfriend would receive. "If I lose, the blame will fall immediately on you." The young pair agreed to keep their relationship secret.

After a year, Gino finally met Adriana's parents. He joined them for a meal and asked permission to court their daughter. They reluctantly agreed. Strict and traditional, Adriana's family forbade her from spending time with Gino alone. Luckily for them, his training and racing schedule was so busy that he could not stop by very often. When he did find time to visit her, the sitting-room door was to remain open at all times. Sometimes Adriana would wave to Gino from the window as he left at the end of the evening. Her mother did not approve. "Too familiar," she scolded. In public, they could only be together when accompanied by friends. Most often they spent time getting to know each other at the pastry shop across from 48. Once in a while Gino even convinced her to play hooky from work and sneak out with him. "Sometimes we would go to the movies, but it was on the sly because I didn't have permission to go," she explained.

Adriana had an endearing independent streak. She worked, drove, and smoked in an era when it was uncommon for most Italian women to do so. But she hesitated about Gino and his career. By its very nature, cycling was an unpredictable way to make a living. The difference of only a few minutes, even seconds, at the finish line had a dramatic effect on how much a cyclist earned. Winners did well, but most others just scraped by. As she weighed the prospect of marrying Gino, Adriana couldn't help wondering whether this was a stable foundation on which to build a family.

Gino realized as much himself. He could envision the future he wanted to have with Adriana. "We would have kids and I would try to win as much as possible, so that they would have a good example. Then we would have grandchildren, our children's children, and I would tell them my stories when I got old. I liked to imagine my future life and I imagined it like that," he said. But racing history was littered with would-have-beens and should-have-beens, hopeful young things whose rise to prominence had been outpaced only by their fall into obscurity. Gino had been a professional for a little less than two years, but was already one of Italy's top racers. The fans knew his name; the journalists argued about how to pronounce it; his fellow competitors had learned to fear it. And yet all of them were asking the same question about his track record: Was this just another flash in the pan, or the start of something bigger?

✦

The answer lay in the Tour de France. Even for wheelmen a generation older than Gino, no other competition was more prominent or lucrative. The race itself was a perpetually fertile field for outlandish headlines; every aspect of it that could be writ large was writ still larger to ensure that it was the most talked-about event in the sport. The length of the course was outrageously long—several thousand miles around France—and it was designed so that the competitors would have to ride over the summits of several of France's highest mountain passes.

Yet for all its shimmering promise, it remained utterly unattainable for the cyclists of Italy. Despite a nearly endless run of attempts, only one Italian, Ottavio Bottecchia, had ever won the race. In the years that followed, the appeal of a Tour victory never faded. The prize money was part of the allure. Successful racers could hope to buy villas in the countryside or cabins by the sea, or to purchase a farm or launch a small business that would support them for the rest of their lives.

Gino, however, was interested in more than mere treasure; the scope of his ambition was decidedly larger. Achieving something that another Italian had already accomplished wasn't enough. He wanted to set a record that had never been attained by any man from any country: Gino wanted to win both the Giro d'Italia and the Tour de France—*in the same year.*

The idea had been raised before by other cyclists, but most experts had dismissed it as dangerous, foolhardy, and perhaps even physically impossible. It was easy to see why. To even attempt to pull it off, a cyclist would be forced to ride more than five thousand miles around Italy and France. To put that into perspective, this would be the equivalent of a cyclist racing against the best riders in Italy from Chicago to Seattle and then racing back from Seattle to New York, but facing a fresh group of international stars. True, there would be a four-week break between the two events. Yet with the schedule of short races, the cyclist's other obligation as a professional, it could hardly be called a time of rest.

The Giro and the Tour. Few men had ever dared to fully contemplate the weight of this challenge; none of them wanted it more than Gino. Still, dreaming about an impossible record could only take a man so far. In 1937, Gino decided to get on his bike and set it.

4

"Italy's Number One Sportsman"

Benito Mussolini rides a bicycle, circa 1928.

AS GINO ROLLED ONTO the national stage as a twenty-one-year-old sensation, he found a country obsessed with sport. It wasn't just the stars and the national champions who dominated the zeitgeist. Across the country, sports had permeated everything and had become such an integral part of everyday life by the 1930s that it was easy to forget that few Italians had practiced them before Gino's birth.

There was of course a small class of professional cyclists. And many Italians used bicycles as their main mode of transport. But the field of ordinary citizens playing sports for the sake of sports was much more limited and had been largely restricted to the well-heeled. All this started to change with World War I, which began days after Gino was born. Military conscription and the medical checkups required to enter the armed forces obliged Italian government officials to recognize the poor health and physical weakness of many of their citizens. Members of the lower classes were found to be the most wanting, plagued by ailments like tuberculosis and malaria and weakened by malnourishment. In the years that followed the war, Mussolini and his Fascist party fixated on this sense of national illness. As they rose to power in the 1920s, they latched on to sports as one of their central propaganda tools for creating a new Italy ruled by a healthy, athletic, and virile "warrior people."

Everyday life would soon reflect this fixation. Physical education became one of the most important components of the school curriculum, with students like Gino taking part in it daily in many parts of the country. Their teachers became "biological engineers and builders of the human machine," and new academies were opened to increase their numbers. The Fascist regime was so adamant about controlling children's athletic training that they even forbade other groups from being involved in this endeavor: The YMCA and various Catholic sports clubs were closed in 1927; the Boy Scouts were denounced as a "grotesque foreign imitation" and shut down in 1928.

Adults were strongly encouraged to dedicate their leisure time to a government-sponsored network of national sports and recreation clubs. Millions of Italians joined, and in just seven years the number of sports complexes in the country grew tenfold. Women began to practice different sports like gymnastics under the auspices of special fitness groups. Men competed in amateur cycling races or joined boxing clubs. A maxim of Mussolini's printed in large letters on the wall of a boxing club in Florence said it all: "I don't want a population of mandolin players, I want a population of fighters."

Even when they weren't playing sports, Italians were bombarded by advertisements and campaigns promising to make the country stronger and more rugged. One popular brand of cigarettes marketed itself as "The Cigarette of Great Athletes." Elsewhere in the country, a moral crusade was launched against the consumption of pasta, which was denigrated for causing "skepticism, sloth, and pessimism." High-ranking government officials weren't immune to the athletic demands of these campaigns, either. At one meeting of Fascist leaders in Rome, Achille Starace, the party secretary, demanded that they all dive from a springboard and swim fifty meters. On another occasion he demonstrated his own athletic prowess as he leaped over a wall of bayoneted rifles.

However newsworthy these activities were, none of them could hold a candle to Mussolini's performances. Playing tennis, driving sports cars, or riding his majestic white horse, he presented himself as an indefatigable sportsman for all to admire. He was all too happy to be photographed baring his chest, whether harvesting grain in the fields or skiing topless in the mountains. It was suggested that he did all of this on an ascetic diet—an improbable claim, given his fleshy frame. (Mussolini was said to forswear coffee, alcohol, and tobacco and survive on just a glass of milk for breakfast, a modest lunch, and another glass of milk and a piece of fruit for dinner.)

The controlling force behind all of this was an extensive propaganda apparatus that was more than happy to gloss over the truth or ignore it altogether. Few Italians at the time would have known, for instance, that Mussolini, like Hitler and Franco, had not been particularly interested in sports in his early life. Nor was it widely understood that photographers and newsreel cameramen consistently shot him from a low angle to lengthen his short, stocky body and draw some attention away from what one Italian historian described as his "big bald head, a pockmarked face and a prominent jaw." Instead, Italians were encouraged to obey their government and place full faith in their leader, "Italy's Number One Sportsman."

✦

As the Italian sports craze continued to ramp up, it couldn't have been a better time for Gino to discover cycling and launch his career. Many of the customers who came into the bike shop where Gino worked as a boy competed in amateur athletic clubs and professional teams that the government endorsed and financially supported. When Gino began competing himself, his first income—the prizes from various amateur and later professional races—often came from government coffers. Once he started winning regularly, the perks only improved. Gino, although nominally conscripted into the military in 1935 alongside the rest of the men in the country, was able to avoid many of his obligations until the onset of World War II.

On a broader level, the national focus on sports brought greater sports coverage in newspapers, even as higher-profile general interest stories about natural disasters or major accidents were being downplayed or silenced altogether by the regime. Increased coverage ensured that the names of budding stars like Gino shone that much more brightly in the public consciousness. Although such fame was satisfying in its own right for Gino, it carried a far more definitive value. In an era before international corporate endorsement deals, most of the earnings athletes like Gino could hope to generate came from appearance fees paid by organizers of smaller races throughout Europe. Those fees were determined by how often a racer won, and how big a crowd he could draw. Gino's prominence in the press therefore had a direct impact on his ability to support himself and his family.

Yet behind this national fixation lurked a political minefield. Absent a war, sport was one of the most convincing ways that the Fascists could promote their ideology outside of Italy. It was a "calling card for the nation abroad," as one historian described it. And so, in the physical culture of Fascism, athletes could no longer be just athletes—they were "blue ambassadors," charged with displaying "glorious actions in sports struggles against the strongest representatives of other races in the world." Their training methods were transformed from ordinary preparation into a de facto showcase of all the advances of Fascist theory and planning; their triumphs abroad were treated as propaganda victories of the highest order. In this political climate, as one Italian historian explained, "a gold medal in any discipline at the Olympic Games, or in the Tour de France, was more important than a thousand diplomatic acts, in as much as to celebrate victory meant to celebrate Italy and Fascism."

Living in this world of Fascist sport, Gino began to find that the decision makers who surrounded him were increasingly driven by political motives. Athletic governing bodies, like the Italian Cycling Federation, which helped assemble national teams and set schedules, were often staffed by high-ranking Fascist party members; the members of the press covering a sport answered to the regime, not to the readers or racers. A star athlete like Gino who didn't share all of the regime's ideological positions thus found himself in an unenviable position. On top of all the normal pressures of high-level athletic training, he was forced to endure the shifting political tides with few steadfast allies.

✦

With his first Giro d'Italia under his belt, Gino was Italy's most promising cyclist heading into the 1937 season. But in March, Gino's year almost ended before it had even started. During a training ride from Milan to Florence, he was caught off guard by a snowstorm. Exhausted by the ride and overwhelmed by the cold, wet weather, he arrived back in Florence with a terrible fever and a phlegmatic cough. Watching his burning temperature rise, his family grew worried. A doctor was called, and his examination yielded a frightening diagnosis of bronchial pneumonia. Little is known about the medical specifics of Gino's case, but pneumonia was still a serious threat to one's life in 1937. "You can imagine [my mother] Giulia's state," Gino said. Given that, the sequence of events that followed could hardly have been more surprising. Not only was Gino deemed healthy enough to race the Giro d'Italia six weeks later, in May, but he was strong enough to win the race.

His victory sent the Fascist press into a tizzy. Gino had not only validated all the hopes they had placed in him, but he had also given credence to the idea that he could bring even greater honor to Italy by becoming the first cyclist to win the Giro and the Tour in the same year. Immediately the Tour de France became *the* discussion topic of the moment. One Fascist magazine summed up everything the race represented to Fascist Italy: "There is no point hiding it: the Tour de France, because of the enormous interest it arouses in all the athletic nations of the continent, is an event of exceptional significance. Winning it would be a clamorous affirmation of great international resonance."

Gino resisted all this chatter and spoke openly about not racing at the Tour. The dream of winning both the Tour and Giro in the same year certainly still burned brightly for him, but his doctor's warnings about his health made him feel that he should put off his plans for another year. Winning the Giro after a bout of pneumonia was incredible enough; trying to win both the Tour and the Giro was asking for trouble.

Il Popolo d'Italia, the newspaper founded by Mussolini that was the official press organ of the regime, pushed back hard. As an opening gambit, its lead cycling journalist gave Gino some benefit of the doubt regarding his pneumonia. He then assured readers that Gino had "to understand that at the Tour de France the national honor of our cycling is at stake," which overruled any of Gino's personal concerns about his health.

Gino still resisted, and speculation continued to swirl that he would decline participating in the Tour. *Il Popolo d'Italia* struck back even more forcefully. In a telling display of the unchecked power of the Fascist press, they invented a story that Gino was holding out for a 200,000-lire payoff from the regime to attend the Tour. They mocked his faith and then used the cold language of war to accuse him of not being patriotic:

> A soldier who defends his flag leaves the trenches, risking his life without thinking of his bank account. He thinks of his Homeland and of his mother and goes. In the land of France, it is a matter of going to defend our flag. . . . Bartali is called to

> represent our sport, our youth, our strength, and all our eyes are on him, many of them rather ill-disposed.

The article ended in a menacing tone, noting that the head of the Italian Cycling Federation, who was also a military general, would visit Gino and ensure his participation in the 1937 Tour.

✦

As Gino waited for this ominous meeting, he could survey the challenging European sports landscape. Two sportsmen of a similar caliber offered models of how he might navigate a relationship with a dictatorial regime that he was unwilling to endorse openly. The first was Max Schmeling, a heavyweight boxer who was riding a tidal wave of support in his native Germany after having defeated the American boxer Joe Louis in a widely followed match in New York in June 1936. Dark-haired and brawnier than Atlas, Schmeling had glided smoothly through the tumult that was German politics after World War I. In the 1920s he had befriended leading figures of the left, like the author Heinrich Mann. As Adolf Hitler and the Nazis rose to power, however, he quickly changed tack and cultivated friends on the right.

Schmeling's shift raised few eyebrows; his saving grace was an enterprising sense of discretion. Where other athletes might have attempted to curry political favor by loudly supporting Nazi policy, Schmeling was tight-lipped. He avoided making any public comments, either positive or negative, about Nazi politics that might upset his professional prospects abroad, likely aware that much of his earning potential rested in his ability to compete in lucrative prizefights in the United States. In his actions and in his private life, however, Schmeling was able to maneuver more freely. To his credit, he chose to shelter two Jewish boys during Kristallnacht, the violent attack carried out on Jews in Germany and Austria in November 1938. Yet he also chose to meet privately with Hitler, a devoted fan, and developed a close friendship with Joseph Goebbels, the Nazi minister of propaganda.

On the other side of the spectrum stood Ottavio Bottecchia, the first Italian ever to win the Tour de France with back-to-back victories in 1924 and 1925. A former lumberjack with Socialist leanings, he had little sympathy for Mussolini or the Fascist regime. Talking with one of France's leading investigative journalists, Bottecchia had spoken freely about his political views and his interest in acting on them in some capacity. Any political work he might have been doing or planning was cut short, however, in June 1927 when he died unexpectedly while on a training ride in northeastern Italy.

The details that emerged about his death were highly suspicious. His cranium had been smashed and several other bones were broken, but his bike was found unscratched some distance away from where he lay. Similarly, the stretch of road where he was found had only the slightest slope, and there were no skid marks or other evidence that a car had caused his death. Despite all this, there was little in the way of an investigation, and the cause of death was hastily attributed to a fainting spell. Such an assessment seemed highly dubious for an elite endurance athlete who had shown no signs of illness during Tours raced under far more arduous conditions.

Rumors spread like wildfire in the absence of any credible explanations. One of the most plausible held that Bottecchia had been killed by the Fascists—if not by members of the Fascist party itself, then perhaps by affiliated individuals looking to bootlick certain officials. This was the theory held by the French investigative journalist who had spoken with Bottecchia, and years later it would receive a certain degree of affirmation. One of the last people to see Bottecchia alive—the parish priest who administered his last rites—told an Italian writer he believed the theory that Fascists were culpable; an Italian émigré in New York would later confess to the murder on his own deathbed. Neither story is wholly conclusive, and so Bottecchia's death remains a mystery to this day.

In the 1930s, however, the shadow cast by Bottecchia's death was more ominous. The circle of competitive cyclists in Italy was close-knit, and word of his untimely death would have traveled quickly. Coming after the high-profile murder of the leftist politician Matteotti, it was no wonder that many sportsmen would draw the same conclusion. In Mussolini's Italy, no man, not even a famous athlete, was ever fully beyond the regime's reach.

✦

When it came to his own political choices, Gino chose to align himself with the Catholic Church, which was perhaps the most powerful constituency in Italy apart from the Fascist party. It wasn't an entirely surprising choice. He had long been a committed churchgoer, and with the death of his brother, Giulio, he had further devoted himself to the activities of Catholic Action. A number of his closest friends were Church leaders, such as the archbishop of Florence, Cardinal Elia Dalla Costa. Above all, Gino's faith had become integral to his everyday life, and it was the root of his determination on the bike, or, as he put it, "It gave me the push to try again."

What was surprising was how zealously and publicly the Church embraced Gino. In the course of just two years, leading Catholic figures elevated him to the highest stature. Journalists of the Catholic press praised him as a "magnificent Christian athlete" and reported his races in the language of biblical ecstasy. Catholic poets wrote long sonnets about him, comparing him to a three-engined aircraft as he rode on his bike. There was even a play written about him titled *Arriva Bartali* (*Bartali Is Coming*), which was performed in small theaters and churches around the country.

If the unifying theme behind much of the coverage of Gino was his faith, the motive for highlighting this piety was rooted more in politics—and the lingering tensions between the Church and the Fascist regime. Rather than openly criticizing a regime that endorsed a culture of violence and machismo, personified by bloody boxing matches and a winking approval of mistresses, Catholic writers and artists tried instead to promote Gino as an alternative icon for Italian youth. Gino, as a pious member of Catholic Action who attended mass weekly and prayed daily, was obviously cut from a very different cloth than the average Fascist athlete. These facts could be easily highlighted, and readers could be trusted to draw the correct inferences about the Church's attitude regarding the Fascist vision of sport.

In large part, this positioning worked. It won Gino, and the Church leaders behind him, the support of the sports press. When, for example, a few Fascist newspapers began to mock all the fawning coverage of Gino's religious devotion by referring to him as *Il Fraticello* or "the Little Monk," it was an otherwise areligious sports newspaper that published a rigorous defense of Gino and his right to active membership in the Church. Some in the hard-line Fascist press might have been tempted to push back, or drop their coverage of the star altogether, but the hard truth of the matter was that Gino had one thing going for him that even the most grudging anti-Catholic critic had to accept: he won races.

In the first half of the 1930s, Italy had no shortage of successful athletes. Primo Carnera became the first Italian ever to win the heavyweight boxing championship, and then declared that his victory was "for Italy and for Il Duce." At the Olympic Games in Los Angeles in 1932, audiences watched as the Italian team, nicknamed "Mussolini's boys," marched in Fascist formation at the opening ceremonies and then went on to win twelve gold medals and placed second only to the United States in the overall rankings. Mussolini addressed the athletes soon afterward: "Four years lie before you. Use the time to prepare well. In Los Angeles, you were second. In Berlin, it's necessary to be first."

The dream of lasting sports dominance never materialized. Carnera lost the heavyweight title, and was soon faring so poorly in international fights that his passport was revoked to stop him from embarrassing the country abroad. The Italian Olympic athletes did no better. When the Olympic Games came to Berlin in 1936, the Italian regime watched as German athletes won more than four times as many medals as their Italian counterparts. This must have been hard for Mussolini to stomach. In three years of power, Hitler had crafted the formidable showcase of athletic prowess that Mussolini had not been able to build in fourteen.

The Italian Cycling Federation officials making plans for the 1937 Tour de France must have viewed all of this with excitement and perhaps even trepidation. At a moment when their sports-obsessed regime was starved for champions, they had Gino, a racer who was blazing a meteoric path to the top of his sport. No single race had ever been so important.

Desperate but stubborn and still recovering from his brush with pneumonia, Gino may have thought about standing his ground and not going to France for the 1937 Tour. But doing so would have amounted to committing professional suicide, if not worse, just as he was within striking distance of his sport's most prestigious title. If he defied the Fascists, they could stop him from competing, thus dethroning him from his vaulted position among the fans. A lesser form of retaliation might have been to reach out to someone in the press to stop the character assassination. Such a request, however, most likely would have been ignored. At a moment when the regime was censoring not just the content of articles but even the smallest details of how the stories were laid out in the newspaper, few journalists would have had the courage to make a fuss over an athlete claiming libel.

If Gino didn't know all of this already, he found out quickly. True to *Il Popolo*'s prediction, he buckled after the visit from the head of the Italian Cycling Federation. Just twelve days before the Tour was to begin, he made a short statement declaring his intention to compete. With that, he packed his bags and got ready for France.

✦

The Tour of 1937 began with more exciting unknowns than most other years in the Tour's history. There was a significant new rule change—described by one modern cycling historian as the Tour's only "truly radical change" in over a century of existence—that permitted the derailleur, or gear-shifter, to be used on all Tour bikes. Riders who had once been forced to dismount and flip their rear wheel to change gears could now change gears on the roll, though they would still need to pedal backward, lean down, and move the chain with their hand or a small lever, depending on their bike's design. Predictably, however, the press spilled more ink on the sensational development of Gino's arrival. Although it was his debut attempt at the race, many reporters in Italy and abroad had already pegged him as a favorite to win.

Even the most exuberant, however, recognized that there were many reasons to be cautious. First, there was a question of competitive endurance. With thirty-one stages fit into just twenty-six days, Gino would face a punishing schedule of races. Second, there were the mountains. For the first time in his career, Gino would face both the Alps and the Pyrenees in the same race. Finally, there was the unavoidable issue of distance. At more than 2,740 miles, the Tour was by far the longest race in which Gino had ever competed—and this distance would come just one month after he had raced some 2,300 miles around Italy.

For all the concerns that some held, Gino performed well in the first portion of the Tour. In the early stages he cycled cautiously, assessed his competitors, and kept the top racers within his line of sight. By the Alps, the first range of mountains to be crossed, he became more aggressive. On the stage from Aix-les-Bains to Grenoble, he summited the imposing Col du Galibier—the Galibier mountain pass—first. Riding confidently, he crossed the finish line with enough of a lead to secure the yellow jersey awarded to the overall leader.

Many in the press took it as a confirmation of their early assessment of Gino. The Italian delegation, who were easily identified by their elegantly tailored suits and monocles, were particularly pleased. An Italian taking the lead before the Tour was even one-third finished offered them an almost limitless opportunity for baroque praise. The *bartaliani,* Gino's most loyal fans, had their own reason to rejoice. A win in the Alps opened up the real possibility that their hero would carry the yellow jersey all the way to Paris. *L'Auto,* the principal French daily newspaper covering the race, summed up the feelings of both groups in the edition that was delivered to newsstands across France on July 8: "Bartali will never be caught. . . . on the contrary, he will increase his advantage in every mountain stage."

✦

Just hours later, everything changed. About halfway into the day's race, the German Otto Weckerling broke away. A group of some thirty racers chased after him, seemingly oblivious to the gentle rain that fell on them. Although it cut through the mountains, the road was wide enough that the men could ride with a few leaders at the front and a large group following behind. A few miles after Embrun, the road narrowed as it crossed a small bridge over the Colau River. Gino, who was riding closely behind his teammate Giulio Rossi, steeled himself for the overpass. The rest of the riders in the group closed ranks alongside him to cross it, each man adjusting a bike that was often just inches from the ones in front of it and behind it.

Whether it was because of the rain or the shifting movement of the group, Rossi slipped and fell. Gino swerved instinctively to avoid riding into his friend. He hit the side of the bridge and was thrown some three meters high, "like a ball into space," over the edge. Falling into a shallow Alpine river below, he was overcome by intense pain and soaked from head to toe by the frigid water that flowed from the mountains.

Above, two of his other teammates swerved to avoid hitting his bike and fell as well. One of them quickly dusted himself off and scampered down to the river's edge. Wading in, he lifted Gino's pale and shivering arm around his shoulder and helped him back up to the roadside. Propping up Gino's bicycle, he coaxed his captain back onto it.

"Get on the bike, Bartali. Get on it. I'm here. We will do the route together, slowly. Don't worry, we're no more than thirty kilometers from the finish. It's over."

And Gino, with his left hand clutching his kidneys, began to pedal. Rossi, whose legs and arms looked "like bloody steaks," was rushed off to the local hospital. To no one's surprise, he quit the Tour.

In Briançon, Weckerling crossed the finish line first. Farther back, Gino did complete the stage, but lost nine minutes because of the accident. "I was mute, physically mute; I raced with my mind alone," Gino explained later. By the evening, Gino seemed to have regained his composure. Although he suffered a painful cough at first, he felt strong enough to continue. The subsequent stages seemed to validate his assessment. His torso was "bound up tightly like a newborn baby," as Gino put it, but he raced competitively through the Alps. He impressed the Tour founder enough for him to remark that he was in "full health and form." Another Tour organizer even predicted a strong performance by Gino in the second mountain series, the Pyrenees.

The Italian Cycling Federation, however, saw it differently. They announced Gino's withdrawal from the Tour for health reasons. Gino would later maintain that the real reason was politically motivated—he was not a card-carrying Fascist. There might be a grain of truth to this. Members of the Cycling Federation may have taken the initiative to withdraw Gino to stave off the possibility of any new accidents that might further embarrass the Italian team and, by extension, themselves or the Fascist Party. Or perhaps their logic was simpler. Seeing the leader's nearly seventeen-minute advantage, they might have dismissed Gino's chances at victory as a hopeless waste of time.

Gino would never forgive them for interfering in his career. "I was crying. I had such great dreams for that Tour and all of them went up in smoke." Gino said. Then he elaborated: "When the doctor didn't want me to race, 'they' made me race; when I should have withdrawn, they made me continue; when, after the four difficult stages, I was getting better, they sent me home." This final indignity would rile him the most. In his autobiography, he would call it the "greatest injustice suffered in [his] career."

Gino shared all of these thoughts when he could speak freely again after World War II. In 1937, however, he had to bite his tongue, swallow the tears, and pack his bags. The Italian Cycling Federation left him to make his own arrangements to get home, and with little money on hand, he had to borrow funds to buy his train ticket. After all the disappointments of France, he found some relief at the train station in Italy when onlookers who spotted him began to applaud him enthusiastically. Speaking to the press, he said he would take some time off to recuperate. And then, already planning the following year's cycling season, he promised to try again to win the Giro and the Tour in the same year.

In a few months, however, he would learn that prominent figures in the Fascist regime disagreed with his plans. In early 1938, Gino met with Mussolini's national sports directors—who supervised all sports bodies, including the Italian Cycling Federation—to discuss the upcoming season. It was the type of stuffy gathering that Gino despised because he had to obtain approval for his training and race plans from government-appointed authorities who didn't actually care about his well-being and "had as much to do with cycling as cabbage with snack time." The authorities quickly made their intentions clear. An Italian had to win the 1938 Tour for the international glory of Italy. Though irritated by their pushiness, Gino started to explain how he would accomplish that goal. "I will do just what I did last year. I will only train for races in stages. I'll do a few little races, more to honor commitments already made than anything else—even if I will try to win them—then the Giro d'Italia and—"

"One moment," the officials interrupted him. "The Giro is long, difficult and hard in and of itself. It's a useless waste of effort and it could be damaging. You are not doing the Giro and you will prepare yourself only to race the Tour."

"What?" Gino sputtered. The Giro—the most important race in Italy? Had he misheard them? "I'm not doing the Giro? I'm perfectly healthy, I assure you; I'm in shape. Listen to me. I know my body and I know how far I can take it. You have always said that I'm a serious racer, right? So then give me this proof of faith."

"No, there's nothing that can be done. We're advising you against it." Their tone left little doubt that this recommendation was an order. "The risk is also ours and we don't feel like taking the risk."

Angry but powerless, Gino acquiesced again. "There was nothing else to say. I had to grin and bear it and be a good boy about it. And yet as the weeks passed, I felt myself unnerved."

✦

The spring of 1938 brought political news that was destined to steal the headlines from sport: Mussolini would host Adolf Hitler for a series of meetings in Italy. The two had met once earlier in the decade, when they had a tense discussion about their conflicting interests in Austria. Time and the exigencies of politics, however, changed matters quickly. By 1938, bristling from the international criticism generated by his invasion of Ethiopia in 1935 and impressed by Germany's rapid military buildup, Mussolini was eager to start anew. He made plans to showcase the nation's military and its resources in Naples and Rome to prove Italy's strength to the Germans. Florence was set as the final stop of the visit. The home of Michelangelo and Botticelli, it was a perfect setting for the more personal task of fostering better relations with a failed artist like Hitler.

Mussolini and his party officials were determined to make it a perfect trip. A committee comprising high-ranking public works officials, an architecture school, and some twenty architects and artists was formed and tasked with carrying out "Operation Florence Beautiful." Buildings everywhere—even Ponte Vecchio—were restored, repainted, and revarnished. Nazi flags were raised in prominent locations, and Renaissance-style banners were hung all over the city, turning one central street into a long tunnel of blue. By the time the work was finished, it was said that many Florentines hardly recognized their own city.

Members of the Jewish community in Italy had reason to be more skeptical about all the preparations. Although they had once been persecuted and marginalized, Hitler's visit came during a golden era of liberties for Jews. After fighting alongside their Gentile countrymen to unite Italy in the nineteenth century, Italian Jews had become fully integrated members of national life in Italy; talented individuals in the community had risen to prominence in the arts, business, and politics. There was even a small group of Jewish Fascists, which underlined the reality that the rabid anti-Semitism that had played such an integral part in Nazism's rise did not have a voice in the early years of Fascism's reign. The fact that Italy was now hosting Hitler seemed to contradict all of this. It also flew in the face of Mussolini's earlier public criticism of Nazi anti-Semitism. Even if it was just a short trip or a routine diplomatic gesture, it was hard to see it as anything but disconcerting.

On the day of Hitler's arrival in early May, all the diplomatic stagecraft and theatrics came to a climactic finish. First, Mussolini arrived by train, showcasing a piece of Nazi military insignia on his uniform. Fifteen minutes later, Hitler arrived on a separate train, wearing the light brown Nazi uniform with an Italian Fascist dagger displayed prominently on his belt. Mussolini greeted Hitler and the two men shook hands vigorously. Later, Mussolini would privately speculate to his foreign minister that Hitler was wearing rouge on his cheeks to disguise his ghostly pallor.

After the formal greetings, the leaders were seated in the lead car of a motorcade of convertibles and began a whirlwind tour of the city. They visited a Fascist shrine and viewed exhibitions of priceless Renaissance masterpieces. A fancy dinner followed, along with a trip to the Florence opera for Verdi's *Simon Boccanegra*. On the streets, crowds were only too happy to yell out their roaring affirmations; preemptive arrests a few days earlier had removed people considered possible threats for protests, violence, or embarrassment to the regime.

Others, notably many Jews in Florence, silenced themselves and steered clear of the celebrations for fear they would be prime targets for violence. One Jewish family, the Donatis, became fearful well in advance of Hitler's visit. They had refused to put a swastika up alongside the Italian flag that usually hung on their porch. A chairman for their building, an official assigned by the Fascist government, intervened and insisted they hang the Nazi flag. On May 22, the day of Hitler's visit, the Donati family fled their home, an impressive edifice built in the style of an old palazzo that stood near the train tracks where Hitler's train passed by. The Donatis hid in the basement of their porter's apartment until the event was over.

Italian Jews could not speak up, but there was one voice of protest that refused to embrace the swastika and could get away with it because the speaker was too visible to arrest. He was Cardinal Elia Dalla Costa, the archbishop of Florence. The cardinal, who was also a friend of Gino Bartali's, was determined to share his opinion on Hitler's visit and decided to carry out a protest by himself. In a rebuke of the Fascists' remodeling of Florence, he forbade any decoration of the city's famous cathedral or diocesan office. Likewise, he had the front doors of another church locked before Hitler and Mussolini arrived to visit it, forcing them to enter through a humble service entry. Finally, he was conspicuously absent from all the official activities that day, choosing instead to spend time in the city's prisons with his fellow dissidents.

It's possible that the Nazi officials picked up on these slights, because their Italian counterparts certainly did. In secret files maintained far away in Rome, Fascist spies duly noted Dalla Costa's anti-Fascist affront in a report they compiled about him. The Fascists in Florence responded with more outright vitriol; they apparently wanted to set the cardinal's office aflame, according to a priest who worked with Dalla Costa. They could take consolation, however, in the fact that the rest of the day went smoothly. At the end of his tour, Hitler evinced his full satisfaction, and there was little reason to doubt his sincerity. It was obvious that no expense had been spared in his honor. When all was said and done, some nineteen million lire had been spent sprucing up the city for his visit at a moment when most average working-class men could hope to earn but one thousand lire per month. It would take the city almost two years to pay off all the debt incurred for an event that lasted all of twelve hours.

The highlight of the trip for someone as interested in architecture as Hitler may well have been the excursion up to Piazzale Michelangelo, the midpoint of one of Gino's favorite boyhood bike rides. Up there, Hitler and Mussolini took in the whole city, with an art historian offering commentary about the city's various buildings and monuments. When they were finished, they could enjoy the piazzale itself, whose "pavement had been temporarily relandscaped to incorporate plantings in the form of swastikas and fasci [Fascist emblems]."

All the diplomatic pageantry came to a close around midnight at Florence's main train station. Mussolini exchanged warm farewells with Hitler as he prepared to board his train and return to Germany. No doubt speaking in his characteristically emphatic voice, Mussolini made a bold declaration:

"Now no force can ever separate us!"

At this, Hitler's eyes were said to have moistened a little with tears.

✦

In June, the Italian soccer team brought sports back to the front pages of newspapers. At the beginning of the month, they went off to the World Cup in Paris with the highest of hopes. Four years earlier, in what was perhaps Italy's last great international sports victory, they had won the World Cup on their home turf. Described as a precursor to Berlin's infamous 1936 Olympics, the 1934 World Cup had been exploited to the maximum for propaganda purposes. The players saluted Mussolini from the field, and their ultimate victory in the event was trumpeted in the press as a triumph of Fascist policy.

In centrist France, however, such heavy-handed politicking played poorly among spectators. Although the Italians would win the World Cup again in 1938, anti-Fascist fans booed them mercilessly when they played part of a match in Fascist black shirts. They were even more aggressive with the German soccer team, pelting them with broken bottles. Predictably, the press in Italy reacted negatively to this treatment. One Italian magazine accused the French of being led by nefarious Bolshevists and suggested that the Italian team hadn't just vanquished another team, but rather a whole "city, a prejudice, a violent injustice."

The antagonism in France could do little to diminish the excitement of the victory celebrations awaiting the players in Italy. A lavish event was carried out in Rome, where Mussolini praised the players during a two-day ceremony attended by several thousand athletes and Fascist party members from across the country. The militant undertones of the proceedings were always readily apparent, with the players wearing full army and navy uniforms as they were photographed with Mussolini for newspaper cover pages.

After the victory at the World Cup, the focus immediately turned to the fast-approaching Tour de France and Italy's highest hope: Gino Bartali. Some days later, in deference to the excitement bubbling around the country, the bridge between the two competitions was made more concrete. In a well-publicized gesture, the soccer players' jerseys were gathered up and given to Gino and the Italian cyclists to carry as good-luck charms to France.

Few gifts could have carried with them a heavier burden of expectations.

✦

The final days before the departure for the Tour were a whirlwind of activity in Italy. The Italian Cycling Federation helped coordinate support staff and organized the team's travel, booking a full first-class sleeper carriage for the racers' journey to France. The coach, Costante Girardengo, met his cyclists and discussed elements of the racing strategy that he had refined over the last few months. Several of the less experienced team members did final training runs in Voltaggio, a small city in the north of Italy. Others, who had just spent three weeks racing around Italy in the Giro d'Italia, made final arrangements before a trip that would take them out of the country for at least four weeks if not longer.

Gino spent his days more quietly. Having been forced to sit out the Giro, he had found himself with more free time than usual over the last few months. But if those long hours should have given him time for rest, they yielded him nothing but anxiety. Agitated and restless, he felt the loss of his brother, Giulio, even more acutely. The only salve was the calm of the Ponte a Ema cemetery, especially at twilight, when few others were around. "It was my most intense period for cemetery visits," he said later. "I was talking with Giulio in order to vent and to free myself from the nervousness that was suffocating me." Again and again, these conversations jumped from the recent past to the present. His last attempt in France had felt rushed and haphazard. With all its frustrations, however, he could take some solace in being sabotaged by forces outside his control. This year, the weight of it all stood on his shoulders alone. Seven years of racing, and thousands of miles in the saddle. A whole nation expecting him to win; several others hoping that he would not. Everything, every thought, concern, and anxiety, led back to one predictable place.

The Tour.

✦

On his final evening in Florence, Gino felt himself drawn again to the cemetery and its cool white stone tombs. It was a balmy night, but the cypress trees were a bit gloomy at that hour. Along the streets, the purple blossoms on the wisteria trees moved slowly in the gentle breeze. Standing in front of Giulio's tomb, with its familiar photo of Giulio atop his bicycle looking back at him, Gino began to say the words spoken so many times before:

> *Dear Giulio, you see what condition I find myself in here. I can't go on. The authorities want me to go race for the prestige of Italy. I am happy that they have chosen me, of course.*
>
> *But if I lose?*

5

Storm at the Summit

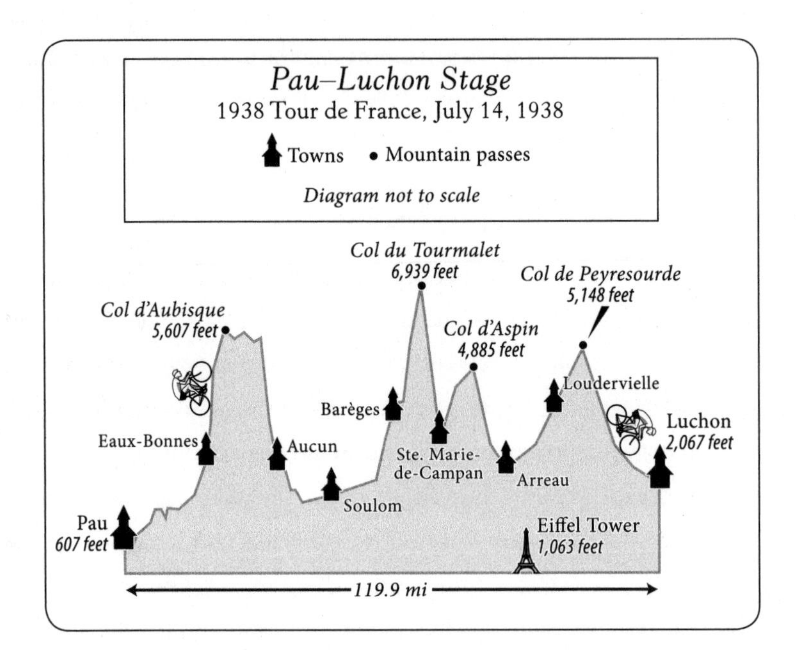

CROWDS CHEERED AS THE Italian cycling team boarded the train in Turin on the evening of June 29, 1938. The following day, shortly after nine, they arrived in Paris. As they stepped off the train, the team was greeted by French members of the press and a small crowd of Italian immigrants. Many of the Italian cyclists posed for photos and chatted with the press while their luggage and equipment were transferred to a private bus. Gino, however, was more reserved. He was overcome for a moment by the memories of his last trip to the Tour and his disastrous fall. But he shook off his melancholy and decided to focus instead on the days ahead. *The past is set,* he thought, *but the future is still unwritten.*

When all their kit had been gathered up, the whole team was whisked off to the luxurious hotel Pavillon Henri IV on the outskirts of Paris. With views of the Seine and Paris, the hotel was a former palace of the *Roi Soleil,* the Sun King Louis XIV, and the locale where Alexandre Dumas wrote his wildly popular novels *The Count of Monte Cristo* and *The Three Musketeers.* The colorful history of the hotel only seemed to bolster the spirits of the Italian cyclists. They were happy to laugh away their time together, with some lounging around in the jerseys given them by the soccer team while others, including Gino, engaged in playful games of soccer in one of the rooms.

Costante Girardengo, the coach of the Italian cycling team, was not nearly as carefree. Girardengo knew the giddy allure of being a famous rider; he had worn that mantle himself. In the 1920s, he was among the first Italian riders to be dubbed a *campionissimo* or a "champion of champions." He won the Giro d'Italia twice, and scores of regional races throughout Italy. At the height of his success, it was even declared that certain trains would stop in his birthplace of Novi Ligure in Piedmont, a sign of respect usually reserved for government officials. But the Tour title had always eluded him. When racing the Tour de France in 1914, Girardengo fell several times, most notably during a stage that ended in the French town of Luchon, compelling him to drop out of the race. World War I would force the Tour into a four-year hiatus; Girardengo never returned to race it again.

Forty-five years old, Girardengo had the bronzed complexion of a man who had spent much of his life in the sun. He was not tall, and his compact frame had grown stocky since retiring—a common occurrence for retired wheelmen, who ate as if they were still riding hundreds of miles per week. In photographs, he occasionally offers a glimpse of his breezy former life as a racer. In one happy picture, he appears wearing radiant white trousers and a pair of white patent leather shoes. But in person, his manner was anything but lighthearted. Stern-faced and severe, his mouth seemed to form a permanent scowl. And getting him to answer a reporter's question was, as one newspaper diplomatically described it, a "superhuman task."

Whether due to his anxious gait or his terse manner of speaking, it was obvious that the task of coaching the Italian team in 1938 weighed heavily on Girardengo. Perhaps his biggest challenge was to unite men who were used to racing against one another on different professional teams into one cohesive national team. Gino, who was captain of the team sponsored by Legnano, a major Italian bicycle manufacturer, would have to learn to ride beside racers who had been his fierce rivals in competitions throughout Italy. An inability to cooperate fully would doom the team's prospects in the Tour.

Beyond these strategic issues, other concerns were decidedly more amusing. One ongoing headache was the team clown, a rider named Aldo Bini. Young and incorrigibly handsome, Bini was a hopeless flirt who had received his first phone call from a female admirer within thirty minutes of arriving at the hotel in Paris. Looking to keep an eye on him, Girardengo put Bini in the room next to his own. He also assigned him a roommate who was older and married—a tactic that did not escape Bini's notice. True to his nature, Bini could hardly resist the possibilities for romance that France afforded him. When the Tour started, he would be spotted kissing and embracing enthusiastic French girls at the finish lines. And one night he was so successful in charming a pair of women who happened to be staying at the same hotel that Girardengo felt compelled to stand guard for hours outside of his room lest Bini try to sneak out.

Bini and the other Italian riders were all too happy to ham it up for the newspapermen, but Gino often tried to avoid them altogether. Still, the members of the foreign press, many of whom considered Gino a favorite to win the Tour, were eager to size him up. They hounded him with questions and photo requests, but the results left something to be desired. With an average height and wiry build, Gino was hardly an imposing figure when photographed. His prominent Roman nose was slightly crooked because it hadn't healed properly after he had fractured it four years earlier in an accident at a regional competition in Italy. (The episode also left his nose with a sun-shaped round scar on the tip.) The rest of his body was quite strong, but he was not overly muscular. He appeared "delicate, nervous and . . . quite fragile," according to one journalist. His limbs were sinewy, and the most prominent features on the thin arms that stretched out from his woolen jersey were the veins. They "remind you of ivy climbing the trunk of an oak tree," remarked another writer. But rarely weighing more than 149 pounds, Gino resembled a slender cypress more than an oak. Always sensitive to his slight appearance, Gino himself claimed to be made of harder wood, "like the olive trees in the fields around Siena where my father was born." No one, however, could deny that his legacy in Italy was imposing, and the fact that he had been deliberately sidelined from the Giro to steel himself for the Tour escaped few in France.

As the start of the race drew near, the anticipation about Gino and all the other racers reached fever pitch. Unfortunately, the first casualty occurred on the opening day of the race. As the ninety-six riders rode from the offices of the Tour organizer, the *L'Auto* newspaper, to the starting line, they were surrounded by a turbulent current of thousands of cheering Parisians. Many were dressed in dapper suits and rode alongside them on bicycles and motorcycles, and in cars. Amid the chaos, a motorcycle slammed into a French rider and knocked him from his bike. He climbed back on and rode with the others to the starting line. He wouldn't, however, make it beyond the second stage as a result of the injuries he'd sustained.

The members of the press flirted with danger as they wove among the crowds and the cyclists on motorcycles and in cars. By 1938, newspapers from all over Europe regularly sent dozens of reporters and photographers to cover the Tour. The rush to score the best photos and stories was as competitive as the race itself, with some newspapers even supplying their own private airplanes to shuttle photographs and stories back to editors. Radio broadcasters were no different, with French channels alone offering almost twenty different newscasts in 1938 on any given day of racing.

Some might have thought that all the attention and the jostling detracted from the race, but the truth was that the press was as central to the Tour as the cyclists themselves. At its core, the Tour was a grandiose publicity stunt, and the competitive spirit between reporters stemmed from the very reason it had been created in the first place: the ambition to sell more newspapers.

✦

On a cold day in November 1902, Henri Desgrange, a former cyclist turned magazine editor, ate lunch with a colleague, a sportswriter named Géo Lefèvre, at the Zimmer Madrid Hotel in Paris. Both wore vests and knee-length black frock coats, and both were at loose ends. Their magazine, *L'Auto-Vélo,* was barely two years old and on the brink of bankruptcy. They needed to improve circulation immediately. As they discussed strategies to remedy the situation, Desgrange and Lefèvre noted how a popular invention—the bicycle—had boosted sales for various other publications for several decades. In 1869, *Le Vélocipède Illustré* sponsored an eighty-mile race between Paris and Rouen. *Véloce-Sport* followed suit, and promoted a three-hundred-mile race between Bordeaux and Paris in 1891. In the same year, *Le Petit Journal* bested *Véloce-Sport* by organizing an even longer event, a 743-mile road race from Paris to Brest and back. All of these competitions had been successful in driving up circulation as spectators along the route and throughout the nation snapped up copies of the newspapers to get the latest updates.

None of this was news to Desgrange, who had stood front and center in the world of early cycling competitions. A former law clerk, he set the first world one-hour record of twenty-two miles in 1893. After he retired from cycling, he continued promoting the sport and even wrote a book about how to become a master cyclist. In 1900, he was hired to lead *L'Auto-Vélo,* a young newspaper trying to upstage its rival, *Le Vélo.*

The conversation at lunch on this day kept returning to the topic of races. Whether in France or in the United States, where thousands of breathless fans filled stadiums to watch the famous six-day cycling competitions, there was something universally appealing about them. Mulling it all over, Lefèvre had a novel idea. What about combining the excitement of the road races popularized in France with the hypnotic appeal of the six-day American events? Fleshing his idea out further, he described a multiday race that traveled through various French cities. Desgrange reportedly paused and then replied, "If I understand you, *petit* Géo, you're proposing a 'Tour de France'?"

Notwithstanding a few hiccups along the way (the Tour's length was reduced from thirty-five days to nineteen because so few people initially signed up), Desgrange's project came to fruition in the summer of 1903. Sixty riders left Paris on a taxing 1,509-mile stage race moving clockwise around the country. Many stages took over twenty-four hours. The start times were scheduled at indecent hours, like 2:30 a.m. in Lyons or 11:00 p.m. in Bordeaux, but timed to the newspapers' publication schedules so that the morning headlines would bear the latest updates. The winner was a Frenchman named Maurice Garin, known as the "little chimney sweep" because he stood five feet three inches and had cleaned chimneys before he became a cyclist.

In its second year, overzealous fans almost ended the Tour before it had even returned to Paris. In Nîmes, in southeastern France, they blocked the race route with a barricade, forcing cyclists to dismount and use their bikes as shields as they fought their way through the crowds. Farther south, fiercely loyal supporters of a local cyclist competing in the Tour tried to sabotage the chances of rival riders by littering the road with bottles, stones, and nails. During one stage, Garin himself was attacked by an angry mob, and during another he declared, "If I'm not murdered before Paris, I'll win the race again." Surveying all of this, the Tour organizers quickly realized that they would need rules to rein in the spectators as well as the riders if they wanted the race to continue.

✦

Desgrange famously said that his ideal Tour would be so herculean that only one racer would manage to finish it. After the success of the first Tours, he tinkered with the race route constantly, making each year's race seem more arduous than the last. In 1910, the Tour entered the high mountain ranges of the Pyrenees for the first time. The course was so challenging that the riders nearly revolted. A French racer named Octavio Lapize, who had won various stages in 1909, was forced to get off of his bike several times because the weather conditions were so dreadful and the road gradient so steep. As race officials watched from the stage finish line at the top of the Aubisque, Lapize screamed at them, "Murderers!" By 1919, only eleven riders of sixty-seven, or fewer than twenty percent of those who started, managed to finish what had become the longest Tour to date, fifteen stages totaling nearly 3,500 miles.

That was a challenging year for the Tour, but 1919 also saw the birth of one of its most enduring traditions. After World War I, severe food and manufacturing shortages prevailed throughout France and Europe. Many teams were barely able to scrounge up racing jerseys, let alone dye to color them. As a result, many riders wore some stitching on the shoulders to demarcate different teams wearing otherwise nearly indistinguishable gray jerseys. Halfway through the Tour, one team director suggested the race leader wear a colorful shirt to help spectators identify him. Created from yellow wool to match the color of the pages of the *L'Auto* newspaper, every leader's jersey, henceforth *le maillot jaune,* also bore the initials *H.D.* in honor of the Tour's founder.

Such flourishes soon transformed the Tour into a national institution. By the 1920s, it was obvious that Desgrange's scheme to attract new readers and advertisers had been a successful gamble. Daily circulation of *L'Auto* (the newspaper's name was shortened from *L'Auto-Vélo* in 1903) had more than doubled from 200,000 in July 1914 to 500,000 by July 1924.

The popularity and commercial possibilities of the Tour did not escape the interest of the bicycle manufacturers who sponsored its different teams. Recognizing the value a Tour victory could bring their brands, sponsors contracted supporting riders to help their aces win. Desgrange was outraged by this at first, and denounced these riders as *domestiques* or "servants." In time, however, he would come to see their value in making the stars of his race shine even brighter.

Although the role would evolve over time, few tasks were ever really beyond the purview of a *domestique,* or *gregario* as they were known in Italy. One of the most important was to ride ahead of their captain to create a windbreak to let their leader draft behind them, allowing him to use as much as thirty percent less energy in his pedaling. They were also expected to chase down opponents and share precious food and drink en route. Some captains demanded even more. One Italian cyclist insisted his domestiques help him as he relieved himself on the bike. (One pair pulled along his bike with him on it, while the other pair found newspapers and water to clean him up afterward.) A French cyclist who lost a toe to sepsis was said to have demanded that his domestique amputate his own toe to better understand his pain. (The captain's toe reportedly remains on view to this day in a jar of formaldehyde on the counter of a bar in Marseille.)

By the 1930s, when Gino arrived on the scene, Tour organizers were already trying to quash some of the more egregious traditions. In May 1938, newspapers published rules mandating that racers eat team meals together at designated locations, a response to various cases in previous years, in which riders skipped out on meal bills during the Tour. Another rule tried to rein in one of the Tour's most beloved rituals, *la chasse à la canette,* in which riders would run into cafés as they were passing through a town and gather as much wine, beer, and other drinks as they could carry, and then run out again without paying. The Tour directors took such misdeeds seriously, and their warnings about breaking these or any of the myriad other Tour rules were comically severe. Fortunately, such interdictions could do little to dampen the spirits of the rambunctious Tour cavalcade.

On July 5, 1938, this caravan left Paris and began its counterclockwise journey around France. The first week of racing was chockablock with the usual jostling as the riders settled into the race. Eight Western European countries had sent teams, but the fans were most interested in the top contenders: the Italians, French, and Belgians. The early stages of the race were largely flat ones, and so the Tour favorites patiently bided their time. Each racer had his reasons for holding back, but for Gino it was a question of following Girardengo's strategy to save his attacks for the mountains. In 1938, the Tour rules had increased the amount of time bonuses awarded to the racer who reached the top of individual mountain passes first. Given that a time bonus shaved off minutes from a cyclist's overall time, Girardengo encouraged Gino to accumulate as many of these as possible.

While Gino held back, no other rider emerged to fill the gap. Whether the other riders were consciously following the same strategy as the Italians remains unclear. It's just as possible that they were simply interested in keeping close to Gino and the other stars. In the end, all the speculation about what tactics the riders were silently mulling mattered little. The mountains now fast approaching would force every rider to reveal his hand.

✦

The stage that Desgrange would call "the most important of the Tour" began in Pau, a village on the northern edge of the Pyrenees. From there the riders would travel 120 miles to Luchon, a mountain town close to the border of Spain, known for its thermal baths. Between these two locales, the riders would travel up and down the Aubisque, the Tourmalet, the Peyresourde, and the Aspin. At 4,885 feet, the lowest of these mountain passes, the Col d'Aspin, was still higher than more than four Eiffel Towers.

But the mountains were about more than just climbs. There were rudimentary roads through desolate uninhabited landscapes, liable to wash away during the first real rainstorm. There were uneven gradients that threw a man off his steady cadence and tired him even more quickly than usual. And, just as night was certain to follow day, the mountain ascents were followed by descents. Bone-shaking rides over gravel and around hairpin turns, descents were the place where a fatigued rider might try to make up time, only to lose control, crash, and "leave meat on the road," as modern racers describe it. In the 1930s, the French press was even less subtle and described this kind of racing as *à tombeau ouvert*—or "open grave." It was hardly a figurative turn of phrase. On a similarly steep descent three years earlier, the Tour had experienced its first racing fatality when a Spanish rider crashed and died.

The mixture of spectacle and danger has an eternal appeal, and so, on July 14, 1938, the crowds came early and they came in record numbers. Buses, cars, and other vehicles stretched for miles up and down the mountains. Many had come from the surrounding areas and nearby cities, but a good number had come from as far away as Paris on a special overnight train arranged for fans to see the stage. One journalist estimated there were up to fifty thousand people gathered in the mountains. "It's unimaginable," he wrote, to see so many fans setting up camp in the barren landscape.

When the racers first set out that morning, Gino rode along with the peloton, his blue jersey lost in the sea of national colors. In time, a series of clouds lifted, and the sun bore down on them, promising a sweltering day of racing. "This stage is one of the worst one could imagine," said Gino. "It is also, in my opinion, the most punishing because it's the first confrontation with the mountains. They arrive just like that. Without any transition, one must climb."

When the gradient of the road increased significantly near the mountain town of Gourette, Gino surprised his fellow riders. "Suddenly, from the small group at the lead, one could see the blue silhouette of Bartali take off magnificently," wrote one journalist. "It was better than a sprint. It was a type of superhuman flight up the terrifying slope." No other racer chased after him, each man consumed by his own climb. Only a Tour organizer's car followed closely behind Gino. It displayed a large banner that admonished "Do Not Push!"—a warning to the drunken spectators who frequently ran onto the road to push straggling racers up the mountains.

For the crowd watching and the caravan following slightly behind him, it certainly appeared as if Gino would need no such help. His pace up the slope was relentless. "One had the impression," explained one reporter, that Gino was "launched by an invisible catapult." Gino was alone when he reached the top of the day's first four cols, the Aubisque.

He rode less aggressively on the way down the other side of the mountain, and lost ground. His two chief Belgian rivals chased after him and caught him. As they got up close, they scoffed at Gino's attempt to break away, chiding him for using the wrong gear. It had been so easy to catch him, they claimed, that they had time to pause and "eat some tender little pigeons" on the mountain road.

Infuriated, Gino charged up to the second mountain pass, the Tourmalet, determined to shake his rivals. When he was about one mile from the top, he tried to push harder. He succeeded in dropping one Belgian rider, but he couldn't shake the other. *Am I not going to be able to get rid of this leech?* Gino asked himself. *I push. He rests. At nine hundred meters from the top, he is still there. I take off sprinting.* Gino finally shook him off and raced into the descent.

The battle up the day's third peak was waged against his own body. Gino stared down the cold face of the mountain ahead of him. He attacked once more, only to be blindsided by fiery pain. "I felt my heart, usually so calm, beating hard and it seemed, looking at my jersey, to have enlarged. My chest was so swollen and my breathing so labored . . . I felt something inside me tearing. I was overcome by a great fear that I would have to dismount."

Nevertheless, Gino kept pushing, trying to maintain his lead. As the climb continued, he felt his mind breaking down, and the battle of voices raging in his head erupted. He began speaking aloud in delirium to the mountain. Like a chant, he started whispering "I can't go on; I can't go on. I can't go on." Then he focused back on the mountains ahead and called them out for what they were: "difficult, mean and made of rock." His chant slowly became a series of prayers that matched the rhythm of his pedaling. "Go, go, go!" Then he added other words to shore up his courage, repeating them as he worked his way along the switchbacks: "Up there it's finished, up there."

The race seemed endless; the chaotic gathering of people, trucks, and cars on the mountain roadside resembled a colorful oasis in the desolate landscape well above the tree line. A few braver souls had pitched tents among the bare rocks. Others enjoyed picnics near parked publicity trucks for companies like Montplaisir Beer. Closer to the road, fans were everywhere. Cheering from the roadside or the hoods of cars, this human mirage would disappear as soon as the racers had passed.

Gino took it all in as he rode by, and only the sharp pains of his body buckling could pierce his dreamlike delirium. His arms and back, hunched now for several hours, ached. His legs were growing weary, and each push of the pedal was painful. The prospect of food and water, which might otherwise have offered some hope, was doubtful. They had long since passed the lunchtime food drop, and any sandwich, banana, or sugar cube that he might have stored in the front pocket of his woolen jersey had already been eaten. He had one small tin water can that offered paltry relief from the climb and the sun. His Italian teammates, who would normally have refilled it at roadside wells, were far behind him in the mountains.

Yet, as he looked back at the other cyclists behind him, he suddenly found solace, even nourishment, in the sport's most perverse pleasure—the suffering of others. The two Belgians in black jerseys were buckling. The dual strain of the climb and their attempt to catch up with Gino was simply too exhausting. With renewed vigor, the Tuscan cyclist crossed the day's third mountain pass, the Peyresourde, first. The yellow jersey was virtually his, and this knowledge powered him on.

As Gino raced down the other side of the Peyresourde, some spectators appeared out of nowhere and crossed the road. Terrified, Gino clenched his brakes. "I flew off my bike as if I had been on an airplane."

Miraculously, he didn't break any bones. But his bike was not nearly as lucky. The wheel broke, forcing Gino to wait for a replacement. Abandoned on the mountainside, he paced angrily as the seconds ticked by. Finally, his team car pulled up.

Gino clambered back on his bike as quickly as he could change the wheel. It wasn't quick enough. Rattled by his fall, he took the descent more slowly than he had planned. The Belgians passed him. Exhausted, scraped up, and covered in mud after seven hours and sixteen minutes on his bike, Gino pulled into Luchon. He was two minutes and thirty-five seconds behind the race leader.

✦

Back in Italy, the day was unfolding in an insidious manner for altogether different reasons. The source of all the trouble lay in a distressing new publication, the *Manifesto of the Racial Scientists,* which appeared the same day as Gino's resounding performance in the Pyrenees. The *Manifesto* was described in depth in the popular newspaper *Giornale D'Italia* and many other publications. Claiming to be a scientific investigation of the Italian race, the document was reportedly written by a group of top Fascist scholars and intellectuals who were temporarily working for Mussolini's Ministry of Popular Culture. Italy's foreign minister, Count Galeazzo Ciano, would later say that Mussolini "practically wrote it himself." Through ten points, it argued why the Italian race was "Aryan, Nordic, and heroic" and stated that "Jews do not belong to the Italian race." And foreshadowing what was to come, it proclaimed, "The time has come for Italians openly to declare themselves racists."

With its publication, the Jewish community in Italy, which numbered some 47,000 along with another 10,000 foreign Jews, could see the first clouds of a changing political climate. Since 1933, Germany had started enacting anti-Jewish laws. In Romania, Austria, and Hungary, anti-Jewish legislation instituted in the first half of 1938 had created a similarly pernicious climate. In Italy, the *Manifesto* was the harbinger of an emerging new era of public and private persecution.

The *Manifesto* would affect the Jewish community most directly, but it also affected Fascist relations with other groups in Italy as well. In a more subtle way, the *Manifesto* represented a significant flare-up in the complex relationship between the Fascists and the Catholic Church. By discounting mixed marriages between Jews and Gentiles and later failing to recognize conversions of Jews to Catholicism, the Fascist regime was violating agreements it had earlier signed with the Church that delineated each other's realms of power. Clearly displeased by it, Pope Pius XI, the head of the Church, publicly criticized the *Manifesto* and the ideology that motivated it three times in the two weeks following its publication.

Perhaps most surprising of all is the fact that the publication of the *Manifesto* and the emerging Italian racism that it represented even transformed coverage of Gino's progress during the Tour. Modern sports fans accustomed to newspapers that separate political and sporting news in distinct sections would hardly expect that the events from one arena would affect developments in the other. Yet in 1938, when Mussolini controlled the Italian press, that was precisely what happened. When the Tour began, one prominent magazine wrote that Gino and the Italians had gone across the border to win "in the name of Mussolini." As the Tour progressed and the *Manifesto* was published, the language became increasingly belligerent. Gino was no longer just a cyclist, but a warrior who "uses his bicycle as a weapon." By the end of the competition, the most prominent sports newspaper and sports magazine in Italy would be heralding his performance as proof of the strength of the Italian race.

✦

The race from Pau to Luchon was followed by a rest day on July 15 that allowed the journalists and fans to digest the performance of the top stars in the Pyrenees. The stage had been so grueling that even a former winner of the Tour de France had to be pushed up a hill by teammates, and then—out of desperation—he grabbed a car to help tow him (an infraction that disqualified him). Though Gino had finished third in the stage, he had improved his overall ranking from eighteenth to second. Most important, many journalists were convinced that they had seen a flash of what was needed to win the Tour. One wrote, "The king of the mountains in the Pyrenees was Bartali. . . . He was deprived of first place by an unlucky break." Another journalist gushed, "He is the great and real champion of the mountains. We were speechless before his allure and before the extraordinary ease of his style, which is harmonious and powerful all at once."

Yet fifteen stages remained in the Tour. Gino fought to take the lead for the next five stages, but in the flatter terrain the yellow jersey eluded him. As he prepared to tackle the Alps, the extra boost he desperately needed caught him by surprise. He was awakened one morning by a knock on his hotel door. When he opened it, he was greeted by his father, who had made his first trip ever to France to see his son race. Gino was astounded. Torello cried as he embraced his son.

The next day in the Alps, Gino was ablaze. His attack came early and his rivals never recovered. He pushed so hard that he thought he could hear his heart pounding in his chest; when he spat on the roadside, he saw blood. He stormed up and down the Col d'Allos, the Col du Vars, and the Col d'Izoard, winning three of the most difficult mountain bonuses. At the top of the Izoard, he was welcomed by a hollering chorus of Italian fans. "It was an uproar. A continuous celebratory yell, every shout was an incitement, a push, a whip," he said. "Every ovation refreshed and cleansed my morale."

By the time Gino arrived in Briançon, the king of the mountains had earned his crown. He finished more than five minutes ahead of the second-place rider and some seventeen minutes ahead of the Tour leader. Bystanders realized they had witnessed an epic performance. "It's true that the sport of cycling has never known such a mountain man, a real phenom, an athlete that comes around once every twenty years, an absolutely unique case," said one journalist. For Gino the stage victory was more personal. "Think about destiny," he said, referring to the stage in the 1937 Tour when he crashed into the Colau River, ending his Tour hopes. "On exactly the same streets where I had been defeated a year before, this year I got my win."

His commanding stage win in Briançon had given him the yellow jersey. He would keep it all the way to Paris. With the result of the race more or less decided, the French press amused itself with short pieces about Gino's personality and his life off the bicycle. Inevitably these focused on his religious observance and regular attendance at mass before races, or small details like the fact that he often ate with a small statue of the Madonna watching him. Gino tried to keep his calm, but his appetite for being teased had only diminished since he was a young boy. "Sir, my faith is a personal, private matter. It shouldn't interest anyone," he rebuked one reporter. "Judge me on the road, speak about my race, about my gears and my weaknesses. That should suffice." Gino might have been more sympathetic had he understood the motivation behind the focus on his religious allegiance. Whereas many in France booed the Italian soccer team for their support of Mussolini, Gino's religious beliefs distanced him from the regime. The French press did not characterize him as a Fascist, as many would try to do in Italy.

While the newspapers hailed his victory as a foregone conclusion, Gino knew how quickly a cyclist's fortunes could change. So he remained intensely focused on the race and kept the journalists and fans trying to guess his mood. If he had performed as he hoped, he was gracious and spoke freely with all who approached him. If he was disappointed or nervous, beware. He would ignore journalists' questions and send photographers away. Inevitably his temper got the better of him. At the starting line of one of the last stages, a group of gushing young girls swarmed Gino as he tinkered with his bike. They wanted his autograph.

"Niente!"—"No!" he said, swatting them away with his hand. "Leave me alone." His flirtatious teammate Aldo Bini was only too happy to swoop in and lead the smiling young women away from his captain.

✦

On the early morning of August 1, 1938, several hundred people lined up outside the Parc des Princes stadium in Paris, where the racers would complete their twenty-eight-day odyssey. The gates opened at nine, and three thousand people flooded through. By noon, twenty thousand spectators sat in the arena and cheered on the arrival of the champions. Many racers rode in wearing new jerseys, white socks, and fresh caps. Not Gino. He did not don the fresh yellow silk jersey that he was given for his victory ride into Paris. Instead he wore the same woolen jersey he had raced in, now caked with mud and dried sweat, and a white cap, dirtied by dust.

For coach Girardengo, the Italian victory was particularly sweet. "I have realized one of the dreams of my life: helping one of my countrymen win the Tour," he said. Through Gino, Girardengo had lived out his greatest cycling aspiration and provided Italy with its second Tour winner ever—thirteen years after Bottecchia had last won, in 1925. Reflecting on Gino's triumph a few days after the Tour, Girardengo momentarily relaxed his stern demeanor and waxed nostalgic about the first time he had ever seen Gino race: "Seeing you pedal, Gino, was one of the first signs of aging for me, like a woman who was very beautiful who watches her daughter the night of her first ball."

Gino, in turn, thanked Girardengo for motivating him through the most arduous mountain stages. "During a moment when my legs started to become heavy or I felt that burning in my stomach, the contraction which marks a peak effort, I heard your voice telling me simply, at once tender and authoritative, 'Gino, Gino . . .' And then soon enough, I felt myself comforted. My legs became light again and I took off again for the summit. You were my father."

In Italy, Gino's victory sent the Italian press into happy hysterics. The triumph was immediately imbued with political sentiment when it was announced that Mussolini would award Gino a silver medal for "athletic valor." Predictably, some reporters used Gino's victory as an attempt to praise Mussolini, with one journalist referring to Gino as "Mussolini's sports ambassador" and another declaring that Gino had obeyed Mussolini's command to win. Others went further, deriding France as a land of "democracy and international pigswill" and linking the Italian Tour victory to the racial ideology underlying the *Manifesto.* According to that interpretation, Gino's victory in Paris was about more than just an athletic triumph—it was proof of the superior quality of the Italian race. "The ovations were not only directed at the triumphant one of the Tour de France. They had a louder and more significant sound. They were exalting the athletic and moral virtue of an exemplar of our race. Gino Bartali's victory surpasses the limit of sports events as clamorous as it is."

The climax for the propaganda machine should have been the victor's acceptance speech. Between the tens of thousands watching at the Parc des Princes velodrome, and the millions listening by radio across the continent, it was the perfect opportunity to try to transform an athletic success into a political one. Gino would have been aware that Fascist officials were expecting him to praise and thank them.

Gino must have wrestled with what to say. After the public squabble about his hesitation to participate in the Tour a year earlier, Gino had witnessed the power of the regime. And between the news coverage in the French press and his conversations with family and friends in Italy, Gino had heard about the recent dispute between the regime and the Church. As perhaps the most famous member of Catholic Action, he knew that his behavior would be closely studied.

In the end, Gino spoke as he saw fit. In his address to French radio listeners, he made a completely apolitical statement thanking his fans in France and Italy, his voice at times nearly drowned out by the spectators screaming in the stands. As one modern Italian historian explains it, "In 1938, everyone knew that they had to thank *Il Duce*. So if Bartali didn't do it, it was a definite political gesture."

His address to Italian radio listeners remains more of a mystery because the recording no longer exists. *Il Popolo d'Italia,* the regime's most prominent mouthpiece, claimed that Gino had spoken about his pride in winning the Tour "holding high the colors of Fascist sport." In a secret report about Gino maintained by the regime's political police, however, an altogether different account emerged of what he had said. According to the agent writing it, Gino "mumbled" instead of praising the regime. Moreover, the report noted that Gino would not have reacted well to Fascist praise because he considered himself a member of "Catholic Action and not Fascism."

If anyone had any lingering questions about where Gino's loyalties lay, his activities the next day might have helped answer them. With reporters and magazine photographers watching him, he went to mass at Our Lady of Victory church in Paris in the early morning. This time he cleaned up and wore a gray suit, a black shirt, and a light-colored tie. He even slicked his hair back. After saying a short prayer, he placed his Tour de France victory bouquet at the feet of a statue of the Madonna. Nearby, a group of schoolchildren had assembled to catch a glimpse of the champion. The church's curate, who had been chatting with Gino, introduced the cyclist to the group: "I present to you Bartali, winner of the Tour de France, who came to thank the Virgin who allowed him to win."

✦

On his return to Italy, Gino received a lukewarm welcome, very different from what he might have expected. The Italian press didn't dare cover the full details of it, but one otherwise apolitical French newspaper sent a reporter who did. Remembering the public celebrations enjoyed by previous Tour victors from various countries on their return home, and perhaps thinking about how the Italian regime particularly celebrated sports, the reporter was amazed to see how little was being done to commemorate Gino's victory:

> An Italian wins the Tour de France, he wins a sensational international victory and his compatriots—who are Latins prone

> to delirious joy—don't react much at all? There's a problem. . . . Not a cat at the train station. No organized reception. Nothing. I don't understand. Let's keep looking. Is this because Bartali is Catholic? There isn't exactly harmony currently between Rome and the Vatican.

Events in the following days seemed to confirm his suspicions. Unlike the soccer team, Gino would not be invited to a flashy photo shoot with Mussolini. At the velodrome in Turin, during his first appearance as a Tour champion before a large audience in Italy, the head of the Italian Cycling Federation was conspicuously absent. The atmosphere was decidedly reserved, though the regime could not snuff out all emotion. As Gino rode his victory lap around the velodrome, his mother sat in the audience wearing a special blue dress for the occasion. She cried softly with happiness.

By early August, the regime's frustration with Gino escalated even further. Fascist officials sent Italian newspapers strict instructions regarding their coverage of Gino. A former journalist himself, Mussolini had closely controlled what newspapers wrote about for years. His Fascist press office, the Ufficio Stampa, would send secret bulletins to the editorial offices of publications with rigid guidelines on what to cover and how to cover it. They even specified the acceptable vocabulary, the type, and the size of the letters. And on August 9, 1938, the Ufficio Stampa made the regime's feelings about Gino astonishingly clear to the press: "The newspapers should cover Bartali exclusively as a sportsman without any useless accounts of his life as a private citizen." Practically, this meant Gino would receive less coverage in the press. It also ensured that journalists could cover only Gino's results and provide none of the extra details and color that helped create the heroes that readers adored.

Of course, in August 1938 no journalist dared tell Gino about the regime's secret orders. If Gino himself noticed a change in his press coverage, he kept his mouth shut. His scorn for the regime had thus far been veiled—he made a statement by the statements he didn't make. But as the winds of war began to tug at Italy's borders, no man would be able to live outside of the tempest that was to come. Gino didn't know it yet, but he was about to ride straight into the political morass his father had warned him to avoid at all costs.

Part II

World War II in Italy
0
MILES
200
0
KM
200
FRANCE
GERMANY
SWITZERLAND
AUSTRIA
HUNGARY
YUGOSLAVIA
Milan
APENNINES
"Gothic Line"
Aug. 29, 1944
Florence
"Gustav Line"
Nov. 30, 1943
Corsica
Rome
Allied advance to
Sept. 25, 1943
Sardinia
ITALY
Allied advance to
Sept. 3, 1943
Sicily
Allies invade Sicily,
July 10, 1943
Territory controlled by Mussolini, June 1940–July 1943
Territory occupied by Allies by Sept. 25, 1943
Territory controlled by the Mussolini-Hitler alliance (the "Salò Republic") after Sept. 25, 1943
Selected stages of German withdrawal to the north

6

From the Stars to the Stables

Cardinal Elia Dalla Costa with Gino and Adriana Bartali on their wedding day, November 14, 1940.

AFTER WINNING CYCLING'S HIGHEST honor, Gino planned to round out his best season to date by capturing the 1938 World Championship title in Holland. The race started a few weeks after he finished in France, and should have been a final feather in his cap after his Tour victory. Instead he suffered an embarrassing loss. He blamed it on a bad team strategy and various bike problems, but the defeat was so humiliating that one secret spy report speculated that Gino had lost on purpose to deny the Fascists a victory and get back at them for their hostility toward Catholic Action.

The spy was wrong. Gino was too proud to cede victories, and he was furious that people could now contest his status as the best cyclist in the world. A few days later he returned home to Italy and encountered even more blowback from fans. Gino was competing in a one-day cycling event in Milan that consisted of several track events. When he rode out into the velodrome for the warm-up, he proudly wore the yellow Tour jersey he had fought so hard to win for his Italian countrymen. The spectators, however, booed him loudly and produced a deafening, shrill noise. Bianchi, the rival of the Legnano team (for whom Gino raced in Italian competitions), had handed out whistles, encouraging people to blow them at Gino for disgracing Italy at the World Championships. Gino bought his own whistle to blow back at his hecklers. "But the noise of them en masse was terrible," he said.

In a fit of anger, Gino ripped off his yellow jersey and screamed at those sneering at him, "Milanese, you are not sportsmen!" He raced wearing his Legnano jersey and won every event in which he competed, even earning himself grudging applause by the end of the night. Despite the wins, however, this experience with fickle fans seared itself in Gino's memory. "The pedestal of fame is neither very comfortable, nor is it very secure," he concluded.

Gino kept competing, and the final races of the 1938 season drew big crowds as they always had of Italians who were enchanted by the "bronzed faces bent over handlebars grimacing with effort, legs that pedal at a dizzying loom . . . people eating while pedaling; a medley of shouts, calls and horns, photographers climbing on the roofs of cars [and] rapid motorcyclists with warriors' helmets."

Yet as normal life and the world of races continued in Italy, serious changes were afoot for the country's minority Jewish community. In Fiume, where Gino's friend Giacomo Goldenberg lived with his wife and two children, the first tremor was felt just after the last sun-kissed days of summer.

✦

On a quiet morning in early September 1938, Goldenberg's six-year-old son, Giorgio, set out for his first day of school. He had endured his mother's fruitless attempts to tame his squirrel's nest of curls for the big day, and his uniform was a starchy reminder that the carefree days of summer were over. After he left the spacious villa that his family shared with their cousins, the Kleins, he kept tugging at the itchy fabric as he trotted toward the schoolhouse. But the pleasant flutter of first-day anticipation made a little discomfort bearable. The classroom would be a disappointing change from the seaside resort where Giorgio and his family had spent their August holidays, but he would finally get to see many of his friends again.

When the schoolhouse came into view, Giorgio bounced a little on his feet and scanned the yard for the nearest classmate he could dart over to for a quick game of tag or hopscotch before the bell rang. Instead, he stopped short. Near the entryway, a teacher stood with a uniformed police officer and the school principal. Giorgio eyed the trio curiously as he headed toward the familiar faces of his schoolmates who were lining up to go inside. He was promptly distracted by the skinny arms of friends flung warmly over his shoulders and the excited jostling that ensued. His attention was not diverted for long. Smiling absentmindedly at the other boys' jokes and laughter, he kept glancing back at the teacher, the policeman, and the principal by the door. He was alarmed and confused to find that as they quietly conferred with one another, they were looking unmistakably at him. Bewildered, Giorgio tucked himself behind the other kids and followed them toward the entrance. He saw the teacher move toward him and instinctively kept his head down, lifting it only when he felt her hand on his shoulder, separating him from his friends. One by one, the teacher pulled aside all the Jewish students who were registered to attend the school. When she had finished, the police officer addressed the small group that had formed. Speaking matter-of-factly, he announced that as a result of a new law, they had been permanently expelled. With that, he forbade them from ever entering the building again. Giorgio watched his friends file in for classes as he gripped his satchel tightly in his small hand and his face grew hot with shame. As he and the other Jewish children were ushered toward the gates, he blinked back prickly tears, stunned and utterly disoriented.

In the evening, Giorgio recounted the day's events to his father. It was a scene that would play out in many homes as Jewish children across the nation discovered that they had been banned from state schools. A good number of families would react to this new regulation with surprise; it represented such a sharp shift from past Fascist policy that it was hard to think of it as anything but a temporary aberration. Even in Nazi Germany, Jewish children were still permitted to attend public schools in September 1938. Other parents were more resigned, having anticipated that something like this would follow the *Racial Manifesto*, which had come out in July of that year. Still others reacted with angry confusion, astonished that a community that had made such sizable contributions to Italian government and culture was now being targeted.

In quick succession, the Fascist Grand Council, a quasi-legislative body that served under Mussolini, approved a series of laws that restricted Jews in almost every facet of their lives. Those like Giacomo Goldenberg, who were born elsewhere and had become citizens after 1919, were summarily stripped of their citizenship and declared foreigners. Italian-born Jews were expelled from a variety of professions and banned from owning real estate above a fixed value. Alongside these more dramatic restrictions, the Racial Laws unleashed scores of small humiliations that revealed themselves over the coming weeks and months. Signs declaring "No Entry to Jews and Dogs" started appearing in certain gathering spots throughout cities and towns, particularly in the north. Elsewhere, local parks, skating rinks, and cafés became off limits. Even those who died were targeted, as it became difficult to publish Jewish obituaries.

The shock of these measures was overwhelming. One Italian Jew who lived through it described the experience succinctly: "We went from the stars to the stables."

✦

As chaos reigned in the Jewish community, little changed for most Italian Gentiles, who went about their daily lives as they always had. Gino was no different. He started the 1939 season with fierce determination and became fervid in his quest to reclaim his dominance in cycling. The first place to do so was the race that meant most to his countrymen: the Giro. But a string of unlucky tire punctures quashed that aspiration. His next conquest should have been the 1939 Tour de France. As a returning champion he was a prime contender. But Gino was dealt another blow by Mussolini's regime when Italy abstained from participating in the 1939 Tour as a result of increasingly hostile relations with France. Gino was robbed of the chance to defend his title. He could scarcely accept it. The government had meddled in his career before, but taking the whole country out of contention was government interference on an altogether larger scale. After a quick rise to the top of the sport at such a young age, this string of losses and disappointments devastated Gino. He started scrambling to find someone or something that could help him win again.

He found who he was looking for at a regional race in 1939 in Piedmont, in northern Italy. His name was Fausto Coppi and he was a "reed-thin lad" who looked "more like a thin, starving goat than a cyclist," according to his coach. There was something delicate, almost intellectual, about Coppi's pointed features next to Gino's boxer's face, surprising given that Coppi had grown up in a family of poor farmers near Turin. A promising young cyclist, he raced under the auspices of a blind and obese coach who grabbed his charges by the scruffs of their necks to assess whether they had pushed themselves hard enough during their training. Coppi was but nineteen years old—five years younger than Gino.

The Tuscan had met Coppi at a small race in Arezzo, but it was in Piedmont that he first witnessed his strength. On the suggestion of his Tour coach, Girardengo, Gino had let Coppi attack first during the climb. During some point in that attack, Coppi's chain fell off. Gino made a break and won the race. At the finish line, he discovered that Coppi had managed to beat back a strong field of competitors to place third. Impressed, Gino encouraged his team's directors to sign the young cyclist. Coppi joined the team that night.

Confident in the group of riders supporting him, Gino dedicated the entire winter to preparing for the 1940 Giro. He pored over the route map and began hatching a strategy on how to win. When the weather improved, he was out on his bicycle targeting his weakest areas, such as his sprints. Soon after, he started scouting parts of the race. As he visited different parts of the course, he carried out his newest reconnaissance strategy of building a list of local restaurants and innkeepers that he could call up to get more accurate information about local weather and road conditions during the race. All this preparation quickly yielded results. In the spring of 1940, Gino launched a blistering sprint during the day-long race from Milan to San Remo and won it. A month later he won the Tour of Tuscany. By the time the Giro rolled around in May 1940, Gino seemed unbeatable. Indeed, the first stage could hardly have been smoother. After setting out from Milan, he was the picture of confidence and crossed the finish line in Turin right after the stage winner.

In the second stage, catastrophe crept up on him. The peloton had set out for Genoa. As the riders wove their way along the mountain roads, a dog darted out onto the race course. Gino crashed into it and was thrown from his bike. When he landed, he was seized by a violent, throbbing pain in his leg. Still he managed to get back up and finish the stage. In the evening, a doctor revealed that he had severely strained his muscle and advised he withdraw from the Giro. Gino refused, but soon realized that he had no chance of winning. The race was wide open again. Coppi, Gino's supporting rider and a first-time competitor at the Giro, rode brilliantly into this vacuum and won. Gino was dumbfounded. He had just recently risen to the top of the sport, only to be supplanted by a rider he had hand-picked for his team.

Years later, when Coppi and Gino were pitted against each other in the biggest sporting rivalry Italy had ever seen, this first match-up would be remembered and described in mythic terms. Among the *coppiani*—Coppi's fans—it would be recalled as the archetypal moment when the brave apprentice first challenged his master. To the *bartaliani*, spurred on by Gino's exaggerated accounts of how he had supported Coppi, it was a moment of nearly messianic sacrifice as the legendary champion forswore his own prospects to propel his younger teammate forward. In June 1940, however, neither Gino nor Coppi had much time to think about it. A day after the Giro finished, Benito Mussolini walked out onto a balcony overlooking the Piazza Venezia in central Rome and announced that Italy had entered the war against England and France. Gino was devastated: "A great tragedy was to befall us all."

✦

A few days after Mussolini's declaration, a group of armed Italian policemen appeared at the home of the Goldenbergs and the Kleins in Fiume. As chance would have it, the Goldenbergs all happened to be out. The Kleins, however, were home when the officers knocked on the door. Signora Klein took one look at them from a window and immediately understood why they had come. In a flurry of panic, she instructed her older son, Aurelio, to escape before they saw him. He immediately jumped out of a second-floor window and slipped out the backyard. The police entered the house as he left and took his parents and younger brother into custody, as part of a nationwide initiative to arrest both Jewish and non-Jewish foreigners residing in Italy.

Upon arrest, people like the Kleins, who were classified as foreign nationals, were taken to the local police station. There they were held for several hours and questioned before they were transferred to a local prison. In the prisons, they were crowded into cells, often alongside common criminals. Many waited for weeks, coping with appalling sanitary conditions and vermin. Then, in small groups supervised by police, they were typically handcuffed and marched through city streets to trains and taken to internment camps.

It remains a mystery where the Kleins were sent. It's possible that they were sent to Ferramonti di Tarsia in southern Italy. Built on a swampy, malaria-plagued site, it was Italy's largest internment camp. It's more plausible, however, that the Kleins ended up in one of the roughly forty smaller camps that were opened to accommodate newly arrested foreign prisoners. Most were located in central or southern Italy, but a few were in the north, in the province of Parma. Hastily set up by local authorities across Italy, these camps were established in large buildings that the authorities requisitioned, including hospices, movie theaters, and villas.

The Fascists set up one such impromptu camp near Gino's hometown of Ponte a Ema in a grand mansion in the Tuscan hills called Villa La Selva. The internment camp was kept top secret. Gino and his neighbors never knew it existed; guards kept any outsiders from coming close. A prison for some 160 people, including a large number of foreign Jews, it was chronically overcrowded and under-supplied. Prisoners were forbidden from working and were given a daily allowance of 6.5 lire for food and other necessities. Most survived on a bowl of watery soup and 150 grams of bread per day. All of this added up to a meager existence, but it was wholly different from the experience of Jews in German-controlled camps elsewhere in Europe, where torture and mass murder became the norm. Jews interned in Italy would not be singled out for brutal cruelty for being Jewish, and they enjoyed the freedom within their camps to set up community institutions like synagogues and schools. None would be turned over for deportation before the Germans took control in the autumn of 1943, despite frequent pressure from Nazi officials.

Giacomo Goldenberg and his family would only discover what their cousins had to endure in the months and years that followed. On the day of the Kleins' arrest in 1940, however, Goldenberg knew just one thing: he needed to get his own family out of Fiume. Packing what things they could carry, they left the next morning on a train for Florence. When they arrived, they made their way to Fiesole, a sunny village that was just a few miles northeast of the city, up on a hill with a scenic view of Florence. On a side street near the ruins of an old Roman theater, they found a landlord willing to rent them a small house.

If the Goldenbergs had hoped to live anonymously in this new locale, they soon realized that plan was not to be. In no time at all, the inhabitants of Fiesole had identified the Goldenbergs as outsiders and Giacomo Goldenberg as a foreign-born Jew. Yet in a striking example of the legal inconsistencies of the Fascist regime, he was not arrested by the local police and immediately sent off to an internment camp. Instead, like many other foreign-born Jews who weren't interned, he was placed under a light house arrest that prohibited him from going to Florence and required him to check in with the local police station once a week.

The relatively favorable terms of Goldenberg's arrest would set the tone for the family's quiet new life in Fiesole. Villagers, while curious about their new neighbors, would prove themselves free of any of the anti-Semitic vitriol that had become so common around Europe and some parts of Italy. Left to live their lives peacefully, the Goldenbergs adapted well to life in the small village. Giorgio started to attend a nearby school organized for Jewish children. When he wasn't in the classroom, he passed the hours playing with local Gentile friends. His mother, Elvira, an Italian Jew, was free to go to Florence as she pleased. Goldenberg, although forbidden from going there himself, was free to host people from the city who came to see him. It was in this context that he began spending time again with his friend from Florence, Armando Sizzi.

One of Sizzi's visits to Fiesole stood out from all the rest, at least for young Giorgio. Talkative and good-natured, Sizzi would regularly bring other members of his family to visit the Goldenbergs, including his young son Marcello, with whom Giorgio had become fast friends. When Giorgio caught sight of Sizzi in the passenger seat of a car slowing down in front of his family's home one day, he raced to see if Marcello had come along to play. As he peered through the windows of the car, however, he was surprised to recognize the driver from the countless magazine covers and sports papers he and his friends were always poring over. It was Gino Bartali.

Giorgio's father stood nearby. If he was taken aback for a moment when he saw the cyclist get out of the car, he could hardly be blamed. More than a decade had passed since Goldenberg had met Gino in Sizzi's shop. Then Gino had been a shy boy who worked obsessively on broken bikes; now he was a confident man who appeared to cope effortlessly with being a national celebrity. In that same time, cruel Fascist laws had pushed Goldenberg from a prosperous life as a businessman in a cosmopolitan port city into the provincial world of a *paesano* or villager.

Goldenberg greeted Gino and Sizzi warmly. The three men began speaking, but Goldenberg barely had enough time to update his guests with his news before they were interrupted by the arrival of a group of curious strangers. In a village where everyone knew everyone else, word had quickly spread among their neighbors that the famous sports hero had arrived. As they heard the news, village children and parents from nearby streets stopped what they were doing, poured out of their homes and the town piazza, and rushed toward the row of cream-colored houses where the Goldenbergs had rented their home.

When they saw Gino smiling and chatting with Goldenberg and Sizzi, some stepped forward to ask for his autograph. Gino was happy to oblige them, and handed out signed postcards of himself that he always carried with him. After securing a memento with Gino's signature, the village children clustered around Giorgio, in awe that his father knew the famous cyclist. They became even more envious of what happened next. Gino reached into his car and pulled out a small blue bicycle that he presented to Giorgio. The young boy was astounded and stared with admiration at the cyclist who towered over him, while his friends pounced immediately on the gift, eager to inspect every inch of the bicycle. "Bartali was a kind of demigod," explained Giorgio.

Of course, even special days like these could not mitigate the war or the restricted circumstances in which the Goldenbergs found themselves. Yet somehow the excitement of a friendly visit and the relative tranquillity of everyday life in Fiesole had helped open a small window of promise. If they could live the war out together in this peaceful little village, the family had a chance of realizing the best possible outcome in a difficult situation.

Ultimately, however, the war extinguished this hope as well. Two years after he arrived in Fiesole, Goldenberg would be arrested and sent off to a distant internment camp.

✦

On October 9, 1940, the war finally muscled its way into Gino's life when he received a notice calling him to active military service. He and Adriana had feared it might happen, but she was still shaken. "Don't worry, I won't end up beneath the bombs," Gino reassured her. His words did little to shore her up, for the situation was starting to feel terrifyingly familiar. Adriana's older brother had also recently joined the Italian war effort. The night before he left, the family gathered for a special meal to send him off. The next day Adriana's brother boarded a ship, along with a few hundred Florentine soldiers, bound for Albania, which Mussolini had invaded the previous year. Out at sea, the boat was bombed and the soldiers all perished. When the news reached Adriana's family, she refused to acknowledge that her brother could be dead. For years she would hold out hope that he would one day appear at her door. Already in a fragile state, Adriana was ill-equipped to cope with losing Gino as well.

As part of Gino's mobilization, he was first required to undergo a routine medical checkup to determine his specific assignment. On the day of his test, he went to the local military office. The military doctor listened to his heart and found it was beating irregularly, a condition that Gino was aware of, but that had never seemed to impede his cycling. Still the doctor was puzzled, and called in a colonel for a second opinion. The colonel looked at the heart rate and rejected Gino as unfit for military service, unaware that he was evaluating one of the nation's cycling stars.

Unsettled, the doctor explained to the colonel that it might look like special treatment if Gino was excused from military service. The colonel relented, and Gino was assigned his post. He became an army messenger near an airplane factory on the shores of Lake Trasimeno, some seventy-five miles southeast of Florence. Compared with those sent to fight abroad, he was undeniably fortunate in his placement.

Still, life in the army barracks was an adjustment for Gino. For one thing, he didn't like carrying a gun. But he became creative and channeled his passions into his new profession. Soon after he started, one of his superiors, a cycling fan named Olesindo Salmi, agreed to allow him to use a bicycle instead of a motorized scooter so he could continue to train. He was also permitted to take frequent leaves to compete in those few races still being held. In his spare time when he wasn't delivering army documents, Gino steered clear of the barracks, where the other soldiers talked anxiously about the fighting in Africa and the fact that Italy was losing in Ethiopia. Instead, Gino passed the hours with religious reading. "I plunged myself into reading the lives of the saints. I frequently read Saint Anthony, Saint Catherine, Saint Thérèse [of Lisieux]." In these books he found an inviting escape from the dreariness of military life and his growing frustration with Mussolini's government. Speaking out in this context would almost certainly have been viewed as insubordination. So "Gino, the chatterbox, had his trap nailed shut," as he explained.

Gino would try to see Adriana whenever he secured leaves to train or compete, but with every visit she was growing more agitated. They both knew his assignment could change without explanation and he could be sent abroad with little notice. Gino grew frustrated because he wanted to protect and provide for her, but his military assignment kept him away. *No one knows what will happen because of this cursed war,* he thought. Gino resolved to remedy the situation by marrying her. His proposal was less a question than a statement of fact. "Better a widow than a girlfriend," he said to Adriana. Though they had talked of marriage, Adriana was surprised. Gino's proposal came sooner than they had discussed. Still, she had made her choice long ago and happily agreed.

In peacetime, this decision would have unleashed a flurry of planning. Few events, after all, can rival the scale of a lavish Italian wedding. A parade of antipasti including fine meats and pickled vegetables is followed by a dizzying number of courses featuring pastas, soups, fish, meats, fruits, and baked treats. After the food is served, fathers and uncles deliver long sentimental speeches over many glasses of wine, grappa, and *Vin Santo,* the special dessert wine used to toast a guest's health.

Adriana's wedding day unfolded in quite a different manner. Gino secured a short leave from the military, and on a weekday morning in November 1940, Adriana and Gino gathered with Cardinal Elia Dalla Costa in his private chapel in the center of Florence. Adriana wore a modest long-sleeved white dress and floor-length veil, which covered soft chestnut waves of hair, draped over her shoulders. Gino donned a dark suit and tie, and the triangle of a smart white handkerchief peeked out of his breast pocket.

Gino stood straight and confident, and Adriana faced him, holding her simple bouquet firmly. Cardinal Dalla Costa watched solemnly as the couple embraced one of the most sacred sacraments in the Catholic faith. At twenty-six and twenty, Gino and Adriana were still young, but as they looked at each other, they couldn't help but marvel at how far they had come since the days when Gino struggled to introduce himself. In front of Cardinal Dalla Costa and a dozen guests, Gino and Adriana declared their love and commitment to each other. And for that moment they lost themselves in the spell of the momentous step they had taken together, oblivious of the world outside the chapel. "My dream from boyhood, for my future, was to have at my side a humble and intelligent woman. God granted me this wish," Gino said.

But the war could not be forgotten for very long. Their wedding guests provided the most obvious clue. Few men were present other than Adriana's and Gino's fathers. Similarly, neither Adriana's mother nor Gino's mother attended. For Adriana's mother, the loss of her son was too fresh, and Giulia was still mourning the death of Giulio, four years later. After the ceremony, the group moved to Adriana's older sister's home, where she hosted a simple reception, serving what small cakes and refreshments they had been able to procure with wartime rationing. The bride was radiant though "the moment was a bit peculiar," Adriana acknowledged later. "We did things very simply."

In the early afternoon the young couple boarded a train for their honeymoon in Rome. The next day the newlyweds were treated to a meeting with Pope Pius XII, a fan of Gino's. Adriana was thrilled, but also exhausted: "It was all racing around. My husband was used to racing, but I wasn't." Afterward they boarded a train for Ferrara, where Gino had a one-day cycling event. While their honeymoon was brief, curtailed by the length of the leave Gino had been able to secure, they added a few extra days the following February in Alassio on the Italian Riviera, ahead of Gino's training in the region. There they had a painting done of the two of them riding a tandem bicycle by the sea, Adriana beaming behind her husband, who for once has forgone his usual muddy racing gear for dapper plus-fours and a jacket. The carefree mood of the painting belies the wartime setting. When they returned home, Gino headed back to the army barracks.

Adriana's first year of married life was shaped by the same austerity that gripped other Florentines on the home front. With the war being fought outside of Italy, and Allied aerial bombings largely confined to northern industrial areas like Milan, Turin, and Genoa, food shortages were the most enduring daily reminder that the nation was in conflict. In beefsteak-loving Florence, meat was the most conspicuously absent item. Where it was available, people learned to make do with much less of it and eat parts of the cow, like the udder and lungs, that they had once discarded. Other staples prone to shortages were similarly replaced with substitutes. Imported coffee was replaced by varying blends of indigenous plants like chicory or barley; eggs were replaced by a powder called *ovocrema*; cigarettes were replaced by rice-paper cylinders filled with dried chamomile flowers.

Despite the shortages and living apart, the Bartalis went on to start a family. Their first child, a son named Andrea, was born on October 3,

1941, nearly a year after their wedding, and was baptized by Cardinal Dalla Costa. This event heralded much joy during a strange period in Gino's life. His day-to-day existence at that time was an unusual hybrid of working as a military bicycle messenger and competing in cycling races around the country. The Italian racing calendar had been significantly reduced, but there were still more than a dozen races in 1941 and 1942. Most significantly, professionals no longer earned any money—their prizes were automatically donated to the war effort.

Gino harbored mixed feelings about these wartime races. On the one hand, they provided an escape from his military duties and they allowed him to hold his tenuous spot in the public eye as a top-flight cyclist. They also allowed him to squeeze in visits with his family after the competitions. But there were trade-offs for participating in these events. Losses had begun to rankle Gino much more than before. After one race where Coppi came from behind to win, Gino found himself in a state of shock. He "went gray as ash. He shook, as if the news weighed more heavily on his legs than the kilometers he had just ridden," described Coppi. Another wartime race crystallized why the sport he loved had become so frustrating. It was the 1941 Giro of Tuscany, raced along the familiar dirt-packed roads and rolling hills near Gino's hometown. Gino eagerly anticipated this race because he was sure to see Adriana afterward and he was primed to win in front of a local crowd for the third year in a row. He started strong and secured the lead early. But at the beginning of the penultimate climb before the finish in Florence, he blew a tire and was forced to stop and replace it. He pedaled furiously to catch up with the others. He came within striking distance when he was stymied again. His chain came off, and by the time he fixed it, all hope of a victory had vanished.

The loss crushed him, but that didn't entirely explain the depth of his unease. Then it hit him. He was "surrounded by people who are thinking only about races, as though nothing were going on, as if the war affected someone else and not the racers," he said. Gino realized that he was part of a charade perpetrated by the regime. Mussolini had recognized that these wartime races were effective propaganda for boosting public morale in Italy during the war. So while the Giro d'Italia had been canceled in 1941, the Fascist regime resurrected the race in 1942. It was still called the Giro, even though the multiweek race had been reduced to a series of six one-day races.

Elsewhere in Europe, the world of racing had slowed down considerably. In bicycle-loving France, the Tour had been canceled since 1940, though the Vichy regime, like the Fascists in Italy, would also organize a faux Tour for propaganda purposes. In Paris, the cavernous *Vélodrome d'Hiver,* a popular cycling stadium where Gino and his fellow competitors had officially registered for the 1938 Tour, was marshaled for altogether different purposes. In the summer of 1942 the French police used it as a giant holding cell for seven thousand Jews (including four thousand children) arrested in Paris. They held the internees there for five days without sufficient food or water before deporting them to Auschwitz.

✦

In the spring of 1943, Gino and his countrymen felt Italy's path change course once more. Mussolini made a last-ditch effort in North Africa by sending yet another contingent of troops to Tunisia in March. This group included Fausto Coppi, whose regiment was captured quickly by the British. Coppi would spend the rest of World War II in prisoner-of-war camps, first in northern Tunisia and then near Naples.

In early July, the Allies landed in Sicily. At the end of the month, on July 25, 1943, a day after the Fascist Grand Council made a vote of no confidence in Mussolini, the King of Italy declared during a radio broadcast that he had arrested *Il Duce*. Spontaneous celebrations broke out around the nation as the news spread. Italians took to the streets en masse, and crowds that had once lauded Mussolini's every pronouncement now cheered his arrest. "It was beautiful," recalled one Italian Jewish woman, an eyewitness and an ardent Bartali fan. "We were thrilled. We said, 'At least this nightmare is over.' "

News of Mussolini's overthrow took longer to reach other Italians. Such was the case for Ubaldo Pugnaloni, an acquaintance of Gino's from the cycling world. On the morning of July 25, he was scheduled to compete in the national cycling championship for amateurs. The race began and he left the starting line wearing a jersey with Fascist insignia (mandated by the government in certain competitions). Pugnaloni raced splendidly and crossed the finish line ahead of all his rivals. When he went to the winner's podium to receive his trophy, he was surprised to find not a single Fascist official left to present him his prize. When Pugnaloni finally realized what had happened during the hours he had been racing, he ripped off the Fascist insignia and joined the festivities.

The official announcements said that the war would continue, but hopeful signs began appearing over the next six weeks that suggested it might soon end. Portraits of Mussolini were removed from public buildings. Streets and schools named after famous Fascists were renamed. A prominent anti-Semitic newspaper editor was arrested along with one of the officials who had been charged with the enforcement of the Racial Laws. The man who had killed the popular Socialist leader Matteotti was found and arrested. Finally, on September 8, 1943, Italians heard the news for which so many of them had longed: Italy had surrendered to the Allied Forces.

Just as they had done some six weeks earlier upon hearing of Mussolini's overthrow, Italians poured out into the streets to celebrate the cease-fire. In Florence, crowds gathered in the city center. Children fluttered little Italian flags as their parents chattered about their plans for the future. Across Italy, many (though not all) prisoners in internment camps were freed. At the camp where Giacomo Goldenberg was being held, the commandant called all the prisoners together and instructed them to leave. Goldenberg returned to Fiesole immediately to find his family.

Gino had his own reason to celebrate. Thinking that Italy's involvement in the war was over, he joined thousands of young men across the country who submitted the paperwork to be discharged from the army.

Thousands of others were less inclined to follow any procedures. They just discarded uniforms and arms and left military bases en masse. Many spoke about girlfriends, wives, jobs, and new aspirations, their minds struggling to imagine a world beyond their regiment. Gino was the same, thinking about Adriana, Andrea, and his hopes of seeing a full racing calendar restored. After three long years of hardship and a summer of uncertainty, nothing could weigh down the infectious air of possibility.

✦

All this euphoria would prove cruelly brief. Unbeknownst to most in the jubilant crowds on September 8, 1943, the Allied forces had far less control of Italy than was understood. The German army seized power, and on September 12, a group of German paratroopers arrived by air in gliders and freed Mussolini from his imprisonment in a ski lodge that had been converted to a jail. He was whisked off to Berlin and made leader of a new puppet regime that would be based in northeastern Italy, near Bergamo. With Mussolini serving as the Italian face of the German occupation, Germany and Italy were declared allies once again.

Soldiers like Gino realized fortune's wheel had abruptly turned once more. Under this new Fascist regime, a large number of the soldiers who had abandoned the army were pressed back into service. They were mobilized to help the German army repel the Allied forces. Many refused and became deserters. Some 640,000 of these men were captured and imprisoned in camps where an estimated 30,000 of them died. A small number became partisans—a group of guerrilla soldiers who helped the Allied forces wherever possible. A third group made the decision to hide from the authorities, moving to the countryside or distant villages.

With a wife and a young son to shield, Gino struggled with how to proceed. He turned to his older cousin, Armando Sizzi, a practical man with a talent for dispensing sage advice. Sizzi would only recommend one option. The Bartalis needed to disappear.

Gino gathered up his family and relocated to Nuvole, an isolated mountain village some seventy-five miles southeast of Florence in rural

Perugia, where he believed few people would recognize him. He moved into the house of a farmer who had never heard of him before, and introduced himself as Armando Sizzi's brother—Gino Sizzi. To be extra cautious, Gino avoided spending any time in the village except to attend weekly mass at the local church.

The farmer was a generous and unassuming man who asked few questions of his new visitors. He left them in peace as he tended the groves and small fields that surrounded his little house. Gino wanted to feel at ease in these new surroundings. He was far enough from Florence that he felt hidden, but still close enough that he could ride into the city as needed. As the days wore on, however, he realized that he was incapable of appreciating the idyllic serenity of the countryside. Instead, the tranquillity left his mind more time to wander and contemplate the dramatic turn of events under way in Italy:

> In this little lost corner where I often refused to read the headlines of the newspapers, I passed some very sad days of idleness. . . . I hesitated from speaking because I believed they would double-cross me. I believed it to be terrible, unbearable, this war regime where one saw police everywhere. Events were turning worse and worse for Italy. . . . I felt all of this would end in a dramatic fashion, in particular for me, despite my strong reserve.

Nightfall brought him no solace. He spent long, restless hours in bed, doing little but churning over his thoughts.

During a tense moment in the village church, Gino realized that his relocation to Nuvole would be short-lived. The parish priest listened to Gino during confession and then watched him during mass. Afterward, he confronted him.

"Are you Gino Bartali?"

Instinctively, Gino started stuttering something and lied. The priest sensed his nervousness and refused to be deceived. Gino, likely realizing that the priest wasn't the only one in the village who had recognized him in church, decided it was time for his family to leave.

They planned to travel to Siena and then Rome, but their progress was halted when one of their connecting trains was delayed and then canceled after an aerial attack. They were stranded out in rural Tuscany until a friend offered to house them. Within a few days they had returned home to Florence. Though they would continue to evacuate from time to time throughout the war, to friends' homes elsewhere in Florence, and to nearby towns when particularly worried about bombings, they had come to a sobering realization: no place in occupied Italy was completely safe.

7

An Impossible Choice

Giorgio Goldenberg.

Elvira, Tea, and Giacomo Goldenberg.

ONE EVENING IN THE fall of 1943, Gino received a mysterious phone call. It was the archbishop of Florence, Cardinal Elia Dalla Costa. Gino was unnerved. The two men had been friends for years, but Dalla Costa had never been one to call just to chat. It didn't help that Dalla Costa kept the conversation short and cryptic. He wanted to meet the cyclist in person at the archbishop's residence in the center of Florence. And it was urgent. Gino didn't press him for more details. He understood that phone calls were liable to be monitored by the Germans or the Fascists, and if the cardinal was being curt, he must have had a good reason.

When the day of the meeting arrived, Gino mounted his bike and started off for the archbishop's residence. In the fields near his home on Via del Bandino, signs of autumn's departure were already emerging. The vines stood in forlorn, leafless rows, their plump, ripened grapes already carried away to nearby cellars. The dry heat of the summer that had nourished them had long since disappeared, leaving behind drab, listless days that slipped quickly into night. Contemplating this time of year in Florence, the author Henry James had once mused, "Old things, old places, old people, strike us as giving out their secrets more freely in such moist, grey, melancholy days."

The dreary limbo between seasons suited the moment. After a summer of hopeful expectation, Florence had moved into an unsettling netherworld between war and peace when Mussolini returned to power in mid-September. At the end of the month, the city had suffered its first war damages when an Allied bombing expedition targeting an important railway station in the eastern part of the city went terribly astray. The bombs pulverized a school, destroyed a pharmacy, and leveled various neighborhoods. Over two hundred civilians were killed.

But as Gino pedaled on this day past the burnt-umber-roofed buildings that made up central Florence, signs of life and activity bustled everywhere. Adults with jobs proceeded with business as usual; most children still attended school. Theaters continued to delight audiences with stagings of Shakespeare and Chekhov, and one of the city's big cinemas offered up Italy's most famous comedian, Totò, in a madcap comedy called *The Happy Ghost*. Behind this façade of normalcy, however, the war prowled. During the day, it lurked behind closed doors in the secret activity of the city's black markets, where desperate Florentines traded their valuables to get a few ounces of cheese or a handful of eggs. It emerged in the late afternoon as groups of women rummaged through the garbage looking for a stray leaf or core to eat after the markets closed. At dusk, it roved the streets again as haggard elderly men began to hunt down the city's vanishing legion of stray cats for sustenance.

Riding into Florence, Gino could forget the bleak undercurrent of war by focusing on the things that hadn't changed, like the white, green, and red marble–clad Duomo cathedral that dominated Florence's skyline. He wheeled toward it and then arced past it and across to the archbishop's residence. Swinging one leg back and over the frame of his bike, he rolled up to the front of the four-story yellow stone palazzo, stepped off, and walked his bicycle to the front gate. He rang the bell, and after a few minutes he was greeted by the cardinal's personal secretary, a tall, white-haired priest named Giacomo Meneghello. After the tall gate shut behind them, Gino leaned his bike against one of the pillars that lined the courtyard and followed the secretary into the residence. The two men walked to the cardinal's study, an inviting room with ornate rugs, intricately designed draperies, and dark wood bookshelves lined with leatherbound tomes. There they found Dalla Costa ensconced behind his desk. Gino stepped forward to greet the cardinal, and the heavy wooden door closed behind him as Meneghello left them to talk.

✦

Although he had lived in the sumptuous archbishop's palazzo for over a decade, Elia Dalla Costa had never lost the wan and searching look of a desert ascetic. Seventy-one years old, he was tall and thin and had gray, close-cropped hair framing a broad forehead. The angular, hawkish quality of his features imbued him with a look of uncompromising severity that concealed a remarkably sensitive personality. Early on, his peers had recognized a profound and reflective quality about his character and faith, and in the latter years of Pius XI's tenure as pope, rumors spread that Dalla Costa was a likely candidate to replace him. Younger priests found him a kind, selfless teacher and a quick judge of character, who left a lasting impression on them, "like a father does on his own sons."

Dalla Costa had spent his adult life tending to the religious needs of his Roman Catholic parishioners, but he wanted to speak with Gino about a secret request from a group of Florentine Jews. This group was part of a larger organization called Delasem (*Delegazione assistenza emigranti ebrei*), which helped foreign Jews pouring into Italy from other parts of Europe. During the early war period, before the Germans arrived, Delasem had worked in the open, legally, as Fascist government officials realized that this relief organization could spare them the trouble of having to coordinate basic services for the new refugees. After the Germans arrived in Italy in the fall of 1943, however, all foreign and Italian Jews (including the members of Delasem) became targets for arrest. The relief work of Delasem's Florentine branch was forced underground and became more difficult to carry out. The growing number of Jewish refugees arriving in the city only taxed the organization further. It became clear that they needed to reach out to sympathetic Gentiles in order to have any hope of helping all those in need. In the latter half of September 1943, they approached Cardinal Dalla Costa.

That decision would prove an inspired one. Dalla Costa had already demonstrated his anti-Fascist convictions when Hitler visited Florence in 1938, and in 1943 he quickly became an effective and compassionate leader of what would emerge as a powerful rescue network. When asked, the cardinal organized nearly all the resources at his disposal. His personal secretary, Monsignor Meneghello, was instructed to help the Jewish relief coordinators. For a short time, Meneghello received Jewish refugees seeking assistance in the diocesan office before moving this activity to a less conspicuous location. Another priest was recruited to reach out to various convents and religious orders scattered around Tuscany. Dalla Costa supplied this priest with a letter of introduction that provided clear guidelines to those throughout the archdiocese. "He told us to peremptorily welcome all the needy that would present themselves at our doors and to offer them assistance and food, without asking anything, not where they came from, nor for how many days they would be staying," said one recipient of Dalla Costa's letter. The cardinal also gave of himself, housing and feeding several Jews in the archbishop's residence before finding them lower-profile housing elsewhere.

✦

Gino would not learn the full extent of the cardinal's wartime activities until years later. As he sat down in Dalla Costa's office on that late-fall day in 1943, it was all an utter mystery. Speaking in his slow, methodical manner, in which he seemed to weigh each word and shape it in his mouth before he spoke, Dalla Costa outlined the problem. Jewish refugees were flooding into Florence. Some had come through the city with the intention of getting closer to the front and the arrival of the Allied forces; others were looking to slip across the Alps into Switzerland or to leave the country at ports like Genoa. Still others were hoping to ride the war out in the city or its outskirts, living under non-Jewish identities.

These refugees needed food, shelter, and false identity documents, the cardinal explained, and he wanted Gino to help him. The cyclist would work as one of the network's messengers, delivering documents and carrying out tasks around Tuscany and its environs. At first glance, it looked like a tailor-made role for Gino. During much of the war, he had been riding the local roads as a military bicycle messenger, and on his frequent leaves from the army, he had been training and racing on them. If anyone knew these roads and had a credible alibi to be on them, it was Gino Bartali.

The danger of the work, however, was inescapable. Dalla Costa was explicit. If he was caught helping Jews, there was a very real possibility that the Germans would imprison him, execute him on the spot, or send him to a concentration camp, where disease, starvation, and torture regularly killed prisoners. The Italian Fascists were no less formidable. Desperate and angry, many hard-line soldiers had formed large gangs that terrorized civilians and searched for Jews hiding around the country. Together the two groups ensured that the threat of being caught helping Jews was an ever-present one.

Secrecy would therefore be paramount. Gino could not share the information that Dalla Costa passed on with anyone, not even his wife. Even Gino himself would be limited to knowing the absolute minimum required to carry out his role. It was essential that no one individual know too much, or even know the other people involved in the network, the cardinal explained, so that no one could give the whole group away if interrogated and tortured.

The cardinal finally raised the question that defined the evening. Would Gino join the rescue effort? Would he be willing to risk his life for a group of strangers?

✦

In nearby Fiesole, Gino's friend Giacomo Goldenberg assessed an alarming piece of news that was spreading through the Jewish community: Jews in concentration camps in other occupied countries were being murdered en masse. In the strictest sense, it wasn't new information. It had been discussed for months on Allied radio stations, and it had spread like wildfire from the letters of Italian soldiers on the eastern front. But when the Fascists alone held power in Italy, the threat had felt more distant, a feeling borne out by the fact that groups of foreign Jews secretly poured into Italy because it was safer than the rest of Nazi-held Europe at that time. With the arrival of the German army, however, the sense of danger became more raw and immediate as the darkest force of the occupation permeated Italy. Goldenberg had felt the first tremors with the Racial Laws in 1938 and the indignity of the arrests of foreigners, including foreign Jews, in 1940. And now, under Mussolini's new German-supported regime, the last supports of his world were fast collapsing beneath him.

Since his release from the internment camp, Goldenberg had heard nothing from his cousins the Kleins, which raised the terrifying possibility that they had been arrested again by the new Fascist regime. His immediate family's situation seemed no less precarious. His address was known to the Italian police; there was no doubt that it was recorded on at least one list. To a man who had learned to expect the worst regarding anti-Semitic behavior, it was no stretch to foresee the Germans getting hold of the list and arresting his family. It was time to leave Fiesole.

Giacomo Goldenberg and his wife, Elvira, began making a series of arrangements and soon realized their family's chances for survival would increase if they split up. They took their now eleven-year-old son, Giorgio, to live at the Santa Marta Institute in Settignano, a religious children's boardinghouse northeast of Florence that had agreed to care covertly for Jewish children, after receiving Dalla Costa's request. Six-year-old Tea, however, seemed too young to live apart from her parents. With her and his wife in mind, Goldenberg began to think frantically about where they could hide.

The problem was finding a place to go. Having lived much of their lives in Fiume, the Goldenbergs had few relatives or friends who could shelter them in Tuscany. The other option, finding a rental apartment, would have put the family at a stranger's mercy. With their identity documents, which listed the family as Jewish, they were vulnerable targets for betrayal. Since the German occupation, an opportunistic landlord, or any Italian for that matter, who turned a family over to the German authorities could expect a reward of anywhere from one thousand to nine thousand lire per person. At a moment when the average factory worker was earning but twenty-nine lire per day, such sums represented breathtaking amounts of money. More tellingly, they revealed the extent of the Nazi zeal for persecuting Jews; the capture of a Jewish refugee was even more prized than the capture of an escaped Allied prisoner, typically worth just 1,800 lire in reward money.

Even an otherwise kindhearted landlord might have thought twice about housing the Goldenbergs and risking a confrontation with the Fascist and German police apparatus. Early in the fall of 1943, sheltering Jews may have only prompted a questioning or a temporary arrest. But in November a group of Fascists had formalized the *Carta di Verona,* which declared that "Those belonging to the Jewish race are foreigners. During this war they belong to an enemy nationality." By early December it became clear that this meant all Jews on Italian soil could be arrested. And anyone who helped them, let alone housed them, was committing a severe and punishable offense. As individuals like Dalla Costa had realized, it was a crime that could be punished by death. Given these circumstances, Goldenberg knew that few Gentiles would be willing to take his family in.

Frantic about his lack of options, Goldenberg reached out to his old friend Armando Sizzi. The two men met one afternoon in Fiesole, and Goldenberg laid out his dilemma. Sizzi recognized his friend's fear and knew that if he did nothing, the Goldenbergs could disappear without warning, arrested and deported like countless other Italian Jews. Before Goldenberg had even finished speaking, Sizzi was trying to work out how he could possibly aid him. As a humble bike mechanic, he had neither the financial means nor the network of contacts to help, but to leave his friend to be hunted down was simply not an option. Sizzi knew the only hope lay with his cousin Gino. As a successful cyclist, he had been able to purchase one house for himself and another for his parents, and had stakes in other residences as investments. And even if he had no space of his own to offer, Gino was a celebrity, a man who had many friends and acquaintances; he knew people.

Sizzi promised his friend he would make some inquiries on his behalf. After arranging to meet again in the coming days, he watched Goldenberg hurry back down the street.

Then Sizzi went back to Florence and asked his cousin Gino for help.

✦

Cardinal Dalla Costa and the Goldenberg family—the weight of it all nearly suffocated Gino. There was no question that he wanted to help them both, but the danger involved was overwhelming. It ate at him, making him more taciturn among friends and downright flighty when Adriana spoke with him. At night, as they lay in bed together, he grew ever more restless and agitated, consumed by the fear of what might happen if he was caught.

The only place that could offer any peace in a moment like this was the Ponte a Ema cemetery. As he sat by his brother's grave, Gino could begin to contemplate the choice that stood before him. He had every reason to help. Dalla Costa was his spiritual mentor—the human face of the faith that Gino had built his life around—and the man who had officiated at his marriage and baptized his son. Goldenberg was a friend, looking to protect his family. It was impossible not to empathize with his situation, and it resonated deeply with Gino's own childhood experience of political tumult. Certainly the scale of the Jewish persecution had been amplified exponentially, but the parallels to what had happened to the Socialists when he was a boy were uncanny. A minority group was being demonized by government-backed voices in the press and scapegoated by government officials. Few men could have better understood the cruelty of such pressures than Torello Bartali's son.

And yet he had two reasons more powerful than any other not to risk himself: Adriana and his son, Andrea. If he was caught helping Jews or even sheltering them, he could be imprisoned and killed by the German authorities, leaving his wife alone to fend for their two-year-old son.

It was an impossible choice. The siren call of self-preservation was deafening, but a nobler impulse beckoned. Other Italians facing the same quandary in other parts of the country would liken it to a battle in which there was no middle ground. Few of them had any illusions about the repercussions if their activities were discovered. But to stand by and do nothing while civilians were being captured and murdered was a choice that many viewed as tacit support of the deportations. And so each individual was left to decide on which side he would stand. "It was something that we all had to do," explained one participant in the broader resistance. "One made the choice to be on the side of the Fascists or one had to defend the people."

Gino wrestled with the dilemma about what course to take. As a man of fervent faith, he turned to prayer for solace as he contemplated his options. He poured out his thoughts to his brother's tomb. Finally, without speaking to his wife, he made his decision.

✦

Cardinal Dalla Costa and the other members of the resistance effort in Florence quickly understood the scope of what they were up against. On November 6, 1943, without warning, German SS and Italian Fascists arrested Jews around the city, many of them foreign-born. At the end of the month, as part of a larger series of arrests, German and Fascist soldiers stormed into one of the buildings of Florence's archdiocese and arrested key members of the Jewish refugee assistance committee, including one of Dalla Costa's most trusted priests and the chief rabbi of Florence.

Rufino Niccacci, a monk and priest from Assisi, happened to come into Florence to meet with Cardinal Dalla Costa at the time of these November raids. As he left the train station and walked toward the archbishop's residence, he was startled by what he saw. German soldiers and Fascists with rifles swarmed the city in trucks and on motorcycles. As he neared the archbishop's palace in the center of town, Niccacci could hear loudspeakers blaring "*Achtung! Attenzione!* All inhabitants outside! No packing, take nothing. You have three minutes." Jews were being rounded up in different parts of the city. On one street, Niccacci came across groups of Jewish families huddled together as Nazi soldiers grabbed parents by the shoulders to load them into one vehicle while they pushed the children with rifle butts, to shuffle them into separate vehicles. A few women clutched their babies to hide them, but the soldiers ripped them from their arms. Some young Jewish men sized up the situation and decided to make a break for it. They didn't get far, crumpling as the bullets hit them. Niccacci hurried along through the city, and the violence only got worse. "I saw a whole family lined up against a wall and machine-gunned because a revolver had been found on one of them," he said. By the time he reached the archbishop's palace, he was distraught and soaked in a panicked sweat.

✦

In his everyday life, Niccacci was the father superior of the monastery of San Damiano in Assisi. With a square jaw and prominent dark eyebrows, he was the picture of youth. He was energetic and strong, a trait he inherited from his father, the operator of a small grain mill. Even the formless brown sackcloth of his Franciscan cassock, tied at the waist with a cord, could not hide his muscular frame. To many people who knew him, however, he seemed an unlikely candidate for the monastic life. As he himself readily admitted, he was rather inclined toward certain earthly pleasures. He relished a good bottle of wine and was the only one in the monastery's community who smoked. At thirty-two years of age, he seemed too young to be the head of a monastery filled with older men.

But when a group of Jewish refugees had arrived in Assisi in September 1943, and the local bishop asked him and another priest, Don Aldo Brunacci, to help them, Niccacci discovered within himself an uncommon reservoir of courage and wisdom. He arranged safe accommodation for them in the guesthouses that the different monasteries and convents in Assisi maintained. He organized the production of false identity documents so that they could evade detection during arrests. And when stopped by the German army or the Fascists, Niccacci proved adept at telling bold lies in order to protect these people who now relied on him for their personal safety.

He had come to Florence to seek the cardinal's assistance in coordinating safe passage out of the country for some of the Jews he had been hiding. When he entered Dalla Costa's study, the cardinal was sitting at his desk with his head resting in his bony hands. The cardinal looked up and composed himself. Niccacci listened as he shared an alarming piece of news: there was no longer a practical way for the refugees in Assisi to leave Italy. The Swiss were turning away many Jewish refugees at their borders; the Germans were keeping a watchful eye on the Port of Genoa, closing off the possibility of escape by sea. Dalla Costa could do little to help those who had taken refuge in Assisi. Niccacci sat gloomily as he contemplated how his trip to Florence appeared to have ended in failure. Then the cardinal slowly outlined an alternate plan.

"You came here to ask my help in establishing a route out of Assisi. I would like to reverse the process—and establish a route *to* Assisi," he said.

"Your Eminence doesn't mean to suggest that all Jewish refugees come to Assisi?" replied Niccacci anxiously.

"Calm down, Padre. No, I don't mean to turn your city into the hiding center for Jews. But I would like to turn it into a counterfeiting center—where you could produce identity cards for the people who need them. First of all for those who are hiding in private houses and are in constant danger. Those people need your help, Padre."

Niccacci balked for a moment, worried about all the new responsibilities he was being asked to shoulder. Slowly he composed himself and agreed to help.

Weighing the task ahead, he asked the cardinal one final question before beginning his trip home to Assisi. "How do you propose, Your Eminence, to forward the photographs to us and pick up the identity cards when they are ready?"

"I have my couriers," the cardinal replied. "The photographs will reach you in a week."

✦

As the afternoon sun sank in the sky, Gino left his home on the outskirts of Florence with some bread and vegetables he had procured from several farmers near Ponte a Ema. The Bartalis didn't really have extra food to spare, but Gino knew the Goldenberg family would have nothing. He walked down Via del Bandino toward an apartment he co-owned on the same street as his home. He let himself in and put the meager supplies in the small kitchen. It wasn't much, but it would have to do. After one final look around, Gino left the way he had come and locked the door behind him.

He then hurried north toward Florence. Having made his decision, he knew there could be no looking back. It was time to bring the Goldenbergs to their new home.

8

The Counterfeiters' Ring

The Brizi printing press.

ONE EARLY MORNING NOT long after Dalla Costa's meeting with Niccacci, Adriana Bartali awoke to see Gino putting on his cycling shorts, jersey, and sweater in the corner of the room. *Where is he going?* she wondered as she sat up in bed. Startled, Gino stopped changing and turned to her.

"Don't wait for me this evening. I'm leaving for a few days of training," he said.

She stared back at him.

"If someone should come looking for me, especially at night, say that I left the house for an emergency."

"Who would be looking for you—at nighttime?" she asked, anxiety creeping into her voice.

"No one," he replied. "But if someone does, just tell them that I'm out finding medicine for little Andrea, who is sick."

Adriana watched as Gino finished dressing himself, adding a pair of long johns over his shorts because the mornings were already getting cold as winter approached. That he would be gone for a few days wasn't what bothered her. She was long familiar with the demands of her husband's training commitments and a racing schedule that took him all over Europe from early spring to late fall. But in these last weeks he had been disappearing more frequently, and the nervous way he had answered her questions alarmed her.

"What are you training for if there are no races scheduled?" she asked.

Gino stopped getting ready and walked over to his wife. "I'm just training," he said, and leaned over to kiss her firmly on the forehead. Adriana's breathing slowed as her husband communicated reassurance in the unspoken language they shared. Gino wanted to be ready when the races started again.

Gino carried his bicycle out of the house and left. Soon he was gliding across Florence's city streets to meet one of the cardinal's trusted assistants. The rendezvous spot changed frequently, but the objective was always the same: Gino was picking up a few documents and a cache of photographs. All would be used to create counterfeit identification papers for Jews in hiding. Although barely larger than four postage stamps placed together, each photo told a story about its provenance. Some had been taken recently, with the black and white tones still crisp but artfully weathered to look older. Others betrayed their true age in their creases, and in the corners still curling from where they had been pulled off genuine identity documents. Gino recognized none of the faces. From old men wearing youthfully stylish suits, hinting at their vanity, to young women staring blankly with world-weary eyes, they were all strangers.

After hiding the photos away in the safest place he knew, Gino began the journey south. It was still early morning, but Florence was already humming with activity. Pedestrians streamed across sidewalks, drawn like magnets to lines outside the neighborhood dry-goods stores, where each hoped to pick over the nearly empty shelves and find something that could tide them over for a few more days. Here and there, soldiers mingled among them, some chatting among themselves while others stood still, watching. The most menacing were the German SS, who wore caps bearing a skull-and-crossbones badge. Gino had seen these men in the city time and time again, but the sight of them always filled him with a mixture of fear and anger. It was just another unwanted reminder that he lived in a police state, where his every move could be followed and questioned. Relief came only when he rode over the bridge above his beloved Arno River. In a few minutes he would leave the city behind and be alone again on the open road.

✦

The trip to Assisi was a lengthy one, some 110 miles along the most direct route, and so Gino had several hours to reflect. If Alfredo Martini or one of his other training partners had been out riding with him, he would think out loud in an unbroken stream of chatter. "He liked to say everything that passed through his head," said Martini when describing these rides. Martini, like Gino's other training partners, loved to train with Gino because Gino would happily let Martini draft on his wheel for almost the entire ride; he was just delighted to have company. "He never stopped talking to me," said Martini, who could barely understand Gino at times because of the wind and his own fatigue, though he never failed to respond "Yes" whenever he could to encourage his friend.

Gino talked about everything except the war. He could spend hours analyzing a strategy he had used in a race years earlier, or share his latest thoughts on the best food to eat before training. But his favorite topics were his rivals, and in 1943 that meant Fausto Coppi, the young upstart who had become a credible competitor in those last races before the war turned more serious in Italy. Coppi seemed to be among the very few who could methodically parry Gino's staccato attacks with an unyielding fluidity that refused to be baited. Inevitably on those training rides, Gino would also vow to win the Tour de France again. He would silence those critics in the cycling community who he believed were quietly starting to whisper that he was past his prime, calling him *Il Vecchio,* "the Old Man," a "grandfather [who had to be] taken for walks from time to time."

But Coppi had been gone from Italy for more than six months, dispatched as a soldier to Africa as part of one of Mussolini's failed military campaigns. Nor could the Tour have felt more remote. Five years after Gino's win, it was nothing more than a dream from a distant, prewar world. And so, in the rare moments of silence when Gino was riding alone instead of with his cycling partners, he wrestled with a growing sense of hopelessness. He was losing his "most fertile years," as he put it, for winning cycling's top honors and earning the prize money that would be critical to support his family. Whatever plans he held for the future were diminishing with every passing month without races.

When he had ridden some seventy miles, Gino came close to Terontola, where he had a little job to complete. Terontola was a typical small Tuscan town with a cluster of ocher-and-tawny buildings, but it held one unusual distinction: it was the transfer point between the main north-south rail line in Italy and one of the regional lines that ran southeast to Perugia, Assisi, and Foligno.

Some five hundred yards from the train station, Gino stopped on a nearby bridge. He was early, and so he busied himself by pretending to inspect his bicycle. As he fiddled with it, however, he watched the train tracks. He was waiting for a train coming in to Terontola from the north, which was thought to be carrying either Jewish refugees or other anti-Fascists fleeing to the countryside and southern Italy. This station was particularly dangerous for them because they often had to switch trains and therefore risked detection and capture when moving across the platforms.

Jewish refugees dreaded train stations because they were exposed to so many possible captors. As one Italian Jew explained, "That's where one was most likely to get cornered. Nazi and Fascist uniforms were everywhere, and God only knows how many secret service trench coats. Most evident were the German military police. They were tall devils, walking in pairs in impeccably fitted and pressed gray uniforms, gloved hands joined behind their backs and simonized boots clicking in slow, synchronized rhythm. A polished metal plate with the engraved word *Feldgendarmerie* hung from their necks by a chain like a wine steward's emblem, and it swung on their chests as they watchfully zigzagged through the crowd."

Gino knew these dangers, and so when the train finally appeared in the distance, he got back on his bike and rode into town to the bar in the Terontola train station. Word of his arrival spread quickly through the station and even the small village itself. The appearance of one of Italy's most famous sports stars in Terontola was an exciting event unlike any other. In the bar, the owner, a friend of Gino's, greeted him; the town tailor, another friend who worked nearby, appeared and offered Gino a prosciutto sandwich for lunch. Around them, people from the train station pushed to get closer to Gino. Many hoped to embrace him or give him a friendly slap on the back. Others wanted to buy their idol an espresso or get his autograph.

In no time at all, the little bar filled up, and Gino was called to address the noisy throng. He offered a few words of friendly greeting, and was answered with loud cheering. All this extra commotion attracted the attention of several of the soldiers in the train station, some of whom likely hoped to get autographs of their own. And for those refugees and dissidents hoping to avoid the Germans and Fascists as they switched trains, it is believed that this planned distraction bought them a few precious minutes of cover.

When it was all over, Gino got back on his bike and headed to the city of Perugia, where he planned to stay the night in a local church.

✦

Meanwhile, in Settignano, the hillside Tuscan town northeast of Florence, eleven-year-old Giorgio Goldenberg rushed out of a local elementary school. His stomach growling for food, he joined a group of his classmates heading back to the Santa Marta boardinghouse for lunch. It was a short walk past a few small farms and a German military post. Within a few minutes they turned the corner past the estate's stone wall and walked through the front gate, a soaring manorial entrance that would have made any giant feel small. Scurrying up a long stone driveway, they came to the ivory-colored four-story building that Giorgio and his housemates called home.

The boys stormed through the front doors and made a beeline to the room where the nuns brought them together for meals. Lunch this day was the same thing they had eaten at lunch every day since Giorgio arrived: a bowl of watery soup and a serving of peas. Dinner, a slice of stale bread and a warm glass of barley coffee, would just be a repeat of breakfast. "For an eleven-year-old child, this was not enough," explained Giorgio.

With such limited rations, food emerged as a constant obsession. Some of the boys became very enterprising. One turned the chore of potato peeling into a chance to gather the discarded skins (covertly pared as thickly as possible) that he later roasted secretly over a small fire built with friends and enjoyed with a pinch of salt. Others turned brazen, strong-arming younger students out of their food, or filling their pockets with bread stolen from the pantry. No scheme, however inventive, offered a permanent remedy; the satisfaction of any morsel, no matter how ill-gotten, inevitably yielded to the gnawing pain of hunger and a renewed struggle to find more.

The nuns did what they could to pacify these little battles, and tried to overcome the inevitable tension wrought by shortages by showering the boys with abounding love. One nun, known affectionately as "Mamma Cornelia," emerged as a figure of particular kindness for the group of about ten Jewish boys who were hidden at Santa Marta's—none of whom knew the others' true religious identity at the time. She helped them avoid any uncomfortable questions when they didn't take communion during mass, by suggesting that their parents were military combatants who would decide about the timing of their children's participation in the sacrament when they returned from the battle front. Attuned to their spiritual needs, she memorized and privately delivered a traditional Hebrew blessing given by Jewish parents to their children. In the evenings, when she visited each boy as prayers were being said in the dormitory, she quietly encouraged them to say the prayers of their own faith in silence. Through all of these acts, her boarding house became a small island of refuge in a country beset by murderous persecution.

Try as she might, however, it was impossible to keep the outside world entirely at bay. The children saw it when truckloads of German soldiers trundled past them as they walked from their boarding house to the school nearby. They heard it in the noisy drone of Allied bombers flying overhead. And they felt it in the loneliness of a visiting day spent waiting fruitlessly at the window, when a boy was forced to accept the reality of his parents' arrest and deportation. At times like that, "hunger was almost a blessing because food was all you could think about," said one Jewish refugee who spent the war hiding in a nearby orphanage.

✦

At dawn, Gino awoke in the Perugian church where he had spent the night. He did his morning calisthenics, as he had done nearly every day since 1936, and checked his bike. The distances between his seat, handlebars, and pedals always had to be the same; if the settings were off by even a fraction of an inch, that could cause muscle strain or pain midway through a ride. When he was satisfied with his bike, he wheeled it out of the church. He put his cycling cap on and set off again for Assisi. In the distance, the sun was just beginning to rise. The world was asleep, but there was a quiet hopefulness to this time of day that Gino had always cherished. It was the time that long races started, when a cyclist waited with nervous excitement to see whether the hundreds of miles of training he had accumulated in his legs would be enough.

Riding out of Perugia, Gino moved slowly at first, "warming up the engine" as he called it, getting a sense of how his body felt. It had been nearly six months since he last competed in what was admittedly just a middling wartime race, yet his legs remained remarkably strong. The ribbon of road spooled out in front of him, beckoning with a gentle descent through dormant wheatfields and silvery green olive trees, whose ripe globes were still being pressed into liquid gold by a bold few. Gino started to push harder. His heart sped up and he started to feel warm enough that he took his sweater off and rode just with his undershirt. The road leveled out, opening up as an alluring temptation. Gino pushed a little harder, sailing through the Umbrian countryside, slightly wilder and more rugged than his home region of Tuscany. Finally he could begin to feel the foothills of the Appenine mountain range under his wheels. Still he was holding something back; a real climb could only be won when every last ounce of strength was in play. Gino looked around and tried to estimate how far he was from his destination—and then he checked his watch and attacked.

Ahead, the town of Assisi rose out of the landscape, a cluster of pinkish white monasteries, convents, and churches perched on the side of Mount Subasio. Imposing and austere, Assisi traced much of its history back to its most important inhabitant, the thirteenth-century Catholic monk and saint, Francis of Assisi, who was revered for his teachings on charity and simplicity. Francis's monastic order had spread around the world and transformed the sleepy outpost of Assisi into a major center of religious activity. Gino knew the town and had visited its churches before the war, receiving a chalice from the local bishop as a gift for the chapel in his home. But he had not come to Assisi today as a pilgrim. He had come to see Father Rufino Niccacci.

He found him at the San Damiano monastery, an expansive oatmeal-colored stone building just outside the town walls in a grove of olive and cypress trees. Gino made his way to the thick wooden side door and knocked on it. Niccacci heard him from his room and rushed down and let him in.

"You'll catch a cold, Bartali!" he said, looking with surprise at the cyclist in his shorts and undershirt, before inviting him in.

"Thirteen kilometers from Perugia in a quarter of an hour is not bad, is it?" Gino replied with a touch of swagger, as he removed his cycling cap. Niccacci led the cyclist to a private room in the monastery.

When he was sure they were alone, Gino began to take apart his bike, and Niccacci watched as he unloaded its precious cargo. Gino loosened the screw attaching his seat to the bike, removed the seat, and pulled out the cache of photographs and documents, rolled up like a scroll and hidden in the hollow frame of his bicycle. Niccacci took the papers, unrolled them delicately, and hid them in a cupboard that held sacred relics in the monastery's oratory.

Turning back to Gino, he said, "Come and have some coffee." The two men walked to the refectory, the catacomb-shaped room of maroon wood and cream stone where the monks took their meals. They sat at one of the long, well-worn wooden tables beneath a nearly life-size painting of the crucifixion as Niccacci served up the monastery's roasted barley coffee. It was simple fare, but Gino was happy to have it. As he sipped his drink, he relayed the news that the cardinal had instructed him to go even farther south. He was to speak with a priest who had contacts with smugglers who might be willing to be paid to run Jewish refugees across the battle lines into Allied-controlled territory. He would stop through Assisi again on his return.

When they finished, Niccacci walked his guest to the side door. The conversation turned to cycling as Gino put his cap back on. "I'll be champion again one day. I'll show them who *Il Vecchio* is," he promised boldly. With that, he mounted his bike and sped off.

Niccacci would keep this meeting and the others that followed it as secret as possible. Still, on at least one occasion, a monk who was uninvolved with the network found out. It happened soon after Gino arrived for one of his deliveries. As chance would have it, Pier Damiano, a twenty-two-year-old member of the order, was coming out of his room when he saw the cyclist standing by the side door. Confused, Damiano stopped and looked at the stranger intently. In a moment, he recognized the face and sinewy figure that he had seen in countless newspapers.

Niccacci swore Damiano to secrecy about Gino's visit. It was essential that the network they had set up continue to function without interruption, because the arrival of Gino delivering photographs could mean only one thing: Cardinal Dalla Costa in Florence needed more false identity documents.

✦

Few things were more important in German-occupied Italy than identity documents. Often little larger than a small folded pamphlet, an identity document typically consisted of a stamped photo and lines of information that detailed everything from the holder's name and address to racial background and skin type (possible entries included "healthy" and "pink"). An ID was used constantly. Renting an apartment, getting food ration books, keeping a job, even just passing an everyday police document check on the streets—everything required an identity document. "A man without identity documents," Giorgio Goldenberg later explained, "did not exist." For Jews in Italy, now enemies of the state who could be arrested on sight, this meant the possibility of detection loomed around every corner of daily life. False identity documents, which hid their Jewish heritage, therefore became integral for survival.

Possession of false identity documents was, however, a grave offense in occupied Europe. A Jewish refugee captured with them would be arrested and probably deported to one of the death camps. A counterfeiter caught making the documents was liable to be executed for his crime. Given such severe punishments, forgers skilled and brave enough to do the work were difficult to find. Good false documents that could pass the near-constant inspections became more precious than gold.

✦

In such a climate of desperation in the early fall of 1943, Father Niccacci had found himself the guardian of an improbable alchemist's secret. On a side street in Assisi he had found a skilled printer named Luigi Brizi. Now he just had to persuade him to risk everything and become a counterfeiter.

Short and portly, Brizi often sported overalls and an Italian beret in his comings and goings about town. At seventy-one years old, he was the aging patriarch of a family that traced its roots far back into Assisi's history. One ancestor, Eugenio Brizi, had been the town's mayor and a noted local ally of Giuseppe Mazzini, a key player in Italy's nineteenth-century battle for independence. Other members of his family had been wealthy landowners, amassing significant holdings of buildings in a nearby town. By Brizi's time, however, the family had slipped inexplicably into a state of genteel poverty. The family's buildings had all been sold off, and the profits spent. Only a street named after Eugenio remained in Assisi, an obscure memorial to the prominence they once enjoyed in the town.

As a young man, Brizi had settled upon the idea of starting a store in Assisi. He chose a small retail space across the piazza from St. Clare's, the basilica dedicated to the thirteenth-century nun who was Assisi's second most important religious figure after Saint Francis. Like many of the stores in Assisi, the space was small, narrow, and, at full width, measured but fifteen feet across. It was poorly lit, and its cold stone walls surrounded a rudimentary wooden floor that looked ready to collapse at any moment.

In the beginning, Brizi had intended to focus on stationery. Over the years, however, he added a small assortment of tourist bric-a-brac—religious figures, medallions, carvings, and the like. The income generated from all this would probably have been minimal, and it certainly wouldn't have gone far in supporting his wife and five children. So he also began offering printing services. Sitting behind a refurbished Felix printer that he set up in a corner of his small store, he coaxed the press like a virtuoso behind a piano and began printing menus, rate cards, and circulars for the town's restaurants, hotels, and churches.

Brizi likely first met Niccacci in this context, although it's not certain. What is certain is that the two men did not meet because of a common affinity for the Catholic Church. Brizi was an atheist, despite living in one of Italy's most religious towns. He had little patience for proselytizers and, like his ancestors, identified closely with the strain of Italian politics that viewed the Church's influence in the nation with skepticism.

It must have been unusual in the Assisi of the 1930s for the head of a monastery to befriend a man who avoided church at all costs, and the fact that it happened revealed something about each man's respective capacity for tolerance. In time their friendship grew stronger, nurtured over its own weekly ritual—a game of checkers each Wednesday, played with a shared carafe of Umbrian wine at a small café in the town's main piazza.

✦

In the fall of 1943, a single conversation would transform their relationship. It happened after Bishop Nicolini charged Niccacci with helping a group of newly arrived Jewish refugees. Each of these individuals needed counterfeit identity documents. One day, after their weekly checkers game, Niccacci reached out to Brizi to help him. As they walked through the narrow, cobblestoned streets of Assisi, the late-afternoon bells began tolling for evening vespers. Niccacci introduced the idea by reminding Brizi of the Jewish contribution to the cause of Italian liberation, aware of the Brizi family's support of Italian nationalism. Niccacci kept speaking, leading Brizi through a brief history of Jews in Italy until finally he reached the end of his meandering monologue.

"Luigi Brizi, are you going to help them?"

"Jews? Here, in Assisi?" Brizi asked incredulously and with good reason. There was no history of a Jewish community ever existing in Assisi.

"Yes."

"How?" Brizi demanded.

"By printing false identity cards in your printing shop. By contributing to the cause you preach yourself—freedom and democracy. By repaying the debts Mazzini, Garibaldi, Cavour, *and* Brizi owed them. By saving their lives."

Brizi was stunned into silence. But slowly Niccacci's words began to take effect as the old printer bristled with the realization that the descendants of Italian patriots were now being betrayed by the very country they had helped establish. Finally he responded.

"I will do it—on one condition. I don't want my son, Trento, to know, to be involved at all. In case something happens to me, I do not want him to be incriminated." The twenty-eight-year-old Trento had just returned to Assisi in early September after fighting for Italy on the Yugoslavian front. Having almost lost him to the war, Brizi wasn't willing to risk his son's life again.

Just days later, Brizi was working on the false identity documents in his store when his son walked in. He tried to hide what he was doing, but Trento demanded that his father tell him what was going on. Brizi resisted at first, but then buckled under the weight of his son's questioning. He swore him to secrecy, and then explained what Niccacci had asked of him. When his father had finished, Trento responded, "I fought for three years on the front, I heard the bullets whistling around me, and at this point I am no longer afraid of anything. If you are doing something, I will do it too. I will help you." The old man reluctantly agreed.

Over the next several hours, father and son labored intently on their creation in the back of the store. Brizi continued to experiment with the movable type and printed samples on different types of card stock. Working on a suggestion that Niccacci had given his father, Trento began crafting the first of several false rubber seals from different communities like Lecce and Caserta that were below the Allied front and therefore unverifiable by the Fascist authorities. Together they made several copies, testament to Brizi's long-held belief that "making prints was like making fritters—the more one made, the nicer they turned out." Finally they managed to craft a workable blank identity document. They filled it out with personal information Niccacci had provided them. When they finished, their first counterfeit identity card was complete: Enrico Maionica, a Jewish refugee who had arrived in Assisi from Trieste in the north, became Enrico Martorana, a bachelor from the southern city of Caserta.

As they were wrapping up, they heard a noise outside the print shop. Brizi signaled to Trento to be silent, and turned off the light. They held their breath and went to the front of the shop. Trento looked outside through a crack in the shutter. They heard a pair of men's voices, the snap of a match lighting a cigarette, and then one man said, *"Danke schön,"* or "thank you" in German. Though there was little light with which to see, Trento recognized the uniforms of the German SS and the Italian Fascist police. The pair had paused for a smoke outside. They moved on after a few minutes.

"What a scare. I wanted to throw everything away," remembered Trento later. Then he reconsidered. Niccacci was risking his life to protect the Jews, and Trento decided that he didn't want to surrender, either. So while it was after curfew, and there were Fascists and German soldiers patrolling the streets, Trento hid the new ID in his pants, and rushed out of the printer's shop. He walked across the piazza, out the archway at the corner, down the steps, and along the descending path lined with cypresses and olive trees to the San Damiano monastery.

When he arrived, Trento pulled the document out of his pants. Niccacci inspected it closely and started speaking excitedly: "My God, you are very good. It's perfect. Tell your father that there are dozens of Jews hidden here, and I will need several identity cards like this one. But please—change the city often. Identical identity cards will arouse the suspicions of the Nazis."

And then, as if sensing the enormity of his request, Niccacci offered a small measure of help. Going forward, he would see to it that the identity documents were filled out with the appropriate personal information such as one's birthplace and parents' names.

✦

As fate would have it, Enrico Maionica, the recipient of the first forged document, would emerge as the last link in the counterfeiting chain. An athletic chemical engineering student, he arrived in Assisi in the fall of 1943 carrying with him a story of persecution that would have been familiar to any Jew hiding in the small town. His trip to Assisi had been a nightmare, hiding from German and Fascist officers swarming the trains, which were overflowing with people and belongings. Some desperate souls rode in the couplings between carriages; others rode atop the cars, clinging to the roofs, only to be killed when the trains passed through narrow tunnels. Once in Assisi, Maionica hid for a period in a boardinghouse run by an order of nuns. Recognizing the risk of being identified as a Jew, he asked Niccacci to help him get false identity documents, and was soon drawn into the monk's counterfeiting ring.

Working out of a back room in Assisi's San Quirico convent with two other Jewish refugees hiding there, Maionica took up the task of finishing the false identity documents that Brizi had created. (In time the three men would expand their operations to include creating fake drivers' licenses and ration cards.) He carefully affixed the photographs that Niccacci had given him to the blank documents. Using an old southern Italian telephone book, one of Maionica's partners picked out the names of people from regions already under Allied control to match the seals created by the Brizis. Working together, the three men typed the new names onto the identity documents with an old typewriter and forged signatures where needed.

When they were finished, the documents looked ready. In a moment of inspiration, Maionica decided that they were missing two things. The first was a House of Savoy stamp, the imprimatur of the Italian royal family that he had seen on many older identity cards. The problem was that these seals were too detailed to be carved quickly by hand, and too rare to be carried by most typographers. Desperate, he visited several print shops in the local area. When he finally found one that carried the stamp, he stole it and used it to place an impression of the Savoy coat of arms on the identity documents and licenses.

As a final touch, he devised a scheme to add one more authentic element to the false cards. He daringly ventured out to a nearby house where several Italian soldiers had taken up residence and persuaded them to sell him the postage-stamp-like tags from their drivers' licenses. Amazingly, many soldiers agreed to his offer to earn a few extra lire, probably since most couldn't drive during the war anyway. With a piece of damp blotting paper, Maionica peeled off the tags and soaked them in bleach to dissolve the ink that had been stamped over them when they were originally authenticated. Once they were dry, he glued them to the false licenses and identity documents that he was making. "I put three- or four-year-old tags to give them more authenticity," he later explained.

When the documents were finally completed, Maionica would hand them over to Father Niccacci. He had no idea whom the monk would give them to, or where they were going. (It was only after the war that he discovered that many were being smuggled into Florence in the frame of Gino's bike). From there, Niccacci would either give the documents to Gino directly or pass them along to the mother superior of the San Quirico convent to hold. In the meantime, they would be hidden until the cyclist came back to pick them up.

Gino's return to the monastery played out much like his earlier trip, but his arrival at the San Quirico convent caused more of a stir. "He would arrive with his bicycle and would ask for the mother superior," explained Sister Alfonsina, who witnessed Gino's arrivals firsthand. "I can still see him. He was strong and had short pants." Another nun, Sister Eleonora, also spoke with him and heard his voice. But she never saw him because, like the majority of the convent's other nuns, she had forsworn contact with the outside world. Instead, her interaction with Gino was limited to what she heard when she was stationed behind the convent's *ruota,* a wooden wheel where items from the outside world could be placed and retrieved, without the attending nun having to see or touch the person on the other side.

With the false identity documents collected and safely hidden inside the frame of his bicycle below his seat, Gino would set off again for Tuscany, hoping to make it home during daylight hours. Given the danger of violating the curfew, a crime punishable by up to a year in prison, it was undoubtedly the least suspicious time for him to make his way home. It was, however, not without its risks. One frightening episode happened when Gino stopped by a café in Bastia Umbra, near Perugia. He left his bike propped against the wall and went inside for a coffee. Something nearby attracted the attention of an Allied plane flying overhead, and it shot a short burst of machine-gun fire in the general direction of the bicycle and the café. The pilot could have been reacting to anything, but Gino was convinced it was the chrome of his bicycle shining in the sun that had drawn the attack. From that moment on, he got in the habit of dirtying up his bike before riding on it so that it wouldn't be so reflective. For someone who was so meticulous about caring for his bike, this felt "sacrilegious," as Gino's son would say later.

Attacks by air, however, were less of a threat to Gino than the land patrols. In the cities, uniformed soldiers could stop anyone at any time for any reason at all. In case the rifles, grenades, and other weapons the soldiers regularly carried didn't evoke enough fear, a newspaper column advised Italian civilians to take these situations seriously: "If you are stopped on the street by any military patrol who says to you 'who goes there?' stop immediately, give your name and last name and wait for the patrol leader. Then, upon request, you can show them your documents. *Be careful not to make any sudden moves*."

In the countryside, these patrols would take the form of roving groups of German and Italian soldiers on trucks and motorcycles. They routinely stopped civilians and searched homes, looking to thwart the partisans smuggling weapons to use in guerrilla attacks. If Gino heard them from afar, he would duck onto a side road or find anywhere he could to hide in a hurry. Once he even dove into a ditch as he saw the headlight of a military motorcycle approaching him on a dark road.

Gino recoiled from these encounters because so many of the soldiers seemed blinded by their poisonous ideology. "I was neither hot nor cold about politics. It wasn't my trade," he said. "I wanted to be a man of sport." But that had become impossible by the fall of 1943. When he was riding with the documents in his bicycle frame, a stop at a military checkpoint filled him with dread because it meant his work could be uncovered.

Yet encounters were almost inevitable, particularly on the outskirts of cities like Florence, where one had to use specific roads to enter the city. So Gino was forced to devise his own way of coping. When he was flagged by a patrol checkpoint, he pulled over. *"Documenti prego"*—"Your documents, please," the soldiers would say. One military man might scrutinize Gino's face closely as another inspected his papers. If they hadn't identified him already by sight, most soldiers instantly recognized his name. If Gino thought they would believe he was still a soldier, he could feign he was doing his old work as a bicycle messenger. If any knew to ask why he no longer served, he could explain that he had resigned to focus on training and winning races that would bring Italy greater glory (betting they wouldn't be aware that all races had been suspended). While many soldiers had been pressed back into service after the Germans took control, or then labeled deserters if they refused, Gino was able to avoid either scenario because the military officer who had eventually processed his resignation papers was a cycling fan.

It was no surprise that Gino found many sympathetic strangers, if not impassioned fans, among the soldiers that worked the patrols in Tuscany and the neighboring region of Umbria. Young conscripted servicemen had been some of his most enthusiastic supporters at his races as he rose to fame in the late 1930s; in the intervening years he had befriended countless other military men in these parts when he worked as a military messenger.

At the checkpoints they still searched him, of course, but, without any bags or weapons on his person, he appeared fairly harmless. Once their suspicions had been allayed, the members of the patrol were freed for a moment from the anxieties of the war to delight in the novelty of meeting one of their nation's most famous sports celebrities. Gino recognized this interest and coyly played to it. Low-ranking privates were delighted with autographs or a well-delivered joke in *toscano,* the distinct local dialect proudly paraded as the badge of Tuscan authenticity. For patrol leaders or any other authorities with a penchant for playing armchair cycling experts, Gino could indulge their pontificating with a sympathetic ear and a few flattering remarks. As his exchange with the soldiers ended, Gino mounted his bike again, with the documents still safely stowed away in the frame. He continued to the city of Florence, where the distribution of the false identity cards could begin.

Most were handed over to one of the cardinal's assistants, who either passed them along to another trusted confederate, or personally hand-delivered them to the intended recipients. Such was the case of the Frankenthals, who became the Franchis, and only found out in the months after the war ended that Gino had brought their false documents to Florence. In rarer cases, refugees received their documents directly from Gino. It was in this way, for example, that the Goldenbergs staying in Gino's apartment discovered their new alias. It would be several years before they learned the incredible details of how their identity cards had been manufactured.

As impressive as the whole counterfeiting relay was, however, mistakes did occur. On one occasion, Gino had gone out to Lido di Camaiore to deliver a set of false documents to the Donatis, a Jewish family from Florence hiding in this Tuscan coastal town. Everything had been arranged beforehand, but when he arrived, the Gentile woman who was sheltering them panicked. Worried that Gino's arrival or delivery of the documents might endanger her own family, she turned him away at the door. Although she would continue to help the Jewish family for the rest of the occupation, they would have to live in daily peril without any identity cards.

✦

The fact that the counterfeiting operation was located in Assisi would prove to be an important asset to the rescue network. Without industry of any kind, the town had little strategic value that might cause it to be targeted by either the German or Allied air forces; the proximity of nearby farms and related amenities like the Niccacci family grain mill meant that food shortages were less acute. Taken together, residents were spared some of the most vicious violence and famine that terrorized the rest of the country.

Yet in their own way, these small comforts were also risks insofar as they made it easy to lose sight of the dangers lurking in the town. The reality was that the German army and Italian Fascists were never far from sight in Assisi. Spot searches of homes occurred; the risk of being betrayed by civilians seeking monetary rewards was an invisible but omnipresent one. As the weeks passed into months and the rescue network found its own rhythm, it was easy to get complacent.

On a cloudy morning in early 1944, Trento Brizi learned the danger of such complacency firsthand. He was working alone on the latest batch of identity cards in the back of the shop, and he had forgotten to draw the curtain separating that area from the front. He was surprised when two uniformed German soldiers entered the store. He swallowed hard. *I'm caught,* he thought. *They have seen me and now they're going to arrest me.* Terrified, he walked over to the soldiers to accept his fate.

In broken Italian, one of the soldiers politely explained that they were hoping to bring home images of Saint Clare to their wives. Trying to contain himself, Trento could barely control his shaking arm as he found two wood carvings. The soldier spoke again and asked the price. "Nothing, a gift from Assisi to our German friends," Trento responded. They thanked him profusely, smiling as they left.

Inside Trento, something snapped. The pressure of making the false identity documents had finally worn him down. A small oversight had almost seen him arrested for a crime that routinely resulted in execution. He could risk his life no further. He knew he had to visit Father Niccacci immediately to tell him of his decision to resign from the effort. He hid his work, left the store, and raced down the cypress-dotted hill to the monastery.

When he arrived, another monk let him in the side door and asked him to wait in the courtyard. As he stood there, he caught sight of Father Niccacci talking to a stranger in a room across the way near the front door. He was a young man with dark hair, combed back, and he was leaning against the handlebars of a bicycle. He was wearing shorts, and the muscular build of his legs was obvious even from where Trento was standing. *I am sure I have seen this man somewhere before,* Trento thought.

The man walked to the main door, mounted his bicycle, and sped off. Father Niccacci started walking toward Trento. Trento was barely able to keep his surprise in check as he realized exactly who the man was.

"But Father, isn't that man—"

"Yes, Trento, he really is the great racer Gino Bartali," Niccacci said, interrupting him. "For pity's sake, do not tell anyone that you saw him here."

Stunned, Trento listened as Niccacci offered a little more explanation to wipe the surprised look off his face. "It will please you to know that some of the documents you prepared have been brought to Perugia and to Florence by [Gino] himself," Niccacci continued. "Speaking of which, Trento, how is your work going?"

"Good . . . good," a starstruck Trento stammered in reply. "By all means, tell Bartali that soon he will have to pedal with more identity cards. And tell him to train well."

Trento returned to his store. Later he reflected on the singular importance of that moment in his decision to continue making counterfeit identity documents. "Yes," he said, "the idea of taking part in an organization that could boast of a champion like Gino Bartali among its ranks, filled me with such pride that my fear took a back seat."

9

Free Fall

Florence devastated by war, circa 1944.

AS WINTER WITHDREW AND spring crept into its place, the Florence that Gino had learned to love as a boy was fast mutating into a monstrous, unrecognizable place. Every day the newspapers displayed lengthy columns written by the German commander in Florence calling Italian workers to German factories. "Germany offers you work, pay, and well-being. Accept!" But few Italians were willing to uproot themselves for a gluttonous war that was devouring men and supplies at an alarming rate. In Florence, twelve thousand workers went on strike, and scores of walk-outs occurred in many other towns throughout Tuscany as well. Protests often elicited brutal reprisals, and several workers who went on strike or refused to do national service were executed publicly. Coupled with the increasing frequency of air raids, such brazen violence made most Italians even more fearful and skittish. Living amid a hungry and angry populace, each day seemed to carry a heightened risk of careening out of control.

In this surreal spring of 1944, Adriana Bartali was distracted by dramatic news of her own. She was pregnant. At any other time this news would have been a source of unconditional celebration for the Bartali family. But with war rations dwindling to the point that many Florentines were malnourished if not starving, these tidings shepherded staggering worry alongside profound joy. Even a celebrity like Gino struggled to track down enough provisions to feed Adriana, their two-year-old son Andrea, and himself. The shelves of the neighborhood stores stood empty and their ration allotments continued shrinking. Olive oil—that treasured staple of any Italian housewife's pantry—no longer appeared regularly, if at all, and when it was available, a quarter-gallon could cost up to a month's salary for a civil servant. Meat had become so scarce that frequently just bones were doled out. But bones could be used to make soup. What passed for bread, however, had become barely edible: a lumpy mixture of potatoes, maize flour, and insects. With an unborn child to consider, the Bartalis' quest to find enough food became even more pressing.

Grappling with her news, Adriana was less worried than might be expected by the fact that her husband had been disappearing over the winter for days at a time. Certainly she had questioned Gino several times about where he was going, especially as there had not been any races since the spring of 1943. Gino never answered, however, so Adriana stopped asking. Time would reveal this silence as one of Gino's most generous gifts to her. Considering her self-described "anxious personality" in even the happiest of days, her fragile state during the war may not have withstood discovering all the risks her husband faced. Moreover, this enforced ignorance helped to shield her from recrimination by the authorities. In the event of Gino's arrest or interrogation, the less she knew, the less culpable she was likely to be found.

Adriana's distress would only have increased if she knew that Gino had been drawn ever deeper into the relief effort. Gino was now also gathering food and clothing for the growing number of Gentile refugees fleeing bombed parts of Italy to shelter in the Vatican and elsewhere. As Niccacci and others helped small groups of Jewish refugees move closer to the Allied line in the south, Gino was asked to scout out parts of the route. He agreed, and rode as much as 270 miles from Florence to report on the placement of German checkpoints. In time, Gino met some of the human smugglers who would sneak the Jews into Allied territory, and was soon negotiating the fees for their services. When a German patrol killed one of these smugglers and arrested another, it was Gino who discovered the news and then relayed it to Niccacci in Assisi.

✦

Down the road from the Bartalis on Via del Bandino, the escalating violence also made the Goldenbergs very nervous. In the spring of 1944, Giorgio Goldenberg's mother decided it was time to retrieve her son from the Santa Marta boardinghouse and have him join his family hiding in Florence. She was right to be worried. Unbeknownst to her, Germans had been arriving unannounced at the boardinghouse hoping to seize any hidden Jewish children. To find them, they brought all the children out into the yard and compelled them to recite a litany of Catholic prayers. Fortunately, Mamma Cornelia had anticipated as much and taught them the requisite prayers. And if any did happen to forget a phrase, they needed only to look beyond the soldiers where she stood silently mouthing the words to make sure that no one tripped up.

For Jews in Italy like the Goldenbergs, life had entered a new nightmare phase. The Germans and their Fascist collaborators ratcheted up the intensity of their persecution, even as it became increasingly clear that they would be defeated in the war. In addition to raiding convents and monasteries, Nazis invaded old-age residences and hospitals looking for Jews. The numbers soon illustrated the results of their murderous zeal. By the spring of 1944, little more than six months into the occupation, more than 6,500 Jews (both foreign and Italian) had been carried by train from Italy to Auschwitz alone.

When Elvira Goldenberg appeared at the Santa Marta Institute, Giorgio was thrilled at the prospect of being reunited with his parents and sister Tea. He soon discovered, however, how dramatically their lives had changed. The house in Fiesole was long gone, and their room in the Bartalis' apartment on Via del Bandino was evacuated for fear of the increasing frequency of German and Fascist raids. In its place, Gino had found them room in the *cantina,* or cellar, of a building a few houses down. This space was barely more than ten feet by ten feet, with a low ceiling and stone walls. There were no windows and the one door was always closed. Dark and cold, the room fit little more than one double bed that the four Goldenbergs shared. There was no electricity or running water.

Life in the cantina was lived on the smallest scale imaginable. Only Giorgio's mother ever ventured out, armed with a water bucket in each hand. With light brown hair and blue eyes, she did not draw any attention in Florence. For Giorgio's father, his sister, or himself, it was too dangerous to leave their underground hideaway. As a result, their days moved between overwhelming fear and boredom. "What can you do if you are closed in a room twenty-four hours a day without permission to go out?" said Giorgio later. "My sister and I sat there counting flies."

Hunger remained a constant obsession. Food was forever scarce and usually consisted of a meager portion of rice, pasta, or stale bread. Most of it had come from Gino and Sizzi, and the rest Elvira Goldenberg found on her expeditions in Florence. In the corner of the basement room, she kept a sack where she saved any leftovers from their meals as supplies for the next day.

Nighttime brought curfew and mandatory blackouts. In the long hours of darkness, any sound, perceived or real, preyed mercilessly on the children's imaginations. For Giorgio, the shrill cry of an air-raid alarm conjured up that indelible image of a sky teeming with bomber planes. For Tea, it was the sound of German jackboots clattering on the stone streets, their metallic thud becoming the terrible soundtrack to her nightmares.

✦

As the violence dragged on, Adriana Bartali felt as if she were in free fall. After nearly four years, the war no longer seemed like an event with a defined beginning and a probable end. Instead, it had devolved into an incessant hallucination, punctured by sudden relocations whenever the danger escalated and they left their home to stay with friends in safer parts of Tuscany. She dreaded the nights when the screech of the air-raid warning ripped through her slumber and, in a mad dash, she and Gino would scoop up Andrea and flee into the fields to join countless others trying to escape the bombs.

"The air reverberated with the heavy roll of engines, like a blanket of sound waves suspended overhead," wrote one man about a bombardment of Tuscany at the time. "The hypnotic droning throbbed and saturated every cubic inch of air." Overhead they could see the bluish Bengal lights—flares used by bombers to illuminate the sites they wished to target. The flares would hover, suspended by parachutes, and for a few seconds everything was floodlit in a ghastly glow, leaving the people below feeling completely exposed and blinded as they cowered in the deep trenches and shelters carved out of the soil in the Tuscan countryside. The planes, invisible in the inky night sky above the flares, dropped a barrage of bombs that screamed through the air until they walloped the earth and unleashed an ear-piercing series of explosions. If Adriana was holding Andrea, she covered his ears with her hands and folded him inside her arms while they crouched and felt the earth tremble as the bombs made impact. Finally, the all-clear siren would sound, but most let it ring for some time before they dared to move. As they cautiously stood up to return home, they could often smell acrid smoke and hear the

An autographed card given to Giorgio Goldenberg by Gino Bartali during one of his wartime visits to Fiesole.

Gino, Adriana, and Andrea Bartali, circa spring 1943.

Jean Robic wins the 1947 Tour de France.

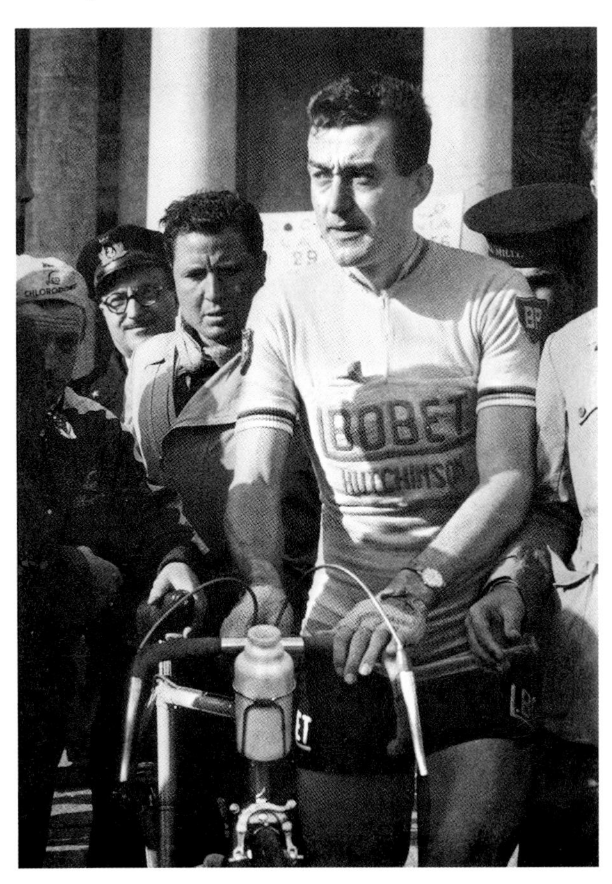

Louis Bobet.

The Goldenberg family, saved by Gino Bartali: Elvira, Giorgio, Tea, and Giacomo.

The Goldenberg family in 2011: Giorgio (top center) and his wife, with their married children, his late sister Tea's married children, and all their respective grandchildren.

BUENOS AIRES, 16 SEPTIEMBRE 1938

Precio del ejemplar en toda la República: 20 centavos

el Gráfico

GINO BARTALI

El extraordinario routier italiano, ganador de la Vuelta de Italia 1936 y 1937, y de la Vuelta de Francia 1938

Gino Bartali on the cover of an Argentinean sports magazine after his 1938 Tour de France victory.

Father Pier Damiano stands by the monastery door where he saw Gino Bartali enter to meet with Father Rufino Niccacci during World War II.

In the family print shop in Assisi where he once manufactured false identity documents, Trento Brizi showcases some of his printing equipment to Dave Catarious and Harry Waldman of the Graphic Arts Association.

Gino Bartali during a trip to Argentina, circa December 1951.

Gino Bartali in his eighties.

sirens of ambulances. They plodded slowly back to their homes, where they would wait tensely until the next time the alarms started wailing.

Daytime was no less lethal. As the Allies inched up slowly through Italy, the bombardments increased in frequency and ferocity and spawned an ever-present anxiety that started to permeate everything until it seemed to assume a life of its own. One early-summer day in 1944, Gino had evacuated his family to a friend's home on a hilltop town southwest of Florence. The front was inching closer to Florence, and they could hear sporadic gunshots and ordnance in the distance. Artillery was particularly treacherous. Unlike the air-raid sirens, which gave people a few minutes of advance warning of aerial attacks, shells could appear unannounced from anywhere, launched from tanks or other land-based artillery, often miles away.

When the initial panic that prompted the evacuation had subsided, the Bartalis found themselves with a welcome lull. Gino, his friend, and Adriana decided to go for a short stroll near the house, a reliable remedy for pent-up nervous energies. The men were soon lost in conversation and walked ahead of Adriana, who lingered a bit behind; walking was becoming more laborious as the child in her womb continued to grow. As she stepped, Adriana heard a loud thud, no more than five yards away from her. A hard artillery shell had pelted the earth. Adriana stopped still in her tracks. Where had it come from? Transfixed, she stared at the shell, and could hear nothing but a lethal silence.

After several agonizing seconds, Adriana carefully exhaled. The shell was a dud. *If it had exploded, I would have been blown up,* she realized in horror. She walked slowly back to the house, ashen-faced. Gino was devastated when he heard what had happened, and realized how close he had come to losing his wife and unborn child.

Somewhere along the line, the collective weight of such concerns about his family and his secret work for the cardinal began to cloud Gino's mind. "Try to line up, day after day . . . without joy, without satisfaction, in a state of depression and continual anxiety," he said. Distressed and withdrawn, Gino grew more and more restless and volatile—telltale signs of a condition known at the time as "war neurosis." (Post-traumatic stress disorder, or PTSD, was not given that name until 1980.) "Everywhere, I felt like I was being tracked," Gino recalled. "I, who sleep very little, didn't sleep at all anymore. I rested the whole night listening to the sizzle of a petrol lamp wick."

Gino was cracking. Given his mysterious trips around Tuscany and Umbria and an alibi that must have grown increasingly questionable as the spring races of the previous year became ever more distant memories of the past, it was becoming clear to anyone paying attention that he was up to something. In the early summer, a volatile Fascist brigand named Mario Carità took notice.

✦

One unhappy day in July 1944, Gino received the summons that he had dreaded for months. He was required to appear at Major Mario Carità's headquarters, the building that most in Florence knew only by its nickname, Villa Triste, or "House of Sorrow," so named for the screams heard coming out of it. Had one of his neighbors tipped off Carità's thugs to Gino's mysterious trips to Assisi earlier that year? Or, worse, had someone discovered the Goldenbergs? Gino grew very jittery. "These were times when life was not highly valued, it was held by a thread and vulnerable to circumstance and the moods of others," he said. "You could easily disappear as a result of hatred, a vendetta, rumor, slander, or ideological fanaticism."

In these uncertain times, no Italian wanted to cross Carità. Less than two months into the German occupation of Italy in September 1943, he had "erupted on the scene like an insane Minotaur to begin his wholesale repressions, tortures, ceaseless interrogations, all of which were accompanied with the most degrading brutality and humiliations," as one historian put it. His surname, Carità, meant "charity," but his behavior was anything but charitable. The major's ambition was simple. He wanted to be "the Himmler of Italy"; Heinrich Himmler, the German head of the Gestapo and the SS, was known internationally for his role running the

Nazi concentration camps. Carità's men, a degenerate gang of two hundred, had ingratiated themselves with the Nazis by zealously pursuing Jews and anti-Fascists. By the time Gino arrived in Villa Triste in July 1944, Carità had turned the torture of suspected enemies of the Fascist and German forces into a grim science.

Just a few miles from the heart of Florence, Villa Triste was not a typically dreary prison, at least from the outside. It was a five-story luxury apartment house made of marble and yellow sandstone in a neighborhood popular with lawyers, businessmen, and other professionals. "The close-carpeted corridors and sumptuously large apartments gave the house the impression of an oceangoing liner, which had docked unaccountably in the midst of a peaceful countryside," wrote one historian.

The polished exterior, however, did little to calm Gino as he walked through the neat courtyard, past a low row of narrow windows, which offered glimpses of the coal bunkers in the basement that had been turned into prison cells. As Gino entered the building, he grew more alarmed. Villa Triste was "a sinister place that aroused terror," as he put it. *How will I ever get out of here?* he wondered as he crossed the threshold.

He found himself in a large entrance hall flanked with tall marble columns, off of which there was a spacious room with a dining table, often littered with scores of empty wine bottles and the remains of lavish feasts if Carità had felt like using a prisoner's inquisition as the entertainment for an evening. On such occasions, he would bind prisoners to a chair and interrogate them, sometimes staging mock executions. He fired his revolver just past the nape of their neck to scare them as he and his guests watched and laughed. Nearby stood a piano, where a monk who had joined Carità's gang was said to play "Neapolitan songs and Schubert's Unfinished Symphony . . . to drown the cries of the tortured."

Most prisoners, however, including Gino, were first dragged downstairs, to the subterranean cellars. Before their eyes could adjust to the dim shadows, their senses were assaulted by the sour smell of old blood and rancid sweat. Their feet crunched as they walked on the floor soiled with a mix of coal debris and blood. Carità liked to terrify his prisoners in advance of their interrogation, and among the first shocks, as their eyes began to focus on the inferno they found themselves in, was the array of medieval torture tools. There were "thick whips, rods of steel, pincers, manacles," not to mention the primitive carpentry tools used "to tear off earlobes of recalcitrant victims." In one room was a heavy wooden triangle, where Carità would splay and tie prisoners and then beat them until their flesh hung in bloody ribbons from their bodies. In another area, medical equipment stolen from hospitals was used to administer electric shocks to prisoners.

Gino glimpsed the horrors that he could expect as he was led into a questioning room to wait for Carità. He sat petrified. As the minutes ticked by, he grew increasingly apprehensive about meeting the man who had become one of the most bloodthirsty Fascist villains in Italy.

While Gino waited, he spied some letters addressed to him sitting on a table. Somehow Carità's squad had intercepted them. Gino panicked. How could he possibly respond if Carità had found any scrap of evidence of his work carrying forged documents or sheltering the Goldenberg family? Helping declared enemies of the state such as Jews was treason. Men had been shot for lesser crimes.

Carità burst through the door. He was a force to behold, with his "frog-like mouth" and "hooded eyelids covering his cold, lizard-green eyes." The major launched into a tirade against the Catholic religion, hoping to provoke the cyclist from the get-go. Gino struggled to stay calm.

Carità snatched up one of the letters on the table addressed to Gino and started reading it aloud. The letter came from the Vatican and thanked Gino for his "help."

"You sent arms to the Vatican!" yelled Carità.

"No!" Gino responded. "Those letters refer to flour, sugar, and coffee that I sent to people in need. I didn't send arms. I don't even know how to shoot! When I was in the military, my pistol was always unloaded."

"It's not true," the major said, fixing his prisoner with a knowing smile.

"It is true," Gino replied, matching the major's steady gaze.

Carità was not convinced. He threw Gino into a cell, leaving him to stew with his worries and listen. For the basement in Villa Triste was a very noisy place. Men and women were dragged kicking and screaming down the stairs and thrown into the coal-bunkers, holes barely nine feet long and six feet wide, which could serve as a prison cell for weeks on end. When they weren't being interrogated or tortured themselves, they could hear the moans and screams of other prisoners as Carità and his men tried to secure information and force admissions of guilt. They put out cigarettes on the faces of prisoners, pierced their eardrums with daggers, and forced open their mouths to pour scalding hot liquid down their throats. If prisoners still didn't confess, beatings continued until people became unrecognizable husks of bloodied, swollen flesh, so battered they had to be sent on to prison hospitals or they would have died in Villa Triste.

Gino knew most of this from rumors that had spread in Florence, and his imagination filled in the rest of the ghoulish details as he waited in the semidarkness, listening to every footstep near his cell, wondering when his time in Carità's torture chamber would come.

On his third day at Villa Triste, he was pulled once more into the interrogation room with Carità and three of his henchmen. Carità asked again about the letters from the Vatican, and Gino repeated his story. Some Tuscan parishes were gathering coffee, flour, and sugar to send to the refugees who had flooded into the Holy City. Gino had helped procure these supplies from various farmers he knew and had them sent to the Vatican.

Carità still wasn't persuaded.

Exasperated, Gino added, "If you want to try yourself, Major, I will teach you how. Give me sugar and flour. We'll make a package and we'll send it in your name. You'll see that the Holy Father will send you thanks." Gino was never one for tact, and he had slept so little in the past three days that he had become testy. But as soon as he said it, he knew that he had gone too far. Carità was enraged.

But before Carità could lay his hands on Gino, one of his militiamen stepped out of the shadows and interrupted the proceedings: "If Bartali says coffee, flour, and sugar, then it was coffee, flour, and sugar. He doesn't lie."

Gino had been so terrified of Carità he had hardly noticed his other interrogators. When he looked at the man who had defended him, he was startled to see a familiar face, framed by a short-cropped head of dark hair. It was Olesindo Salmi, the same man who had been his military supervisor in Trasimeno and had authorized Gino to use a bicycle instead of a scooter for his military duties. Salmi had taken a big risk by defending Gino, a suspected anti-Fascist, but he had waited until he was sure Carità had been unable to rustle up any further damning evidence.

Gino didn't know any of this, and just sat astounded by Salmi's words. He was even more astonished by what happened next. Carità finally relented. Gino was to be released. His fame had certainly helped save his skin, but Carità was also distracted by bigger worries than Gino. The Allies were moving closer to Florence by the day.

"We'll meet again," Carità sneered menacingly as he left, instructing Gino to remain in Florence.

"I hope I never see you again," Gino said quietly as he left the building.

✦

Gino returned home to find his pregnant wife a nervous wreck. Adriana had known full well that many men did not emerge alive from Carità's clutches, and, given young Andrea and her pregnancy, she was even more panicked about losing Gino. She could scarcely believe he had survived and evaded the notorious torture that scarred so many who spent any time in Villa Triste.

Gino and his family were now living in downtown Florence in the home of his friend who owned the *pasticceria* across from the department store where Adriana had once worked. The Florence that surrounded the Bartalis in July 1944, however, couldn't have been more different from those innocent days in 1936 when Gino had first courted Adriana. The Germans were determined to wreak as much havoc as possible before the Allies arrived. So they blew up seventeen of Florence's pasta and flour mills, and destroyed the city's two main telephone exchanges with corrosive acids and then smashed them with crowbars. At night, they soaked the bases of railway tracks in gasoline and set them on fire. All over the city they plundered goods ranging from beds and binoculars to specialized medical equipment from doctors' offices. And they commandeered vehicles of every description: ambulances, hearses, even the three-wheeled garbage carts used by the town dustmen. Florence reeled in response to this desecration. Garbage and horse carcasses rotted in the streets, attracting flies, and it was not unusual to see people walking their dead in pushcarts to a garden behind the University of Florence where bodies were being collected and sprinkled with lime to prevent the spread of disease.

At the end of July 1944, the German army was in full retreat. Rumors circulated that the Germans planned to destroy Florence's bridges to slow the Allies. A directive from the German commander in control of Florence at the end of the month left little doubt. Those who lived in neighborhoods along the Arno were ordered to evacuate their homes by noon on July 30. Gino grew very alarmed. Though their hiding place wasn't in the evacuation zone, they were still less than half a mile from the Arno.

Chaos followed close behind as thousands of Florentines scrambled to find a place of refuge. Those evacuees without friends or relatives created a sad parade through the streets as they traveled with whatever they could carry to designated gathering centers, one less than a mile from the Bartalis, the famed Pitti Palace in the Boboli Gardens. A correspondent from the *Manchester Guardian* described the scene on the ground: "It is as if a cross-section of London's population were camping out in Kensington Palace, sleeping on the floors of the royal apartments, among the old masters and bits of period furniture, cooking picnic meals while the Germans snipe intermittently from the roofs of Barkers and Derry and

Toms' and lob shells on Bayswater Road. Only this morning two civilians were hit by snipers."

On August 3, the Bartalis heard the news that terrified all Florentines. The German commander of Florence issued his final injunction, declaring a state of emergency for the city: "From this moment on, it is severely forbidden for anyone to leave their houses and walk along the streets and in the squares of the city of Florence . . . the patrols of the German Armed Forces have orders to shoot people who are found in the streets, or who show themselves at windows." By nightfall, Florence was shrouded in darkness. The Germans had completely destroyed the city's main electricity station, so the blackout was ubiquitous.

Behind shuttered windows and closed doors, the Bartalis waited in tense anxiety. Soon after the clock struck ten, the silence was broken by a terrific, crashing explosion. "The sky toward the Palazzo Pitti was magnificently turned to crimson," wrote one resident near the Arno. Gino could feel the house trembling. As the thunderclap of blasts continued, young Andrea awoke with a start. "What is it, Papà?" he asked his father. "Sleep, sleep," comforted Gino. "It's a thunderstorm." For over seven hours the deafening clamor of detonating explosives ripped through the air as each of Florence's beloved bridges was destroyed.

All except one. A huge load of explosives had been placed in the houses at either end of Ponte Vecchio, the oldest bridge in Florence, and the only one lined with alcoved shops. During the middle of the night on August 3, they were detonated. Tiles, bricks, and shutters flew everywhere. Florence's crown jewel survived, but was completely impassable as a result of the huge piles of rubble at either end. This disarray was deliberate. Hitler had reportedly ordered that all of Florence's bridges be destroyed except "the most artistic one."

✦

The wreckage rattled everyone, including Gino. "The spectacle of Florence was devastating," he said. The area covered in rubble on either side of the Arno extended some two hundred yards. Gino knew there would be more violence along the river when the Allies finally arrived by land. So he decided to move his family again, this time to Adriana's parents' home on the northeastern outskirts of Florence. She needed a less tumultuous place to spend the final weeks of her pregnancy. Her parents would help calm her.

But one night, shortly after they had arrived, Adriana began experiencing contractions. She and Gino were both frightened, as it was too early. He jumped onto his bike and began cycling to the heart of Florence to find a doctor. It was after curfew and getting dark, and the destruction was inescapable, particularly near the Arno, where the Florence of Dante and Petrarch lay in ruins. Somehow, despite all the damage and chaos, Gino found a doctor and they raced to Adriana's bedside. The scene that met them would haunt Gino for the rest of his life.

His second son was stillborn.

Adriana's condition was serious, and Gino spent the night terrified that he might lose his wife as well. The doctor did his best, and by the next morning Adriana had turned a corner. Gino was relieved, but his anguish over his dead child was overwhelming. In a daze, he visited a nearby friend, a carpenter, who built him a tiny coffin.

Back home, he sat quietly with Adriana, then gently picked up the wooden coffin holding his stillborn son and carried it to his bike outside. Cradling the coffin under his arm, he pedaled south through battered Florence. He passed close to Campo di Marte, where thousands of Florentines, who had been evacuated from their homes near the Arno, were camped out. The houses in the neighborhood nearby lay in flattened ruins, bombed months earlier. He rode past groups of people huddled around makeshift fires and near handcarts overflowing with belongings that they had pushed through town. Every so often Gino would make eye contact with one of them, and as he stared at them, the tired and vacant defeat in their gaze was inescapable. Finally, Gino made it to the cemetery in Ponte a Ema. He biked up the winding, wisteria-lined path to the main white stone building, where he dismounted and carried his dead son, tenderly placing the small coffin in the family crypt next to his brother Giulio's.

When Gino returned home, the image of his young son remained seared in his memory. He had been a small baby, but his features were well formed. He and Adriana had planned to call him Giorgio to honor her brother lost at sea. Gino and Adriana consoled each other, but they would not speak of this to others for years.

✦

On the morning of August 4, 1944, the first Allied tanks neared the south bank of the Arno. In the heart of the city on the other side of the river, a small group of Florentines emerged from their hiding places. They made a rush for the southern bank, only to be killed by a series of mines planted by the Germans. Other Florentines would soon fall beside them, killed by Fascist snipers still roaming the city.

Although it would be a full week before these last Fascist holdouts were expunged from the area, even they couldn't stop the news of liberation from slowly starting to spread across the city. On Via del Bandino, it was announced by the hopeful shouting of local boys, *"Gli inglesi son arrivati!"*—"The English have arrived!" Sitting in the cellar with his parents and sister, Giorgio Goldenberg crept cautiously out to investigate. He was startled to see a British soldier standing right on the street beside his building. On the soldier's shoulder, he saw a Star of David. Giorgio didn't speak any English, but wanted desperately to communicate with this man whom he recognized as an ally. So he started singing, at first quietly and then loud enough so that the soldier could hear him. He sang the melody of the *Hatikvah,* a popular Hebrew song that would later become the national anthem of Israel.

The soldier recognized the song and burst forth in an excited flurry of English that Giorgio did not understand. Giorgio dashed downstairs to find his father and bring him to street level. His father and the soldier began to speak together in Yiddish. Giorgio watched them happily, a feeling of relief washing over him for the first time in years. "For me, this was the end of the war," he said later.

The Bartalis heard the news of liberation on August 11 with the ringing of the bells atop the Bargello, the "people's palace" in central Florence. Once the partisan scouts were certain the streets were safe for civilians, they sent a courier, a young woman, to spread the good news to Florentines installed in the town hall and at a few other key locations. Sprinting through the city, the courier was seized by simultaneous joy and anguish, capturing the tense mood of the city:

> My heart seemed to want to burst, I felt desperate and happy, down and full of energy. In front of the lowered blinds of the Bizzarri Chemist I stopped, lost: the bell of the Bargello, silent for four years, had rung out once, and in that silence seemed to be magic; there it was again, a second time, I lifted my eyes up and another miracle happened: slowly on the tower of the Palazzo Vecchio the tricolor [Italian flag] rose. I knelt down crying on the pavement while one by one the shutters in the square opened wide, a woman from a low window shouted to ask me:
>
> "Have they gone?"
>
> "We're free, free," I answered, sobbing and opening my arms.

✦

In Assisi, the celebrations had started earlier, and its normally staid residents rejoiced with fervor. When the first Allied tanks rolled into the town on June 17, 1944, the bells of all the churches and monasteries started tolling. From the basilica of St. Francis, a monk started playing "God Save the King" on the organ, and the music wafted throughout the city. On Via San Paolo, an old Fascist poster displaying one of

Mussolini's slogans had been ripped down. In its place, a new banner, crafted by Luigi and Trento Brizi, had been lifted: "The Jews of Italy have Italian blood, Italian souls, and Italian genius."

✦

As the wave of liberation slowly traveled toward the northern borders of the nation, the bittersweet legacy of the war started to become more fully apparent. Italian Jews and their foreign counterparts emerged from the shadows and began to understand just how much a small group of heroic Gentiles had helped them. In Florence and its environs, an estimated 330 Jews had been saved by the efforts of Cardinal Dalla Costa and his associates. Another estimated three hundred Jews had been saved in Assisi and Perugia. Gino Bartali had sheltered the Goldenberg family and had transported critical documents between Tuscany and Umbria (if Gino or Dalla Costa kept a record of how many identity documents Gino carried, neither of them ever told anyone, so this figure remains unknown).

The news of these rescues, however, was inevitably leavened by sadness as a fuller picture emerged of all those who had perished. By the end of the war, some fifteen percent of the Jewish community in Italy had been killed. Compared with other countries in Europe where the German occupation had started much earlier, the death toll was significantly smaller. Nevertheless, it couldn't help but evoke uncomfortable questions for those willing to consider them. In little more than eighteen months, nearly seven thousand Jews had perished, including the Goldenbergs' cousins, the Kleins. Although the primary architects of this murderous campaign had been German, they had been more than ably helped by a small group of committed Fascists and a larger segment of the population that was willing to abet the crime with its silence.

The story of how it had all happened would remain untold for several decades. Instead, Italians in liberated Italy would try to put the past behind them and focus during those final months of the war in Europe on securing provisions and slowly starting their lives anew. Gino was no different. Hoping to restart his career, he tried to cobble together enough new bike supplies so that he could start racing again. Unfortunately, few in Tuscany had any of the necessary equipment to sell him. Frustrated, Gino resigned himself to making a trip all the way to Milan on an old bicycle.

When he got to the city, Gino was startled to come across the corpses of Mussolini and one of his lovers, strung up by their ankles in a gas station in Piazzale Loreto. Below, thousands of Italians gawked at the executed leader who had ruled their nation for over twenty years. "It was an obscene spectacle, a savage testimony of the cruelty of the times," Gino said later. In that moment he simply tried to avoid looking at the frozen gaze of the gruesome suspended cadavers. *This is not the Italy I dreamed of for myself and for my family,* Gino thought. Wearily, he soon made his way home to Florence. As the war in Europe drew to a close six weeks later, Gino would join his countrymen in the monumental task of rebuilding, ever haunted by all that had been lost.

Part III

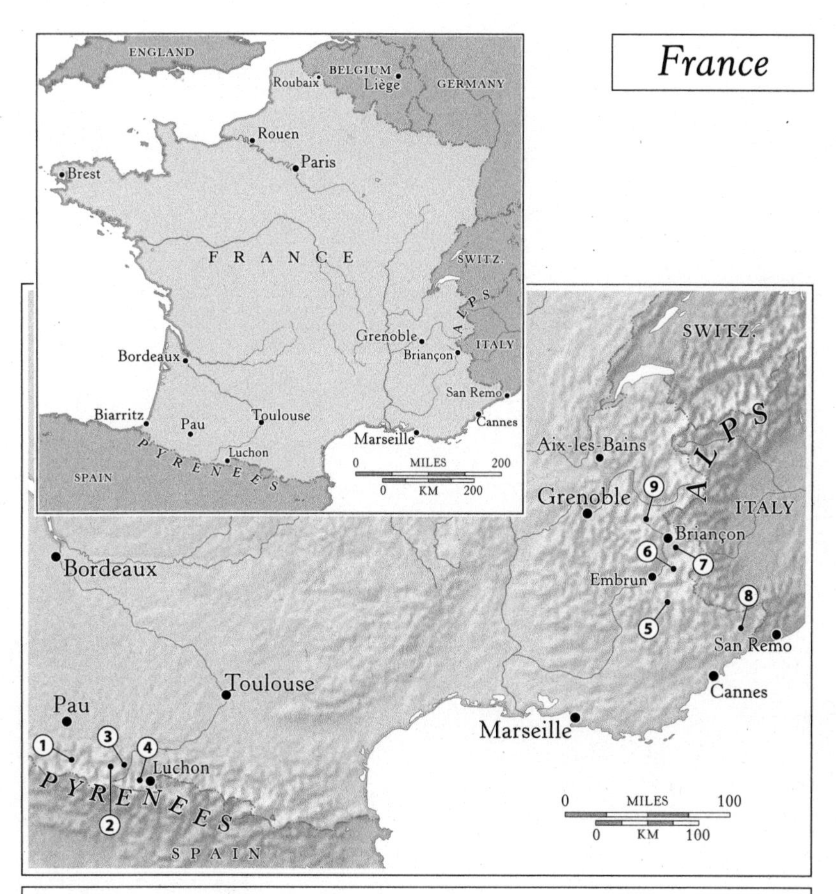

Mountain Passes (Pyrenees)		Mountain Passes (French Alps)	
1 Aubisque	**3** Aspin	**5** Allos	**8** Turini
2 Tourmalet	**4** Peyresourde	**6** Vars	**9** Galibier
		7 Izoard	

10

Ginettaccio

Gino Bartali and another cyclist enjoy a smoke.

IN THE MONTHS FOLLOWING the liberation of Florence in August 1944, Gino finally started to sift through the rubble of his life. Thirty years old, he had a wife and a three-year-old son to support, not to mention two aging parents. Like many of his fellow cyclists, Gino had burned through his savings during the war, when there was no chance of drawing income from the sport. "What we had earned from '35 to '40 had gone up in smoke," he explained. On a deeper level, the physical hardship of this era had changed him. It was not just the prizes he might have won during his prime years as an athlete—the Tour was canceled between 1940 and 1946, and the Giro between 1941 and 1945—but the war itself had scarred Gino. "I think that all that time, more than just lost, is to be thought of as a negative force," he explained. "You feel like you have gotten much older than if you could have led a normal life."

If Gino felt old, he looked even older. His thick, wavy hair had thinned and receded well beyond his temples, and his forehead had become permanently creased with leathery furrows. His eyes were sunken, emphasizing his nose, which seemed chiseled out of rock with rough strokes. He was just easing into his thirties, but could have passed for a man at least a decade older.

Although Gino had not earned anything from cycling for years, he knew that he couldn't start over in a new job. He had no trade or education, and he feared the financial hardship that his father had endured as a day laborer. "He taught me that poverty tastes bitter when you're twenty, and feels like salt in an open wound when you're forty," Gino said. If he was to build a new life for himself and his family, he had to race.

Banding together with a small group of fellow cyclists, he started traveling around the country contacting other racers and staging small races. Few had cars or trailers to carry their equipment, so they made their way "like clowns in a traveling circus," in one cyclist's banged-up old truck that could hold ten riders and their bikes. The scenes that awaited them on the road were heartrending. In villages, locals wore the remnants of discarded military khakis; nearby cemeteries brimmed with the freshly dug graves of the war dead.

Gino and his fellow racers traveled from sports club to sports club looking for any and all cyclists willing to race against them. But as the country reeled from the physical destruction of World War II and debilitating postwar inflation, it was a challenge to find the *tifosi*, those fervent Italian fans who had grown up following the races. "The triumphant years of the prewar period—the championships, the Giro d'Italias, the hard-earned wins—were far away. It seemed like they had been lost in that deafening uproar that had shattered nature and souls," said Gino. "People had forgotten about us. They had other things on their minds, and those who still followed sports considered our generation already 'old.' So we had to struggle a great deal to make our comeback."

They survived on prizes that were as ad hoc as the races themselves. The victors won chickens, pigs, furniture, wine, and—most useful of all—cash, gathered in a hat from fans along the route. Racers often shared the spoils of their victories with their teammates, families, or even hometowns. During one competition, Gino arranged to be paid with gas pipes. Bombs had destroyed many of the gas lines in Florence, so Gino asked for pipes if they won to donate to a gas company in Florence. "We were all really hard up," he said.

In the rush to start competing again, however, he greatly underestimated how much racing fitness he had lost. During the first event after the war, a medium-length race in a small industrial town near Florence called Prato, Gino had to make a humiliating withdrawal, because he was physically unable to complete the course.

This disappointment and others that followed it wounded Gino, cementing his deeply felt sense of injustice that the war had deprived him of his best racing years. This latent feeling of indignation started transforming Gino, already prone to a lack of diplomacy, into an acerbic personality who complained and criticized, and was liable to flare up over any slight, perceived or real. In short order, this testy temperament earned him his most lasting sobriquet—*Ginettaccio,* or "Gino the Terrible"—from reporters and fans who would learn to expect his barbs.

But in that moment, after the race in Prato, Gino was stung by paralyzing frustration. "I ended up completely demoralized. Any kind of dignified resumption of our activity seemed impossible," he said. When he returned home, he pedaled back up the familiar road to the cemetery in Ponte a Ema to visit Giulio's grave. As he sat there for a long while, he was reminded of the promise he had made soon after Giulio died—to honor his memory by becoming a champion. "Then I found my strength again," he said. "I had a wife, a baby, and parents. I had to keep going for them."

✦

While competitive cyclists like Gino were grappling to find their legs after the war, the bicycle had become more important to everyday life than ever before. People biked to get food, share news, and find work. In the early months, when civilian manufacturing was still nearly non-existent and public transit was in disarray, bicycles were often the only way to travel significant distances on roads that had been pulverized by the violence of war. They were ubiquitous, "the inseparable companion of the peasant, the worker, the professional, the clerk, the student, the housewife, and our rosy-cheeked girls," as one journalist described them.

Even when manufacturing did recommence and major roads were repaired, cars were prohibitively expensive for everyone but the wealthiest. Three years after the war had ended, the cheapest car for sale in Italy still cost almost five times the annual salary of the average worker. (In modern terms, this would be equivalent to seeing compact cars with a price tag of nearly $150,000 instead of their actual cost of about $13,000.) In contrast, a new bicycle cost the average worker just a month's wages and there was an extensive secondhand market where a used bike could be purchased for much less. With these economics, it comes as no surprise that in 1947 there were some 3.5 million bikes on the road in Italy and just 184,000 cars.

One film, Vittorio De Sica's Academy Award–winning *Ladri di biciclette* (released as *The Bicycle Thief* in the United States in 1949), best captured the centrality of the bike in postwar Italy. The film starts with the protagonist, Antonio, waiting in a long queue for jobs. When he finally gets to the front of the line, he is offered work on the condition that he has a bicycle. On his first day of employment—putting up posters around Rome for a movie that starred Rita Hayworth (herself a Bartali fan in real life, and vice versa)—his bicycle is stolen. After several fruitless efforts to recover it, Antonio makes a pathetic and failed attempt to steal a bicycle for himself.

From the beginning to the end of the film, bicycles permeate life.

They are the prerequisite for work and a way out of the endless queues of the unemployed. They are the subject of fantasy—Antonio's son's room is adorned with photos of the famous cyclists of the period. And they are also a spiritual symbol of the dignity to which man can aspire in his workaday life—hope and integrity fashioned from metal, gears, and rubber.

In film and in real life, a bicycle in postwar Italy, far more than a simple means of transport, served as an anchor—a connection to the world—in the way that cars and mobile phones now unite people to one another. The bicycle was considered so integral to the lives of all Italians that stealing a bicycle was always viewed with particular severity by the judicial system, according to Oscar Scalfaro, a former Italian president and judge. Like stealing a horse in the United States or the United Kingdom in the eighteenth and nineteenth centuries—a crime punishable by imprisonment or, at times, death—stealing a bicycle in postwar Italy was not just theft; it was an act of forced isolation that stripped a man of his livelihood and exiled him from the world.

✦

If bicycles shaped the rhythm of everyday life in postwar Italy, it was poverty and endemic joblessness that defined its spirit. Economic coverage in the newspapers of the era was as optimistic as a retelling of the story about the plagues of Egypt. Headlines and articles were filled with jarring statistics. Six hundred thousand agricultural day laborers went on strike in the fall of 1947 in the Po Valley. Shortages made Italian gasoline three times as expensive as it was in France, and almost four times as expensive as in the United States. The unemployment rate for industrial workers in central Italy (including Tuscany) rocketed past sixty percent.

The numbers told only part of the story. Gino and his teammates saw the face of poverty everywhere they raced. War had reduced entire city neighborhoods to rubble. Women tried to heat food over haphazard cooking fires set up in the streets. Grizzled, weary men stared somberly as they sipped coffee from old tin soup cans. In Ventimiglia, a small town in northern Italy, an American journalist was dumbfounded by the sight of a pizzeria destroyed during the war where "half-naked children crowded together on the dusty rim of the broken walls and in the holes that had been windows."

Florence lay in shambles. Along the Arno River, where Gino had swum as a child, sat piles of rubble, the remains of the many bridges bombed by the retreating Germans. Nearby buildings and medieval towers stood in various states of collapse and disrepair. The Jewish synagogue had also been disfigured; it was damaged while being used to store German trucks, and another part of the building was dynamited.

In the face of such wreckage nationwide and with few opportunities for employment, some 750,000 Italians went to work temporarily in France, Belgium, and Switzerland. (Tens of thousands of other Italians would leave Italy permanently.) The work that awaited them in those countries was inevitably the most grueling—mining for coal, working in the fields or forests—and the wages tended to be low. Living in pitiable conditions and unable to speak the native languages of the countries in which they worked, many Italian workers quickly found themselves scorned by the locals—even if they had been officially invited and contracted to work by the same locals' governments.

Collectively, these enduring miseries, the everyday hardships and indignities suffered at home and abroad, made an already strained political situation downright volatile. Complex, emotionally charged questions shadowed every aspect of public life. What to do with the monarchy? How to craft a new constitution? What to do about individuals who had been involved in the previous Fascist government? What course would Italy take in the postwar era?

And—perhaps most important of all—who would lead it?

Two men emerged as viable candidates for the task. The first was Alcide De Gasperi, a severe sixty-seven-year-old former librarian whom one journalist described as "utterly honest and sincere, painfully humorless and uninspiring." He was the leader of the Christian Democrats, a large centrist party that was allied closely with the Roman Catholic Church. He was also friends with Gino, whom he had met through mutual Catholic acquaintances in the 1930s. De Gasperi's rival for the job was Palmiro Togliatti, the heavyset leader of the Italian Communist Party, who was so charismatic that even an otherwise unsympathetic, right-wing American magazine acknowledged him as "Italy's most brilliant politician."

In the months that followed the war's end, both men promised the public that they would restart Italian industry and put the nation back to work. While their immediate aims were similar, their international alliances stood in stark contrast. Along with the Catholic Church, the Christian Democrats were closely allied with the United States. The Communist Party, although officially not antireligious, was more closely aligned with the Soviet Union. With these associations as a backdrop, perhaps the biggest question of all facing Italy was not about domestic policy, but which side the country would pick in the emerging Cold War. The decision taken would "influence the course of European history for perhaps a hundred years," in the words of one prominent American reporter.

All of this would come to a head as Italians prepared for their first free parliamentary elections in a quarter of a century. They would endure a bitter political campaign that lasted almost half a year, and on April 18, 1948, they would make their choice.

✦

Gino's appetite for politics had only decreased during the war, and as competitive cycling started up again, he was relieved that government officials no longer questioned his every decision. "Now I didn't have to worry about the authorities," he said. "I could train and follow the methods that I judged to be the most opportune, based on my experience and the advice of my doctors and coach."

The 1946 season kicked off with the traditional season-opener, the Milan–San Remo classic. Despite racing over treacherous war-damaged roads and riding through a critical mountain pass in complete darkness because electricity had not yet been reconnected, the race was declared a success. A few months later the Giro was resurrected after its six-year hiatus (few counted the Fascist version of several one-day races during the war as a real Giro). Nicknamed *Il Giro della Rinascita,* or "the Giro of Rebirth," the race also reignited the rivalry between Gino and his former teammate Fausto Coppi. Gino headed into the race, buoyed by the happy personal news of the birth of his second son, Luigi.

Fans hoping to see a suspenseful battle of the cycling titans were not disappointed. The pink leader's jersey changed shoulders many times, and Coppi wore it heading into the final stage. The winner did not emerge until the final minutes, when, in an upset of sorts, Gino managed to beat Coppi by a scarce forty-seven seconds. He felt indomitable. "Yes, I had become *Ginettaccio,*" he said, "but 'Giant of the Mountains' was a nickname no one would yet take away."

But by the end of the second postwar season and the beginning of the third, Gino was coming up short more and more often. Journalists and fans took note. The inconsistency in his performance couldn't easily be explained by a fluke injury here or a bad race there. Instead, it was something far more perplexing. His imminent decline as an athlete seemed manifestly obvious when he would wheeze in at the end of one race. But then he would suddenly find his stride again in the next competition, and muster up a measure of the old fire.

The most obvious culprit for this erraticism seemed to be some rather dubious medical advice from his physician at the time. In 1946, Gino began to notice a change in how his heart was behaving at the beginning of races. Specifically, he felt that it was beating more regularly but less frequently than it had before the war. "I was slow to get in gear, my body was numb," Gino explained, like a "racing car" with a cold motor. Although the change in the regularity of his heart rate is still puzzling, we now know that a low resting heart rate is a perfectly normal side effect of prolonged cardiovascular endurance training, and starting more slowly comes naturally for many cyclists with aging. Nevertheless, Gino was worried about how it was affecting his ability to race, and so he visited his doctor. Amazingly, the doctor shared his concern and encouraged him to have a couple of cups of coffee and a few cigarettes before every race to speed up his heart. With such official sanction, Gino was soon drinking as many as twenty espresso coffees a day. Smoking in turn evolved from being a pre-race pick-me-up to a reliable salve for all his anxieties. "The cigarette that I had avoided for so many years ended up being my most faithful companion in certain moments. For racers like me, a mouthful of smoke offers a brief and modest consolation during the difficulties of a race or during moments of melancholy in our solitary life as vagabonds of the street—surrounded always by an immense crowd, but always essentially alone with our thoughts and with our worries," he said later. Along with an emerging penchant for staying out long into the night with friends, consuming copious amounts of Chianti, Gino was slowly abandoning his prewar asceticism, and was living "more of a life of a normal person than of a cyclist," as one teammate described it.

Another possible explanation for his poor results was his training. After the war, Gino was toying with a few new ideas in his preparation. On at least one occasion he tried training at night, riding in front of the family car while his wife drove behind him and illuminated the roads with the car headlights. He also began experimenting with another novel tactic—rearranging his bedroom furniture so that his bed was aligned exactly on the north-south axis. He was convinced this would better protect him from what he believed were the pernicious effects of magnetic waves.

By and large, however, he followed essentially the same strategy he had used in his twenties. He built up the length of his training rides over the season until he was out riding nearly every day, and covering as many as 250 miles per training session. In contrast, modern training theory suggests that adding recovery days into the mix would have served an older athlete such as himself much better. An older racer is affected most by a loss in his explosive, top-end ability for hard accelerations rather than by any decrease in his overall endurance. In fact, some evidence suggests that muscular endurance improves to an extent with age as the muscles become more efficient at processing lactic acid and long years of training increase the number, size, and kinematic activity of the mitochondria, the energy plants in muscle fibers. Thus, Gino was right to build up some level of distance in his regimen, but then a focus on shorter and more intensive rides would have better rebuilt his lost sprinting strength, that instinctual hard push that gave his attacks their teeth during climbs.

In any case, Gino was losing—and taking the losses personally. The booing and heckling that every rider encounters began to cut him more deeply. Speaking with a journalist, he lamented how ignorant the spectators were of all the training that a cyclist undergoes to compete with the best, regardless of how he places. He called the crowds ungrateful and temperamental, offering "total glory for the winner, total indifference for the one who loses." All of this seemed a seismic shift for the rider who had avoided criticizing spectators in the press because his popularity among them directly affected his livelihood.

At the 1947 Giro d'Italia, the situation turned from bad to dismal. During a stage in the second half of the race, Gino zeroed in on a fan at the sidelines who taunted him with an anti-Catholic slur. Although he was the leader in the general classification at this point, on course for winning the whole competition, Gino hopped off his bike mid-race. He walked over to the fan and struck him, and then calmly mounted his bike again and rode off. He still managed to win the stage, but it would be his last day at the top. Fausto Coppi overtook him in the rankings in the next stage, and, a few days later, won the race altogether.

✦

Gino's career was clearly sputtering, but that did not stop the Christian Democrats from using his name to mobilize support for their candidate, Alcide De Gasperi, as they revved up a fierce political campaign ahead of the 1948 national election. There was a certain logic to their rationale. Beyond the two men's friendship or the promotional value of Gino's popularity, the men had much in common. Both were devout Catholics and both were fighting very public battles against more charismatic younger opponents—a parallel so powerful that it would lead one journalist to memorably describe Gino as "De Gasperi on a bike." He elaborated, "With a crushed face and not at all handsome, without lyrical flights or rhetoric, [Bartali] shows in pedaling, the calculated patience and tenacity that De Gasperi inspires in governing." As the election neared, the Christian Democrats went even further and asked Gino if they could add him to the Christian Democrats' electoral list, which meant that if they won, he would likely hold office in Rome as a deputy. Gino politely declined.

The Catholic Church also drew on Gino's fame as it outlined what it believed was at stake in the election. In the fall of 1947, Pope Pius XII addressed Italian Catholics gathered in St. Peter's Square with an appeal that linked themes from Gino's life to the Bible:

> It is time to put ourselves to the test. This difficult competition, which Saint Paul spoke about, has begun. It is a time for intense effort. The winner can be decided in an instant. Look at Gino Bartali, member of Catholic Action. Often he has earned the right to wear the much-sought-after "jersey." You should also participate in a championship of ideas, so you can achieve a much more noble form of victory.

The meaning of the Pope's message was "unmistakable," according to one Italian cultural historian. The Catholic faithful were being warned to stand guard, and be "ready to struggle for their faith against the menace of Communism just as Bartali battled his way to victory."

Closer to the elections, tens of thousands of lay members of Catholic Action were mobilized to get out the vote for the Christian Democrats. In cities they walked from apartment to apartment, and in the country they rode by bicycle from one isolated hamlet to the next, knocking on doors to plead with people to support their cause. A small group of clergy complemented this work by directing a moral suasion campaign.

Dramatic films warning about a Communist victory were screened around southern Italy by trucks carrying film projectors. They offered alarming—and likely staged—scenes of what might happen if the Communists won, including images of them ransacking churches and pushing bells down from belfries. In places where few residents had ever seen a film, the production was mesmerizing.

✦

Some four thousand miles away, in the United States, one small group of people was watching the Italian campaign even more closely than most Italians—a new outfit called the Central Intelligence Agency. In late 1947 the CIA received its first orders from the National Security Council to carry out "covert psychological operations designed to counter Soviet and Soviet-inspired activities." With the battle brewing between the Christian Democrats and the Communists, Italy represented a very high-value target in the escalating conflict that came to be known as the Cold War.

Geography explained much of its importance to the United States. Italy was in the heart of Europe, and when it came to the flight path of a plane or a missile, Turin (in the northwest of Italy) was closer to London than it was to Brindisi (in the heel of the boot of Italy). Whoever controlled Italy had all of Western Europe at its doorstep. Naturally, members of the Italian Communist Party rejected the suggestion that they would immediately hand over all power to Stalin and the Soviet Union if they won. The Americans, however, didn't trust them. They believed that an Italian Communist electoral victory might set up another opportunity for a Soviet coup, as had happened just months earlier in Czechoslovakia.

Yet the task of actively influencing the outcome of a foreign nation's elections seemed like a dangerous one, especially to the American field officers charged with carrying it out. Nevertheless, secret authorization was given for an Italian campaign that would represent the CIA's first-ever mission. Tellingly, it was never approved by Congress and it was "illegal from the start," according to Mark Wyatt, one of the CIA agents assigned to the task.

Covert field operations in Italy ran a gamut of activities. The agency created forged documents, books, and leaflets, all aimed at sabotaging the Communist Party. Above all, there was cash—an estimated ten million dollars of it. Millions were funneled "into the bank accounts of wealthy American citizens, many of them Italian-Americans, who then sent the money to newly formed political fronts created by the CIA," according to one leading American journalist. There were even provisions to prevent the IRS from raising its eyebrows about the flow of cash: "Donors were instructed to place a special code on their income tax forms alongside their 'charitable' donation."

And when illicit bank transfers were insufficient for the task at hand, there was a more direct way to get the money to its intended recipients—in black suitcases. In the kind of scenario that would later dominate Hollywood movies, barely trained CIA operatives met with high-profile Italian politicians in rooms at Rome's luxurious four-star Hassler Hotel and handed over bags of cash, intended to defray campaign expenses. Wyatt later acknowledged: "We would have liked to have done this in a more sophisticated manner. . . . Passing black bags to affect a political election is not really a terribly attractive thing."

For all its activities and money, the CIA's work was just one part of a larger American effort in Italy. Other government officials worked with various Italian-American organizations to implement a wide-reaching public campaign to win over the hearts and minds of Italian voters for the Christian Democrats. Americans with Italian roots were encouraged by local churches, newspapers, and other organizations to write some ten million letters, postcards, and cablegrams that were sent to Italy with various terrifying messages. ("A Communist victory would ruin Italy. The United States would withdraw aid and a world war would probably result.") Hollywood also took up the Christian Democrat cause. Italian radio stations aired a one-hour program to raise money for the orphans of Italian pilots killed during World War II, and stars ranging from

Frank Sinatra to Academy Award–winning actor Gary Cooper recorded messages of support that were broadcast throughout the country.

Russian Communists, working on behalf of "Uncle Joe" as Joseph Stalin was nicknamed by some in the American press, staged some stunts of their own. They released Italian war prisoners in a bid to gain sympathy, and supported Communist newspapers in Italy. They also gave money. Although the total amount remains unclear, one reporter estimated it was several million dollars.

✦

With all this foreign money and attention swirling about, Italy turned into "a sort of European Wisconsin, full of political hoopla, Tammany ward-heeling and high-pressure campaigning from the outside world," according to one American journalist. Even the leaders of the parties were willing to discard propriety and wage battle in the muddy trenches of personal insult and slander. De Gasperi denounced Togliatti and accused him of having the "cloven foot of the devil." Togliatti was no better, smearing De Gasperi as a Fascist. He was even reported to have offered something of a vague death threat to De Gasperi, publicly predicting that De Gasperi would meet a violent end like Hitler and Mussolini.

By mid-April, with the elections just days away, the carnival-like atmosphere of the campaign screeched to a loud finale. Italian politics dominated the front pages of newspapers in every language in various countries. In England, discussion of the election had become so popular that Lloyd's of London was reported to be offering odds on it, with De Gasperi favored three to one. In the United States, where De Gasperi and Togliatti had become household names, the *New York Daily News* asked the question on everyone's minds: "Italy Picks Uncles Today; Will It Be Sam or Joe?"

In Italy, there were some signs that many average voters saw themselves as helpless in the face of all the foreign involvement. When asked by an American reporter how it felt to be a voter in Italy, one Italian replied skeptically, "How do we feel? How do you think it feels to be the rope in a tug-of war? Does the rope ever have a chance at winning?"

✦

In the end, the Italian people gave a clear verdict. The Christian Democrats won a landslide victory that handed them an absolute majority in the Chamber of Deputies. Gino immediately sent a telegram to congratulate De Gasperi on being elected the prime minister of Italy: "With sincere thanks I underline my devotion to you and send deep wishes of good luck for the great victory of democracy. GINO BARTALI." The message was printed up as a poster and displayed publicly in various cities.

De Gasperi soon formed his new government, but it was obvious that tensions persisted. The great problems of the day, massive unemployment and endemic shortages, remained unresolved; many Communists were embittered at having lost the elections. In June 1948, it all came to the fore during the speech of a prominent Communist in the Chamber of Deputies. He boldly accused priests, sympathetic to the Christian Democrats, of encouraging Calabrian women in southern Italy to go on a "bedroom strike" and cease sexual relations with their husbands so as to motivate them not to vote for the Communists. A Christian Democrat deputy shouted his rebuttal: "You Communists find your recruits only among criminals and women of ill repute." The Communists wasted no words with their reply, charging across the Chamber almost as one to attack the Christian Democrats. Within seconds, dozens of out-and-out brawls had erupted in what was described as "the worst fight in parliamentary history." Inkpots were thrown and stenographers' desks ripped from the ground and used as weapons. Even a Communist woman deputy was said to have joined in the brawl, hitting several bearded Christian Democrats.

When order was finally restored some ninety minutes later, three deputies were found to require medical care and several others were left with bloody noses and black eyes. An uneasy truce was established, but few could ignore the deplorable state of relations in the Chamber. With all the work to be done and with all the lingering hostility between the parties, it was clear that a dramatic change was needed. Nevertheless, it was surprising and almost sacrilegious when a plan was proposed in the ensuing days to do the politically unthinkable—and force the deputies to shorten their summer holidays.

✦

Coppi: 21 votes. Bartali: 1 vote.

As the new government took shape in the summer of 1948, Gino wrestled with the aftermath of an altogether different selection. Earlier that year, when the leaders of the Italian Cycling Federation, along with their international counterparts, voted on the greatest achievement of the past cycling season, Gino had faded almost completely from sight. With his 1947 Giro victory and a string of other wins, Coppi won twenty-one of twenty-six possible votes, proof positive that he was "Italy's greatest cyclist," as one leading Italian newspaper editor described him. Gino got just one vote, tying for last place with an essentially unknown rider.

In the press write-up following the award ceremony, nothing was said about Gino—probably because no one knew what to say. Poor results could be dismissed, and a few errant episodes did not a pattern make. Yet Gino had not done anything to win himself any support in a deadlocked court of public opinion. Where some saw an aging athlete growing increasingly desperate, another group, a devoted but shrinking contingent of *bartaliani,* hung on to the flickering prospects of a renaissance.

Gino knew that the only race that could settle the debate was the one that had consumed him for the last decade: the Tour de France. It was the Tour where he first won cycling's crown; it was the Tour where he would have to return to reclaim it.

11

Les Macaroni

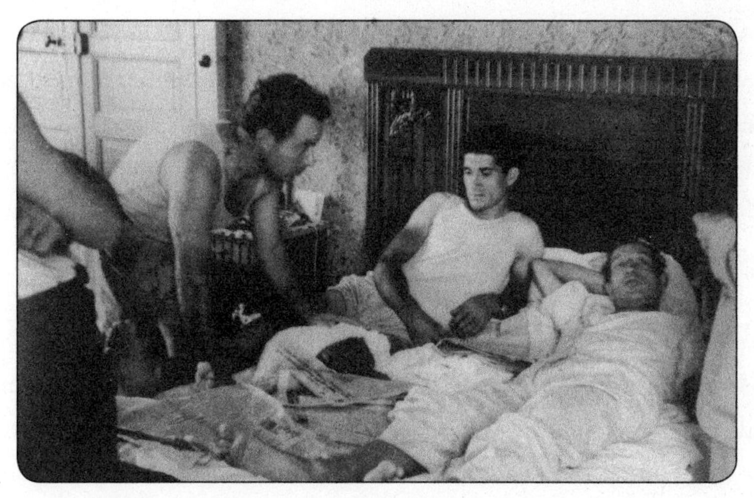

Gino Bartali and teammate Giovanni Corrieri enjoy a rare moment of rest during the Tour de France.

PLANNING FOR THE TOUR de France began in the early months of 1948, and speculation started immediately about who would lead the team. "Lots of discussion, lots of writing, lots of hidden politicking," Gino explained. When Gino emerged as a favorite because he had last led the Italian team to victory in France in 1938, Fausto Coppi quickly made his dissatisfaction clear in an interview with the French press. "I would really like to compete, but I would prefer to race against Bartali and not with him, for reasons that you can surely understand." Having beaten Gino in various races including the Giro d'Italia, Coppi felt he had proved that he shouldn't have to serve as a domestique for another racer, and certainly not Gino. Others didn't see it in the same light, and merely chalked up Coppi's response as the latest illustration of his deep rivalry with Gino. When it became clear that Gino would definitely captain the Italian team, however, Coppi surprised many fans when he declined to participate in the Tour altogether. He would debut at the Tour another year, and on his own terms.

Losing Coppi as a supporting rider was a big blow, and filling out the rest of the team roster was even more difficult. After the war, very few men who had raced before it returned to compete at the highest levels. Yet most of the younger riders, the new generation, had raced only two seasons to establish themselves as professional racers. This inevitably created a gap in the talent development process, leaving a shallow pool of candidates from which to shape a team. The final group that was selected reflected this reality. There was but one other racer besides Gino who had raced at the Tour before the war.

The issue of coaches would prove no less thorny. Gino approached his former Tour coach Costante Girardengo and asked him to lead the Italian team to France. Girardengo considered the proposal seriously. Still, at fifty-five years old, he felt he was too old to go back to the Tour. He declined Gino's request with a less than ambiguous warning. "Ten years have passed—that's a lot." Without Girardengo or Coppi, Gino and the Italian Cycling Federation were forced to become a little creative. For a coach, they turned to Alfredo Binda, the temperamental former cycling star Gino had idolized as a boy.

The Italian press viewed these developments with concern and wanted to hedge their bets. On the one hand, many could sense the national interest in the event, such as one reporter who suggested everyone in Italy was thinking about "nothing but the Tour." Yet newspaper publishers with tiny postwar budgets did not want to invest too many resources in a lost cause, and so their actions reflected their abject pessimism about Gino's prospects. When all was said and done, Italian editors would send only fourteen journalists to France to cover the Tour. In contrast, nearby Belgium, which had a significantly smaller population and newspaper readership, would send some fifty reporters, to say nothing of France, which would assign two hundred reporters to cover the race.

The Italian racers, or *les Macaroni* as many of the French fans referred to them, were scheduled to travel to France on June 26, 1948. In the days before the departure, each man made his final arrangements. Gino did some training under the supervision of his professional team, Legnano, whose director remained guardedly optimistic about Gino's prospects. Speaking with the press, he declared that Gino wasn't thinking about anything but victory at the Tour. And then immediately, as if he sensed that he was somehow tempting fate with such a comment, he insisted that Gino, just shy of his thirty-fourth birthday, would be ready to sign a paper declaring an end to his racing career if he won.

In Florence, Gino spent some of his last days in Italy with Adriana, Andrea, and Luigi, knowing that the Tour and the schedule of velodrome appearances and mini-races that followed would keep him away from home for the next several months. Speaking with Andrea, who was a few months shy of his seventh birthday, Gino was reportedly caught off guard when his son asked him a simple question.

"Papà, what gave you the idea to go do the Tour de France? You're too old now. You're going to get a beating." Although Gino must have realized that his son was just parroting something he had heard, it still must have been a blow to his confidence to know that even Andrea seemed to have lost faith in him.

On the morning of June 26, the team gathered at a hotel in Milan to do their final inspections. In the late afternoon, they made their way to the city's main train station. Surprisingly, very few fans were gathered to send them off. One man who did appear was the Legnano team director, bearing two gifts. The first was a large tart for the journey, and the second a bar of soap for each man to use throughout the Tour, an item he thought would be impossible to procure in France without ration booklets.

On the train, they made an unhappy discovery. Someone at the Italian Cycling Federation hadn't bothered to book the first-class sleeping carriage tickets that the team usually reserved so that they could rest during the overnight journey. It was an astonishing oversight that only underlined the skepticism in the cycling community about Gino's Tour prospects. Gino tried to save face by offering to pay for the first-class tickets on the spot, but they were sold out. Frustrated and resigned to a sleepless night, he and his teammates settled into their cramped quarters, sitting eight people to a compartment.

In the second-class section of the overnight train to Paris, one of Europe's most famous athletes began his long journey back to France.

✦

The 1948 Tour would be heralded as the first truly European Tour of the postwar era, but it was not the first time that it had been raced since the cessation of hostilities. Already in 1946, Tour director Jacques Goddet had attempted to restart the event. For all his best efforts, however, he was unsuccessful. The government refused authorization, given the extraordinary quantities of food and gas required to carry out the competition. At first it even hesitated to sanction the 1947 edition for the same reasons. In the end, it relented because, as legend has it, the French longshoremen threatened to go on strike if it did not occur.

As it turned out, the Tour of 1947 was rife with labor unrest and other challenges. Tour communications were all conducted by telegram because a national postal strike had left mail idling in post offices. More important, there was a demonstrable lack of international variety among the racers. Neither Germany nor Spain participated in the Tour. Italy did not send a team either, abstaining for a combination of diplomatic and commercial reasons. Goddet fretted about Italy's absence because it meant that the Tour would have one less superpower, reducing the international prestige of the event, and potentially endangering its postwar renaissance.

Still, Goddet was too entrepreneurial to give up so easily. Though stymied at the official level by the decisions of the Italian government and the Italian Cycling Federation, an undaunted Goddet quietly worked just weeks before the race to cobble together an Italian team of his own, composed largely of Italian émigrés living in France and whatever second-tier racers he and his colleagues could entice to join. Many of these Italian riders fared surprisingly well; two would finish in the top five. This achievement was particularly impressive given that they had come together at the last minute, with some team members literally cycling across hundreds of miles of France just to get to the starting line.

The 1947 Tour introduced the public to a new generation of cyclists—many of whom would return in 1948—who were presented as being at least as eccentric as their prewar predecessors. One racer was said to call home after each stage to speak to his dog. Another was a viscount of Piedmontese nobility, who claimed to be racing the Tour as a lark, with little concern for whether he finished first or last. A third was said to rest his bike in his bed during the Tour, while he passed the night on the floor beside it. When he fared worse than expected in the race, it was reported that he went home and chopped his bike up in disgust, burying all the pieces in his garden.

Of the one hundred men who raced the 1947 Tour, there were but two revelations, whose stars would shine even more brightly a year later when Gino returned. The first was a scrappy Frenchman named Jean Robic. With his dark aviator sunglasses and the white kerchief he wore over his head on sunny days, he might have passed for a member of the French Foreign Legion, but for the fact that he stood only five foot three inches and was prone to crying when he did poorly in a race. Nevertheless, he was hardly wanting for courage, or, at the very least, bluster. Though he was an unknown racer from one of the lesser-ranked regional French teams, he publicly promised to win and bring his wife the yellow jersey. A little more than three weeks later, during the last stage of the 1947 Tour, he seized the overall lead with the help of a teammate and won the competition.

The Italian press insisted that he had cheated by drafting behind a car in that critical stage, but nothing came of their accusations. Robic celebrated his victory with the extravagant purchase of three cars and the promise to purchase a fourth if he won again in 1948. His wife got his yellow jersey, and the nation got a new champion. Robic quickly became a common figure in the French press, with his face being used to peddle products as varied as shaving cream and bicycle seats. By 1948 he was omnipresent and seemingly omniscient. Like a solemn monarch, he helped send off the organizers who inspected the course before the Tour. When the route was publicized, a photograph of his face appeared in the center of the Tour maps circulated by the press. If there was any suggestion that all this attention had turned a prickly personality into one that was downright Napoleonic, Robic would not consider it. "These detractors, I will amaze them this year, I swear it!" he declared.

The other great discovery was an Italian rider named Aldo Ronconi. To be sure, he wasn't an entirely unknown element. Anyone who followed Italian cycling closely would have known that he had been a supporting rider for years, first for Gino and later for Coppi. At the 1947 Tour, however, he proved that he was a star in his own right, and earned himself a nickname befitting his new status—"the Emancipated Slave." His background was colored with many of the same hues as Gino's. He had come from a poor family that was deeply religious. Indeed, his brother was a Catholic priest who was not above disguising himself as a mechanic to get around Tour regulations that forbade family members from riding along in the Tour caravan.

By the spring of 1948, Ronconi found himself chafing in his role as a supporting rider to Coppi. He complained in the international press about having to sacrifice his own chances for Coppi as part of his duel with Gino. When Coppi declared he wouldn't participate in the 1948 Tour, it was announced that Gino would captain the Italian "A" team and Ronconi the "B" team (Italy and Belgium, both cycling superpowers, were allowed to send two teams each to compete as separate entities). Ronconi saw his opportunity and made no bones about his ambitions: "After the Tour, I will be able to race for myself."

✦

The 1948 Tour promised its audience an expanded slate of European stars and, above all, spectacle. At a moment when food shortages were an ongoing concern, the Tour was a celebration of unimaginable extravagance. In the lead-up to the start, newspapers around France left no mouth-watering detail unreported as they covered all the provisions required for the three-week competition. Highlights from the long list of foods that would be consumed included nearly 1,200 pounds of pasta, 1,500 whole chickens, and 200 pounds of chocolate. Thirty thousand bottles of wine, beer, and water were also requisitioned because "without wine," one journalist declared, "the Tour would not be worthy of being called the Tour de France." Even the otherwise staid Tour pharmacy was imbued with an air of indulgence when it was announced that it would carry six thousand tablets of aspirin and some twenty-six gallons of eau de cologne, which was thought to have some medicinal value when applied during massages.

Once the Tour started, it fell to the publicity caravan to carry on the spirit of excess. In all, there were some forty-five sponsors who had each paid several thousand francs to promote their wares to the public in the parade that preceded the racers in each stage. On some trucks, like the one promoting "Royal Mint Bubble Gum Américain," smiling attendants showered spectators with small packages of gum. On others, new machines were outfitted to run ongoing displays. A laundry detergent manufacturer equipped a truck with a special washing machine that allowed the public to watch as it cleaned the racers' muddy jerseys. Another sponsor, O.C.B. Rolling Papers, paraded a machine that could cut and fold cigarette rolling papers before everyone's very eyes. Inevitably, the most popular advertisers were the liquor companies, which hosted spirited parties featuring popular French singers in the evenings after various stages.

Advertisements in the newspapers and magazines jumped on the festive bandwagon, too, showcasing the heady new era of postwar prosperity that was just a purchase away. A food company heralded a modern world where vegetables could be stored and enjoyed year-round as frozen foods. A cologne company advertised a new offering called Après le Match ("After the Match"), which claimed to eliminate the need for a shower when applied after a sweaty sports competition. And a chemical company advertised a new miracle household insect repellent called DDT; its novel aerosol can promised to turn killing bugs into a "game for children."

The bill for mounting the Tour would be footed by the cities and towns where the stages were raced—each municipality would pay dearly for the privilege of playing host, at a moment when many municipalities were still struggling to rebuild after the war. When the caravan did roll in, however, there were few signs that anyone begrudged the expenditure. In fact, the only vocal critic to get any press coverage at all was the American film starlet Hedy Lamarr. She was angry that all the activities surrounding the Tour had diminished the coverage of her own arrival in Paris. The rest of the country appeared happy just to have a distraction and a chance to enjoy the impromptu local holidays that were so often declared to celebrate the Tour's arrival.

A few individuals would attempt to exploit all of this enthusiasm for less than noble purposes. In Toulouse, a defendant on trial for collaborating with the Vichy regime offered one of the more shameless examples of opportunism. Having learned that the judge, plaintiff, and lawyers had all postponed his trial so they could enjoy the Tour's arrival in their city, he asked to be released from jail for the same reason, and promised to return to his cell as soon as the race had finished. In Marseille, it was reported that a serial killer nicknamed *Pierrot le Fou*—"Pierrot the Madman"—was planning to sneak out of France by taking advantage of the Tour's first visit ever to Italy. One theory posited that Pierrot might don the attire of a cyclist and then hide in the scrum of the peloton as it crossed the border leaving France. The difference between fear and excitement has always been a question of relative distance, and so this storyline, too, became fodder for endless titillation and speculation around France, even if the actual Tour participants might have been a little unnerved at the possibility of having France's number one public enemy riding in their midst.

✦

For all the excitement, the first half of the 1948 Tour unfolded largely as might have been expected. Robic, whom the press had nicknamed *Biquet*—"Little Goat"—for his agility in the mountains, took the lead in the climbing competition in the first series, the Pyrenees. Ronconi raced consistently and was viewed by his competitors as one of the strongest cyclists in the competition.

Gino also fared well enough in the beginning, even winning three stages. But by the time the Tour had embarked on its second half, it was obvious that he was starting to suffer. Part of it could be chalked up to a few unlucky breaks, the kind of mishaps that befall every rider. Still, some wondered whether the wear and tear of several consecutive days of racing would put greater distance between him and the leaders. One Belgian writer, who felt Gino had already lost his place among the top contenders, described him as "a very normal, second-class rider." A French reporter was more targeted in his diagnosis of why he was failing. He speculated that Gino had lost *le jump,* that critical capacity for a final strong push that defines a great climber.

Everyone else was more interested in talking about another rider entirely, a young Frenchman named Louis Bobet, who, one reporter joked, could pass for Gino's nephew. Twenty-three years old, with movie-star cheekbones that could have been carved from marble, he was "*Le Pin-Up Boy,*" as one French newspaper called him, and a Tour director's dream come true. He combined an unexpectedly strong performance on the bike with a confident gait off of it—the unlikely fusion that brings new fans to the sport and sells newspapers by the hundreds of thousands. His fellow racers, and initially a few journalists, however, were jealous and skeptical. Many took to calling him *Louison,* or "Little Louis," a pet name coined by his mother, in a less than subtle suggestion that he was not yet seasoned enough to come out from behind her apron strings.

Others, who grew more numerous as his days with the yellow jersey extended, saw something more substantive in his rise from a lesser-known supporting rider to the de facto leader of the French team.

The final judgment about Bobet would be rendered in the Alps, the second series of mountains in the 1948 Tour. To get there, he and the other racers would have to summit the Col de Turini, a 5,272-foot mountain pass along the route from San Remo to Cannes. The press referred to the Turini as the first Alpine mountain ascent, even if technically it fell during a section that wasn't considered a mountain stage. This was the first year it would be raced, and therefore few journalists knew what to expect from it. With a narrow, twisting road to the top that had asphalt only in parts, it was certain to be grueling. A younger rider who wasn't used to racing on such poor road conditions could easily buckle. Add a bout of fatigue or dehydration, and the possibility of an accident or an injury grew exponentially. It was not surprising, then, that the press was highly skeptical about Bobet's chances. "We doubt that Bobet can cross the Turini properly. This mountain pass is such a difficult challenge that a real catastrophe could ensue if Bobet is not supported [by his teammates]."

✦

At midday on July 13, with the temperature inching over 100 degrees Fahrenheit, the riders faced destiny. Gino felt strong: "On that stage, I realized that I had achieved my best physical shape, and maximum ease in my pedaling. My muscles worked like the gears of a clock."

Halfway up the Turini, Gino found himself side by side with Bobet, ahead of everyone else. A rumor had been circulating that something was wrong with Bobet, but no one knew for sure what it was. Gino considered breaking away, but hesitated. "Everyone would say that yes, I had done well," Gino reasoned, "but that I had kicked in a half-open door, given that Bobet was sick and had not been able to compete on equal footing." Besides, as far as Gino was concerned, Bobet was too green to be a real threat. "I thought he was a wild card, a young man of great potential who had wanted to draw attention to himself." Gino was confident he could bide his time.

It took but a few moments for his optimism to disappear. Rolling over a nail on the road, Gino's tire popped. Bobet took full advantage of the situation and sped off. "Bobet didn't have anything but a little boil on his foot," Gino later discovered, "and as soon as he realized that a nail had pierced my tire, he spurted ahead like an elf." With a support car nowhere to be found and his teammates far behind, Gino bent over and began to change the tire himself. In the time that it took to replace the tire and inflate a new one, a small group of riders from France and Luxembourg rode past him. Gino was livid.

"I was in a black mood," he said. "I had let myself get played like a novice." What was most infuriating was that Gino had grossly underestimated his young rival, a tactical error that a cyclist of his experience should have never made. "Of course, if I had known that Bobet was strong on climbs too, I wouldn't have let him take all of that advantage."

When he was finally able to ride again, Gino chased after the group of riders who had passed him. Desperately pumping his pedals, he raced forward with all the energy he possessed.

And then he stalled.

Maybe it was the heat or maybe it was the thought that Bobet had outwitted him. Or maybe it was the realization that even at a moment when he felt as strong as he had felt in recent years, his body was no longer responding under pressure. The French reporter was right.

He was losing *le jump*.

Ahead, Bobet was a model of strength and intelligence. He reached the summit of the Turini mountain pass first and claimed the time bonus. By and by, he prudently eased up and allowed the small group of riders behind him to join him. Riding with the group, he would be able to draft off the other men and preserve himself for the stages that followed.

Those waiting for some auspicious sign to memorialize the importance of the moment were not to be disappointed. Just past Cagnes, the conductor of an express train to Paris riding on the tracks beside the cyclists spotted them. Within a moment, he had slowed down the train so that the passengers, and even the mechanic, could rush to the doors and windows to gaze at Bobet, riding confidently toward the glittering coast of the Riviera.

The end of the race was little more than a formality. In Cannes, Bobet glided past the beaches, palm trees, and grand hotels that lined the main boulevard, *La Croisette,* and won. The press was euphoric, and the reporters who had once doubted him got religion. "Le Pin-Up Boy" became the "Uncontested Hero."

Several agonizing minutes later, after the victor had been kissed, photographed, and paraded, Gino crossed the line, surrounded by a phalanx of anonymous riders. He had lost ground instead of gaining it, which meant he had ridden himself right out of contention. In total, he was now twenty-one minutes and twenty-eight seconds behind Bobet in the general classification.

But there was something greater than just the loss at work—the stage had revealed a different racer from the one who won the 1938 Tour. When exposed to the Tour's hardest challenges during the eighty hours the cyclists had raced thus far, some fundamental cracks in Gino's strength were beginning to show. Jacques Goddet, the Tour's director and éminence grise, offered the verdict rendered by many in the press corps. "For those of us who rode beside the racer in our cars and our motorcycles, we believe we can discern his true pain. Bartali will not win the '48 Tour. It was the Turini that affirmed it."

12

Four Bullets

A mass protest in Milan, one of many that erupted across Italy on July 14, 1948.

JULY 14, 1948, WAS a sweltering day in Rome, with the kind of searing sun that melts asphalt and forces people to scurry to the shade. In the Chamber of Deputies, the Italian equivalent of the U.S. House of Representatives, politicians were debating a proposed law to round up many of the firearms still lingering in private homes around Italy after the war. The ruling coalition of the Christian Democrats was advocating the measure as an important step to increase public safety. The Communist Party, however, was more skeptical. They were less than eager to confiscate the very weapons with which the Italian partisans had helped wrest their country's independence from the Germans during the war.

For Palmiro Togliatti, the bespectacled leader of the Communist Party, it was a morning like any other. Clamorous and colorful discussions erupted in the chamber; more hushed and routine meetings were conducted in the offices that surrounded it. At half past eleven, Togliatti decided he wanted to visit a famous local *gelateria*. Perhaps he wanted to get an ice cream. Or perhaps, like the millions of other Italian cycling fans, he simply wanted to read the newspaper to find out what was happening with Gino Bartali in France. Whatever it was, he decided to set off for Giolitti's, which had made its name serving up gelato with flavors ranging from hazelnut to watermelon and everything in between. He was accompanied by Nilde Jotti, a female colleague whom *Time* magazine described as "warm-eyed" and "full-bosomed." She was also his less-than-secret mistress.

As they walked out the glass doors of the Chamber's side entrance onto the street, a young man in a blue jacket brushed past them. Within seconds, the young man reached into his jacket for a revolver that was tucked in his belt. The revolver got stuck for a moment, but he quickly jerked it out and started firing. Togliatti instinctively raised his handkerchief to protect his face.

The first bullet grazed Togliatti's ear. The second hit him on the left side and went straight through his body and out his flank. The third bullet was much more treacherous. It traveled between his ribs and hit his left lung. Togliatti staggered, and a journalist who happened to be nearby rushed to grab him under the arms as he tumbled down to the ground near a parked car. A fourth bullet was fired, but missed its target. Togliatti was still conscious but seriously wounded and bleeding heavily. "Jotti! The bag!" he managed to say, alerting her to check whether his documents were secure. Then he asked whether the gunman had been stopped. Jotti, who was unharmed, threw herself on the body of her lover to shield him from further injury and screamed, "Arrest him! Arrest him!" Togliatti was rushed to the hospital. Within minutes, news of his shooting reached the Chamber of Deputies and spread across Italy, launching a maelstrom of violent chaos. The mysterious would-be assassin who had unleashed it all, however, stood by indifferently and allowed the police to arrest him without protest.

✦

His name was Antonio Pallante, and wild rumors quickly spread through the nation about what had motivated this twenty-four-year-old to shoot the leader of his country's opposition party. Some voices on the left accused him of being part of a larger government plot to suppress the Communist Party. Voices on the right speculated recklessly about it being an inside job; even more reasoned voices, such as the *New York Times,* argued that the Communists would exploit the incident to "incite riots and the mobilization of the mob." Others circulated the rumor that he was a paid assassin, working for an infamous Sicilian bandit. Still others suggested that he was a Nazi sympathizer, a charge Pallante himself would vehemently reject. The most notable possession in his bag, a copy of Hitler's *Mein Kampf,* suggested otherwise.

When the first photos of the criminal were published, Italians must have felt a disconnect between the crazed gunman they imagined and the boy they saw in newspapers. With a pale, round face and soft brown eyes, Pallante hardly passed for a cold-blooded killer. One newspaper journalist described him as "dreamy." Nor did any of the details that emerged about his family offer any clue about his motivations. He had grown up in Sicily, and his mother spoke of his deep religious convictions. He had spent four years in the seminary while he weighed the possibility of becoming a Catholic priest. His father, a forest ranger, described him as a mild and obedient young man who hated weapons. He did note that his son grew angry easily when challenged, but volatile tempers were hardly unique to Sicily, or to Italy for that matter.

There was nothing to suggest that Pallante was visibly disturbed in the days leading up to the attack. A stranger who met Pallante on the train ride to Rome had found nothing abnormal about him. One of the last people to spend any time with him was a friend who had shared a room with him in a boardinghouse. He and Pallante had chatted about several topics, but there was nothing Pallante said that offered any hint of his sinister intentions. In fact, Pallante appeared most interested in discussing a subject that had nothing to do with politics at all—Gino Bartali's chances at the Tour de France.

In the police interrogations that followed his arrest, however, a different picture of the would-be assassin emerged, a misshapen one of secrets and double lives. For several years he had flitted haphazardly between political parties in Catania, a city on the east coast of Sicily. He was supported by money from his father, who had sold a portion of the family land to fund his education. His father believed that his son was studying law at university.

Pallante was fiercely patriotic, but his political sympathies were confused, shifting, and erratic. There was but one constant—a deep-seated hatred for Togliatti. In Pallante's twisted logic, Togliatti was not only responsible for some of the reprisal killings carried out by the partisans at the end of the war, but was now plotting to hand Italy over to the Soviet Union.

In early July, Pallante had asked his family for more money so he could return to Catania and finish his undergraduate thesis. With the money in hand, he did return to Catania, but only long enough to purchase five bullets and a .38-caliber Smith & Wesson revolver. He then began his long journey north. Once he had arrived in Rome, he tricked a Sicilian deputy into giving him a pass to watch proceedings in the Chamber of Deputies so that he could study Togliatti's routines and behavior. At first he tried to lure Togliatti into a private meeting by sending him an urgent and mysterious note. When that message went unanswered, Pallante decided instead to try to shoot Togliatti when he was out in the open. On the morning of the fourteenth of July, he waited nearly thirty agonizing minutes by the side entrance to the Chamber of Deputies.

Even after he had committed the act and he had begun to understand the enormity of what he had done, Pallante was unrepentant. As he sat in police custody, he spoke calmly about shooting Togliatti. "I have always thought that his suppression would be healthy for Italy, but it was only three or four months ago I came upon the idea for the first time of committing the assassination myself."

✦

In France, the morning of the fourteenth was unfolding in a happier manner. The nation was celebrating Bastille Day, France's Independence Day. In Paris on this day everyone was a *boulevardier,* eagerly strolling the city's vast avenues in search of amusement. In the morning they could enjoy the grand military parade in the Champs-Élysées, where the president of the Republic was set to appear as the guest of honor. In the afternoon, the city's various national theaters offered free matinees for all the Frenchmen luxuriating in their day off work. By evening, Paris would be set ablaze as fireworks were launched from various locations. When their embers dissipated into the darkness of the sky, the city below them would keep glowing, as all her finest monuments, bejeweled with thousands of tiny lights, illuminated the night skyline.

On the French Riviera, Cannes also buzzed with holiday fervor. In the turquoise waters of the Côte d'Azur, snow-white and cream-colored yachts idled lazily in the sun. On the beaches, children built empires of sand, and more than a few women, the pretty young things that are never in short supply in Cannes, could be seen modeling France's shocking new tribute to bathing-suit minimalism—*le bikini.* Nearby, young couples strolled under the date-palm trees that bordered *La Croisette,* the city's most famous boulevard. This long green chain of droopy palm leaves was complemented by the occasional mimosa tree whose petite yellow flowers released a light, fruity scent with a hint of mango, which local *parfumeurs* bottled and sold so that visitors could savor the Riviera long after their holiday was over.

Bastille Day was a day for wine and happy picnics, and in Cannes these simple pleasures took on a charming elegance of their own. Picnic baskets brimmed with Provence's most succulent treasures—the myriad types of olives and tapenades that are specialties of the area, and various fruit *confits* and *calissons,* delectable local confections made of almonds, melon, and sugar. The wine lover was certain to relish his own delights. Provence is famous for her rosés, but on a national holiday champagne was de rigueur for any red-blooded Frenchman with the means to purchase it.

Of course, anyone who cared to look closely in 1948 would have noticed some shortages. Many store shelves were still empty, and like everywhere else in France, in Cannes many food staples remained under tight rationing. The city itself also seemed a little worse for wear. The war had turned the stream of tourists seeking sunshine into a dribble, and Cannes was short of money.

But when the Tour rolled into town, Cannes spared no expense. Whole parts of the city had been cordoned off to prepare for its arrival; a prominent tribune stand was built at the finish line so that the area's top politicians could see the race's finale. The cyclists, used to simpler lodgings elsewhere in France, were put up in the most opulent hotels. These weren't just luxury hotels, they were some of Europe's best—the type of establishments typically reserved for the world's wealthiest, "the Maharajahs and the blondes" as one journalist termed them. In an inspired act of beneficence, the city and Tour organizers had reserved rooms in one particular hotel, arguably the finest of them all, for the Italian team. It was the Carlton, whose two prominent cupolas were said to be designed to resemble the breasts of the city's most famous courtesan.

Rest days like this one offered an extended opportunity for celebration, although they were officially intended by Tour organizers as a day of quiet recuperation before and after a tough mountain stage. Various catered receptions would be organized, and fashionable clubs would invite cyclists to be guests of honor at their parties. Bands at nightclubs would play to all the visitors who had followed the Tour into the city. There was no doubt that the more earnest cyclists would spurn all such engagements. But it would hardly be surprising to find at least a few of them enjoying the festivities. After 1,700 miles in the saddle, no one could begrudge a man a canapé and a couple of cocktails.

✦

In Room 112 at the Carlton, the day was shaping up to be a quiet one. While Gino had gone sightseeing with his teammate Giovanni Corrieri during an earlier rest day, he planned for a more tranquil day in Cannes. The morning had started well enough. Gino had enjoyed a sleep-in and a late breakfast, the twin delights of Tour cyclists on rest days. The daily mail pile had yielded its own pleasures in the form of a pair of notable telegrams from Rome. One came from Monsignor Montini, passing on blessings from the Pope in the Vatican. (Montini himself would later become a pope.) The other was from Italy's prime minister, Alcide De Gasperi, thanking Gino for a short greeting that he had sent and wishing him luck for the following day's race.

When the members of the press began to gather in his room for their daily debrief, Gino's expression quickly soured.

"Always the same questions!" he barked angrily at the twenty or so reporters who surrounded the bed where he rested. The Italians and other riders frequently gave interviews from bed because when they weren't racing, they wanted to do everything they could to let their legs recover. Corrieri, who was lying in bed just inches away, was silent as Gino mocked the journalists' questions.

"So, Gino, will you win the Tour? Your setback in the general classification doesn't frighten you? What are you planning to do?" Gino asked sarcastically.

Gino was in one of his moods, which was no news to anyone, least of all the journalists who had been following his every movement for the last couple of weeks. But their questions did seem redundant, if not impertinent, given how many had already written him off in their respective publications.

The Italian writers, both those in Cannes and those following the

Tour via telephone updates and radio broadcasts, were particularly vocal in their criticism. As could be predicted, most attributed Gino's poor performance to his age. As an older racer, *Il Vecchio* lacked the endurance needed to keep pace with younger cyclists over three weeks of competition. "While I felt really good, everyone was going around saying that I was a finished man: an old man who still knew how to defend himself but that it took more than that to win the Tour," Gino later recalled.

Other Italian journalists were more pointed. One of them blamed Gino's poor performance on his cherished status with the *bartaliani*, his fans. "Bartali is embraced by too many people. Too much love always leads to sin." Others faulted Gino for inviting Adriana to spend the night with him two days earlier when the Tour stopped over in San Remo, Italy. For Gino, it had been a rare occasion to see his wife during a two-month absence from home, and he insisted angrily to the press that the couple had slept in a bed together with their son lying between them. For hardened wheelmen, however, the presence of women and the possibility of intimate relations, no matter how absurdly remote, could spell nothing but trouble for a racer.

The lead journalist on the cycling beat of Italy's most prominent sports journal *Gazzetta dello Sport* was the most memorable critic as he pronounced, "Bartali, the old king of the mountains, is no longer the king today." He put Gino's shortcomings in the context of Italy's recent history: "These are bad times for monarchies, and kings also pass away in the world of sports. It is wars that knock the world over, and athletically, it's the great racing battles that replace the important champions of the past."

The French press was surprisingly more sympathetic. Gino repaid them in kind when he offered one journalist an exclusive interview in which he outlined three major reasons for his poor performance in the Tour. First, he complained that he was competing not just against one French team, but many. He was right. There were several French regional teams in the 1948 Tour in addition to the French national team.

Second, Gino claimed that he felt "alone" because his teammates weren't strong enough racers to support him when he needed it.

Both excuses might have been technically accurate, but neither held much water. The Tour had for many years featured multiple French teams. In fact, during his victorious 1938 Tour, Gino had raced against three French teams without any incidents of unfair collusion between them. And if Gino felt that his teammates were weak competitors, he had no one to blame but himself—after all, he had helped select them.

Gino's most important complaint was that the national cycling federations that governed the sport in each country should force their best racers to compete in the Tour. In Gino's words as reported in the French sports newspaper *L'Équipe,* such a mandate was necessary because the Tour was a "race with international impact where the honor of each country is in play." The question wasn't which Italian rider Gino would have wanted the Italian Cycling Federation to oblige to ride in the Tour and help him. That was obvious: Fausto Coppi. The real question was how a man who had been so emotionally scarred by the Fascist government's interference in his own fledgling career could now demand that the current government interfere in another man's career. As he wrestled with the prospect of losing the Tour and fading into irrelevance, Gino was openly considering abandoning one of his most cherished personal convictions. As Coppi's long shadow cast its pall over him in Cannes, Gino hit a new low.

✦

Just a short walk away, at the Hotel Victoria, the French team was spending the rest day in much better spirits. Jean Robic, the ruling showman of the team, was particularly boisterous—and for good reason. He was a day away from one of his favorite stages, the race from Cannes to Briançon, and his performance thus far in the Tour had been excellent. In the first round of climbing in the Pyrenees, Robic had succeeded in challenging Gino on the Italian's favorite mountainous battleground. The press had taken notice. In Robic, one reporter proclaimed, "Bartali has found his master." To be sure, Robic had his own concerns. There was still a sizable gap between him and the Tour leader, his teammate Louis Bobet. Yet it was nothing that couldn't be made up in a stage or two. In the previous year, Robic had come back from a similarly large setback and won.

Robic was ready to celebrate, and his plans reflected that. Like a young starlet at a photo shoot, Robic would spend much of the day posing for the cameras of the national media. He hammed it up for photographers while milking a goat at a nearby farm. He also rode a donkey on the beach and then made a trip to a local hospital to speak with several sick children about the Tour. Other racers and onlookers might have thought that Robic was overexerting himself the day before the most grueling stage in the Tour. But for Robic, these activities were rather tame as far as his rest days were concerned. During an earlier rest day in Biarritz, he had borrowed a motorcycle from someone in the Tour caravan and gone for a joyride with friends. He was later spotted in a local casino. A few days after that, when the Tour stopped for a rest day in Toulouse, Robic was delighted as fans mobbed and cheered him in his hotel. When he slipped out the back door of the hotel to explore the city's market, he was spotted again, this time by a group of stocky female fishmongers. They seized him and hoisted him up to their shoulders, parading him around the cheering crowd for the better part of an hour. The revelry continued at Toulouse's city hall, where Robic and several other riders were praised again at a public reception. Though it wasn't yet noon, several bottles of champagne were opened.

Aldo Ronconi, the captain of the Italian "B" team, likely spent much of the rest day as he had spent his other rest days, writing postcards to his friends, family, and fans. After years toiling in both Gino's and Coppi's shadows, it was a delightful novelty to be writing to his own fans. It didn't hurt, either, that there was a lot of good news to report to them. Ronconi had enjoyed some flashes of brilliance in the flats and was holding his own in the mountains. Like Gino, Ronconi had struggled during the last stage. Still, as he sat in his hotel room in Cannes, he could take pride in the fact that he was the top Italian racer in the general classification. The rider who had come to France to show his countrymen that he was Gino's equal was now on track to defeat him.

Other riders spent the day on more routine tasks. One French rider planned to get acupuncture to help a sore knee. Two other French racers helped a third with his personal grooming and shaved him as he lay in bed. One Belgian racer was known to spend a few hours of his rest days in a bathtub filled with vinegar because he thought it would help his muscles limber up. Another Belgian racer would spend part of the day cleaning his clothes, a ritual he performed every day. His roommate, however, was less fussy and was happy just to turn some of his dirty clothing inside out and get another wear with less effort.

The most talked-about rider, Louis Bobet, the Tour leader, all but disappeared. Unlike other rest days, such as the one where he ended up at a cocktail party hosted by a ravishing actress, Bobet had decided to spend the whole day in his hotel room. Tempting as some of the day's festivities might have sounded, there was just too much to lose by tiring himself out. Still, Bobet appeared to be in undeniably good spirits. He had won the previous day's stage and kept the yellow jersey that he had worn for eight of the past twelve that had been raced. He was returning to full health as an injection of penicillin seemed to have cleared up the few painful boils that had appeared on his legs—boils that the press had matter-of-factly attributed to "overtiring, too much eating, and perhaps abuse of performance-enhancing substances."

After a good night of rest, he could spend this morning quietly thinking about how far he had come. In some two and a half weeks, a baker's son from Brittany had become a household name in France. His wife had become a fixture of the press. Police protected him at the finish lines from adoring fans; loyal admirers showered him with gifts, like the pound of unsalted butter he would receive that day from his hometown. Articles from different corners of Europe anointed him France's newest crown prince of cycling. No matter where he looked, Bobet could not escape one fact: his life had changed irrevocably. After years of training and sacrifice, Bobet finally grasped the imminence of his victory in Paris.

And then he got very, very nervous.

✦

In Italy, the situation turned from bad to bleak. Togliatti was rushed to the operating room for emergency surgery, led by one of the nation's leading surgeons. Christian Democrats, Communists, and journalists congregated in the waiting area. "This is the worst possible thing that could have happened," said Prime Minister Alcide De Gasperi, as he raced to join them at the hospital. Though likely in extreme shock and delirious with pain, Togliatti was still conscious. But he was losing blood rapidly, hemorrhaging internally, and had already needed several blood transfusions. At a quarter after one, he was anesthetized and surgeons began the arduous work of trying to remove the bullets from his body.

Outside the hospital, the news of Togliatti's attack swept across the country as radio stations posted radio bulletins and newspapers printed special editions. This information sent the country into chaos. Work in factories and many offices stopped almost immediately. Protesters gathered in the streets, ripped up pavement, and crafted barricades to stop police. "A wind of panic" menaced the country, wrote one journalist. In Rome, "the city wore the livid mask of fear," reported another. In Milan, factory workers took over their workplaces by force. Other workers did the same in Turin, and even held hostage some thirty managers, including the managing director of the Fiat car factory.

The shooting of Togliatti brought all the dissatisfactions, frustrations, and divisions in postwar Italy to the fore with chaotic results. If Togliatti died, everyone feared what would befall Italy. As his condition remained uncertain, the country teetered closer to the brink of revolution or civil war. Public protest meetings that were held in most of Italy's major cities quickly turned into riots. In Venice, a group of radical Communists seized a radio broadcast station and attacked an oil storage center. In Pisa, a pistol-toting Fascist hijacked a horse and carriage and opened fire on a crowd of workers, until he was dragged down and beaten to death by the crowd. In Taranto, protesters hurled rocks and bottles of gasoline at police. In Rome, demonstrators gathered in the large piazza in front of the office of the Foreign Ministry. Rioters made several attempts to break into the building, and the police fired shots into the air to scare them off. In Genoa, a group of radicals seized full control of the city government.

In Gino's hometown of Ponte a Ema, there were loud demonstrations in the streets. Many people in the crowds were crying, according to one pair of longtime residents, the Grifonis, who witnessed the events. "We were out of our heads," recalled Tullia Grifoni. "This news really upset us." Across the Arno River in Florence, angry protestors stormed the offices of the Christian Democrats and plundered them. Another political party that sympathized with elements of the Fascist platform fared even worse. Protesters forced their way into its offices, burned files, and then threw the office furniture out on the street. In a more remote and hilly part of Tuscany where Gino liked to train, a group of armed partisans took to the mountains and began a bloody battle against the army and the police.

In the USSR, radio stations in Moscow announced that Stalin and the Soviet Communist Party were "outraged" by the attack on Togliatti. Across the Atlantic, the CIA and the State Department would have found out about the shooting in the early morning. For officials who believed that Italy's choices would affect the fate of Western Europe, it must have been a terrifying moment as they followed developments from afar. At 8:55 a.m., the terror came much closer to home when an anonymous caller, who police believed was motivated by Togliatti's shooting, phoned the switchboard of St. Patrick's Cathedral in New York City and said, "I am a Communist. The cathedral will be blown up at a quarter to twelve."

A national tragedy had become a potential international crisis.

✦

Most of the Italian press in Cannes started packing their bags as soon as they heard the news from home. Gino caught sight of them as they were checking out of the hotel. Convinced they were leaving early because they thought the Tour was lost, Gino jumped up from his chair, where he had been chatting with his teammate Corrieri, and charged over to confront them. They barely had time to tell him they were returning to Italy before Gino interrupted them defiantly:

"Go! Go home!" he shouted. "I know what you're thinking: I'm old. You came here and tired yourselves out for nothing. There's no point in following Bartali's race, that poor old man, eh? But I'm warning you: a stopwatch won't be big enough to record the amount of time by which I'll beat the others. And don't come back to interview me when I have the yellow jersey!"

The anger in Gino's pale blue eyes quickly dissipated when the journalists explained that their departure had nothing to do with him. He thought immediately about his wife and sons in Florence. He tried calling them, but could not get through.

Details of the attack on Togliatti would trickle in as the day wore on. Yet already the parallels to a painful episode that had shaped Gino's childhood were eerie. As an eleven-year-old, Gino had received his first lesson about the dangers of politics when he helped his father hide his Socialist pamphlets after his employer was murdered, just one of several high-profile leftist figures to be killed by the Fascists. For Italians, it had been a pivotal moment as the nation was kidnapped by a dictatorship, and later war and destruction. With Togliatti's shooting, the country seemed to be retracing its recent history and falling back into another cycle of murder, chaos, and repression.

With little to do but wait, Gino stewed anxiously for the rest of the afternoon. One final problem remained: his coach, Alfredo Binda. Compared with all the troubles at home in Italy, it was a small issue. But it was a small issue that bothered Gino a lot. After the previous day's disastrous race, Binda had opened up to the Tour's organizing newspaper with several caustic comments about Gino's prospects, saying, "Bartali is no longer young enough to endure the repetitive tests of a Tour de France. He races well and he conserves energy, but he no longer recovers quickly enough. Tomorrow he may accomplish a great feat . . . but he will suffer the effects the following day."

Binda chalked up Gino's lagging performance to his decision to race both the Giro and the Tour in the same year. Gino hadn't performed well in the 1948 Giro, and Binda now thought he was too exhausted to succeed at the Tour. Such criticism wasn't news to Gino, but that didn't make it any less hurtful. Binda had betrayed the private relationship between cyclist and coach, and had done so for the transparent goal of improving his own reputation in the French press.

Gino tried to remain resolute. After a quiet meal with his teammates, he led them all out to the beach to play a few rounds of *terziglio,* an Italian card game. The ten men consumed a large cake decorated with an Italian tricolor ribbon, a bottle of vermouth, and a couple of packs of cigarettes. They were a little more lively for a time, but inevitably everyone fell back into their thoughts. Gino was no better, his mind turning to a strange new feeling that had started eating away at him a few days earlier. It was tough to put a finger on what exactly was agitating him. Perhaps it was the news from Italy. Or perhaps it was his disappointing results or the fact that the racers he was struggling to keep up with weren't even teenagers when he last raced at the Tour. Or maybe it was the fact that his thirty-fourth birthday was only four days away. Whatever it was, he couldn't help feeling that he was finally succumbing to the one doubt his critics kept raising.

He felt old.

✦

As the afternoon wore on in Italy, the situation continued to deteriorate. Physical damages to private and public property around the nation kept mounting. Scores of people had been injured in riots and several had even been killed. A nationwide general strike was announced and set to begin at midnight. Industry-specific strikes were not a new phenomena in postwar Italy, but this strike would incorporate almost every industry, including the postal service and telegraphs and, for the first time in twenty-five years, the railways.

In private meetings, Communist leaders urged their members to keep calm, to ensure that any action the party took would be deliberate and considered, rather than a rushed reaction to provocation. Leading Communist deputies were dispatched around the country to pacify regional party members, union leaders, and their membership. The same men who had once preached fire and brimstone in the Chamber of Deputies now found themselves trying to douse the ravaging flames of discontent. No one envied them their task. The Communists had been such obvious and public victims of an unprovoked attack that it was really no surprise that some of their more radical members had been calling for retribution. Still, in private, more than a few of them must have seen the cruel paradox of the situation they found themselves in. The *New York Times* explained, "Indeed it is an ironic twist to the event that Togliatti was shot down while leading the Communists in a Parliamentary battle *against* the Government bill calling for the collection of unlicensed arms. This would disarm the Communist partisans, but it would also make assassinations more difficult."

The Christian Democrats struggled with their own troubles as they tried to navigate the actual logistics of how to stabilize the country. For Prime Minister De Gasperi and his ministers, the day was filled with a chaotic flurry of meetings, updates, and impossible decisions. Italy was declared to be in a state of serious public danger, and all public gatherings were soon banned. A mandatory curfew was established, and 250,000 members of the army and police were alerted for possible deployment to secure the country.

At some point in this day of extraordinary measures, an unusual idea was hatched. Italy's most powerful politicians realized there was someone outside of politics, and of Italy for that matter, who might help. According to France's newspaper of record, *Le Monde,* De Gasperi discussed the possibility of sending a telegram to this person with his foreign minister. In the end, the prime minister decided to make a phone call instead. No one could doubt that the situation warranted it, but many would be surprised when they found out whom he was calling. It wasn't Harry Truman in Washington or Joseph Stalin in Moscow. It wasn't even Pope Pius XII, across the river in the Vatican City.

It was Gino Bartali.

"Do you recognize me, Gino?" De Gasperi asked, reaching Gino in the early evening.

"Of course I recognize you, you're Alcide. Please excuse me, Mr. Prime Minister . . . we used to be on familiar terms," Gino responded.

"And we should continue to be," De Gasperi said.

Gino listened, utterly perplexed. A minute earlier he had been sitting with his teammates on the beach, and now he was speaking with the leader of his homeland. The two were far from strangers, having known each other since well before the war, moving as they did in similar circles of Catholic activism in Italy. The two had also exchanged friendly telegrams earlier in the Tour. Still, none of that made this phone call any less surprising.

"Tell me, Gino, how are things going there?"

"Well, tomorrow we have the Alps . . ."

"Do you think you'll win the Tour?"

"Well, there's still a week to go. However, I'm ninety percent sure I'll win tomorrow," Gino responded, as he wondered what reason De Gasperi had, given all of the current problems at home, to be worried about him and a bicycle race.

"You're right, Gino. It's true that there's a week to go. But try and make it happen. You know that it would be very important for all of us."

"Why?"

"Because there is a lot of confusion here," the prime minister responded.

"Don't worry, Alcide. Tomorrow we'll give it our all." For all his knee-jerk confidence, it was a long shot and Gino knew it. With nothing else to say, the prime minister ended the call. Gino hung up the phone and swallowed. De Gasperi was asking a lot, to be sure. But even more had been asked of Gino before, and he had delivered. Steeling himself for the challenge ahead, Gino returned to his teammates on the beach.

When he found them, Gino dropped to his knees and began silently drawing the following day's racecourse in the sand. Conventional wisdom suggested that they should reserve their energy for the final climbs. Given the uncertainty about how the team would fare in the mountains, it seemed safest for the Italians to bide their time and see how their opponents attacked. In turn, Gino could then count on his teammates having enough energy to support him on the final mountain, which would help improve his overall chances. With several days of mountain stages awaiting him after the following day's race, prudence demanded that an older racer conserve himself.

Prudence wasn't an option Gino wanted to consider. With his finger tracing through the sand, he outlined a risky strategy of continuous attack. Instead of waiting until the decisive climbs later in the day, the Italians would strike right at the beginning. Rather than waiting to respond to their opponents' first move, they would attack first. Instead of having his teammates to support him, Gino would charge up the mountains by himself.

Elsewhere in Cannes, the other Tour riders made their final arrangements. Bobet took his dinner in his room and was fast asleep by nine. Robic and four other teammates only finished eating dinner at ten, at which point they began a lengthy final inspection of their equipment, cutting into the precious hours of rest before they needed to wake, well before sunrise the following day. The Italian team took a short constitutional to walk off the cake and vermouth and then retired to their respective rooms. After changing into their matching striped pajamas, Gino and Corrieri prepared for bed. Flitting between nervousness and giddiness, Gino kept chattering away until the wee hours of the morning. Corrieri, however, did what he always did. He turned off the light, rolled over in bed, and fell asleep.

13

A Frozen Hell

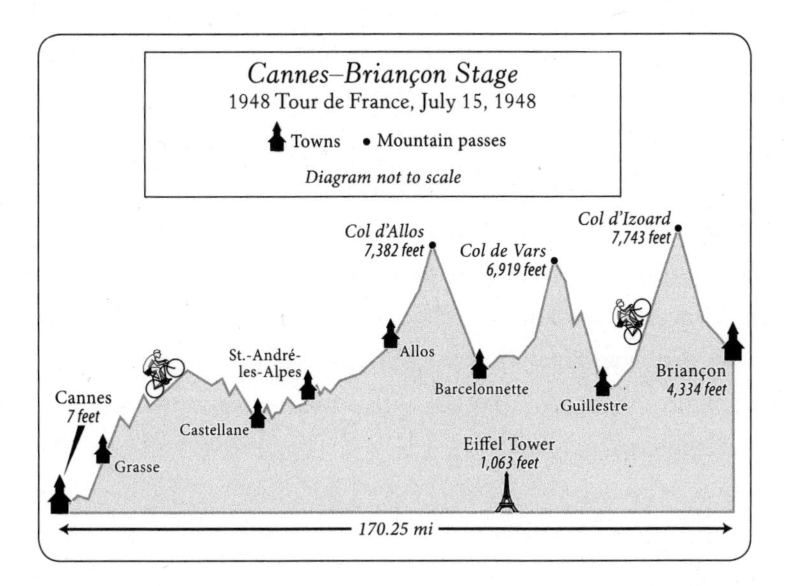

GINO AWOKE WELL BEFORE dawn. Giovanni Corrieri, his roommate, watched him. There was something strangely reassuring in what he saw. Gino was silent and lay calmly in bed, in striking contrast to his frenetic banter the previous evening. His bike rested nearby, propped against one of the hotel room's walls. Like the cowboys in his favorite movies, Gino had insisted on spending the night beside his horse.

After a few minutes had passed, Corrieri climbed out of bed. He walked over to the window and opened it up. The shattering staccato of rainfall poured out on Cannes's tawny beaches below as a short-lived storm pounded the surface of the Mediterranean into a choppy froth.

The Alps stood prominent in the distance, looming behind Cannes's clusters of whitewashed and pastel buildings. Their peaks jutted thousands of feet upward, a jagged gray barrier that prevented passage to the world beyond. Behind them lay Italy, fractured and heaving in violent national protests.

Gino would soon begin a ten-hour race through the Alps against the world's best cyclists, wearing nothing more than a thin woolen jersey, a pair of shorts, and a cloth racing cap. If the rain continued in the Alps, the high altitude would turn it into snow and sleet. The crude dirt roads that had been hewn into the mountains would easily yield to this torrent of precipitation, leaving the cyclists to navigate the steep Alpine ascents and hairpin turns in a perilous river of mud.

There was little to say or do. Both men just watched the rain fall in silence. In time, Corrieri turned to his teammate, looking for a comment or at least a gesture acknowledging the situation. Gino caught his glance. Already picturing his opponents struggling hopelessly against the elements, he responded to Corrieri with a most unexpected reaction. He started laughing.

✦

The loudspeakers crackled to life at four o'clock in the morning. As Tour officials made their final preparations before the day's race began, a mass of colorful vehicles and figures assembled at the starting line on Cannes's main thoroughfare. Each settled into its place like a veteran member of a cacophonous orchestra. In the front, drivers idled the motors of the forty-five trucks in the Tour's commercial caravan of sponsors. They each had paid several thousand francs to promote their wares to the crowds expecting the riders behind them. After the publicity cavalcade and the riders came the press corps: 311 members of the media had gathered to follow the day's race. Most had joined the expedition more than two weeks earlier when the Tour began in Paris. Print journalists rode in cars emblazoned with the names of Europe's most famous newspapers. A few were chauffeured so that they could type as the race unfolded, punching out their articles on typewriters mounted onto the passenger-side dashboards. Others took notes by hand and relayed them at the end of the day to their editors by telephone. Still others saddled up on motorcycles, where, like the photographers, they could weave dangerously among the racers. The most daring of these rode back and forth through the whole procession like the radiomen who ferried updates to the broadcast stations.

A vast line of Tour support cars lined up behind the press corps. Each team had a small truck to shuttle replacement pieces and backup bicycles, along with a flashy Renault sedan for the coach and commissioner to ride along in. The Tour organizers carried their own supplies around in a massive eighteen-ton tractor-trailer nicknamed "the Dreadnought," which was equipped with a pharmacy and an office complete with desks and filing cabinets that had been bolted to the walls to secure them. Two humbler vehicles rounded out the Tour caravan. One was an ambulance, whose three female nurses, the only officially sanctioned women in the convoy, were charged with tending to the needs of riders with lacerations, road rash, and broken limbs. The other vehicle, known as "the Broom Wagon," swept up the broken spirits of the Tour—those riders, and there were always a couple during most stages, who decided they could race no farther and needed to be carried to the finish line.

One final vehicle, known universally as "Car Number 1," would occupy the place of honor directly behind the racers. It was a convertible sedan and the personal car of the silver-haired Tour director, Jacques Goddet. He had his own driver so that he could take in the whole race standing, clad from head to toe in khaki. His dark eyes peered out from underneath a sturdy pith helmet, and he watched over the entire convoy with the solemn gaze of a British general launching an expeditionary force in Africa.

✦

"Cannes has never awoken this early," it was said, and for one dapperly dressed coterie, it had never gone to sleep at all. Long before the sun had even countenanced the idea of rising, a large crowd had stumbled out of Cannes's finer establishments, her glittery nightclubs and casinos, and descended noisily upon one of the city's main boulevards. Among them were the stars and crew of a French film about Buffalo Bill.

Few in this illustrious crowd seemed to be fazed about walking to the starting line of the day's race as the brief rainstorm petered out; fewer still seemed perturbed about doing so in their evening finery, clutching bottles of champagne. If such behavior crossed the line into boorishness, no one seemed to mind. Perhaps it was the fact that many of them were from the ethereal world of the movies. Or perhaps it was just a question of geography. On the Riviera, the wealthy and besotted have never worried too much about the trivialities of propriety.

The rest of the spectators, the mere mortals, flowed in like the morning tide. They came alone and they came in crowds. Some came by foot, and a great number came by bicycle. Couples rode together wearing matching shirts, while other fans rolled in on two-, three-, and four-person bicycles. If previous stages were to be any indicator, there were likely even a few Franciscan monks riding about, though the familiar noise of their cassocks flapping against the wheels of their bikes would have been barely audible. It was drowned out by the happy chatter of young girls that bubbled out from under bright-colored umbrellas, carefully positioned to protect the bobbed coiffures that were in vogue.

They all mixed together in a loud and splashy display of humanity. On the sidewalks, small children chased each other around while their parents chatted with other adults. Migrant Italian workers shuffled among the French citizens for whom they were building houses and roads. Some people milled about in the street, squinting to see through the forest of umbrellas whether the big-name racers had appeared yet. Others laughed at the hundreds of paper pamphlets that were being handed out by Tour officials, with their preposterously stern warnings against helping racers up the mountains. Some of these were straightforward: "Pushing: It's cheating." Others were more philosophical:

"Those racers who struggle today in the hills ardently desired to race the Tour. They freely chose their lot."

Many people struggled to secure a good spot from which to watch the action that would soon unfold. The early birds took up places on the curb. Everyone else improvised. They stood on benches, cars, crowded balconies, and rooftops. Young boys peered out from the tops of store awnings; a few even shinnied up lampposts.

To some, all this frantic activity seemed unnecessary. The day's 167-mile racecourse would provide more than enough space for everyone to congregate. And congregate they did. From Cannes all the way to the finish line in the mountain village of Briançon, the sides of the road swarmed with clusters of people. The flatlands and mountain summits filled up quickly, and it wouldn't be long before a few zealous supporters would dot the forsaken climbs through the Alps. Whole towns closed down as fans made a day of it, anticipating for hours on end that thrilling moment when the stars would appear and then speed off, visible for less than a minute. In the meantime, they waited. If the weather obliged, the bold could be counted on to write colorful messages to their favorite racers in chalk on the sections of the road that were paved, each encouraging word measuring several feet across. The Italian fans, whether working in France or just visiting for a few days from Milan or Turin, were never afraid to write large patriotic proclamations in Italian: *Viva l'Italia! Viva Gino!*—"Long Live Italy! Long Live Gino!" The rest of the spectators were happy just to pass around bottles of wine, cheering loudly, even boisterously, as they watched the antics of the local children, decked out in cycling uniforms and helmets, who were competing in short races for prizes donated by local storekeepers.

Everywhere, they waited.

✦

At the Carlton hotel in Cannes, each member of the Italian team made his final preparations. Aluminum water bottles were filled and placed in their holders, seat heights measured to an eighth of an inch for the umpteenth time. Bike frames were checked and rechecked. Anyone who cared to look would have noted that Gino had opted for slightly thicker tires. They were undoubtedly heavier than his regular tires, but Gino hoped that they would compensate for their weight by giving him some added traction in the mountains.

When everyone was satisfied with the state of their equipment, they sat down together for a team breakfast. Gino devoured an imposing pile of eggs, meat, and bread with marmalade, and washed it all down with several cups of coffee. Discussions around the table were few and far between. It was as if the boisterous mixture of laughter, gossip, and bravado that usually accompanied the Italian team had been swept away with the rain. To be fair, the conditions hardly seemed conducive to even the most superficial of conversations. At five in the morning before a long day of climbing, few subjects seemed worth wasting the energy needed to speak about them. Most members of the team, including their captain, were lost in reflection about the events taking place in Italy.

"How is Togliatti?" Gino asked a journalist.

"He's been operated on. I heard on the radio he's still alive," he responded. Gino was somewhat calmed, but this update did little to relieve the other Italian riders.

A few silently contemplated the uncomfortable question posed by the Tour director in a column that he wrote for one of France's most popular newspapers. "Bartali fights the final battle of his career. After a defeat in the Tour, what's left for this champion, overtaken by Coppi?" Others mulled over their own diminishing future prospects. The 1948 Tour winner would take home 600,000 francs, and even more from appearance fees in races afterward. Nearly all the other racers would return home with nothing to show for their efforts but their disappointment. Gino understood this. Finishing his meal off before starting on one of the American cigarettes that he reserved for moments of importance, he broke the uneasy silence that hung in the room.

"Let's think about the race, guys, it could be the last." It was no rousing call to arms, just a simple statement of the facts.

No one responded.

✦

At the Hotel Victoria, Bobet did his own final inspections. Like Gino and many of the other racers, he had adapted his bicycle for the day's stage, opting to exchange a heavy pedal axle for a hollow one, which would allow him to ride more quickly because it was lighter. To most onlookers, it seemed an unusual decision because a hollow axle was decidedly less robust. With a large lead over both Robic and Gino, Bobet had no need to race so aggressively. In fact, he could afford to lose the stage and even a few minutes of time—as long as he avoided any major disasters that might prevent him from shining in the flats that would follow the Alps. But Bobet wasn't in the mood for conservative racing. Perhaps it was anxiety—there are few shoulders on which the yellow jersey rests easily. Or perhaps it was vanity—winning in the Alps would have exorcised those remaining demons in the press who still doubted him. Whatever it was, Bobet planned to race for victory alone.

Robic must have smiled when he checked over his own equipment. For once, his leather helmet would be an object of envy in the peloton. This signature accessory had made him the butt of countless jokes because few others regularly wore anything beyond a cloth cap. Cycling was always a dangerous sport, but in the mountains, where the roads were often little more than gravel and mud, it could be deadly. Just weeks before the Tour, a Belgian racer had died during a descent in the Tour of Switzerland, in which Robic had competed. Later, in the Pyrenees stages of the Tour itself, one of Gino's teammates was struck by a swerving car, and another car, a press vehicle, slid off the road into a ravine, killing one passenger and seriously injuring the other.

At least one team of racers followed Robic's example and insisted on wearing helmets for this and every other mountain stage. Other riders adopted equally unorthodox measures to protect themselves throughout the Tour. One French rider, an outspoken Communist, had been spotted secretly dipping a medallion of the Madonna into holy water for good luck on the climbs, moments after making a big show of turning his back to a bishop during a mass for the racers.

With all their final preparations completed, the French team headed for the starting line in the center of Cannes. The Hotel Victoria faded quickly from sight and with it the inscription that their coach had left in its guest book: "With the hope that the hours spent here will allow us to keep the yellow jersey until Paris."

✦

"The weather is unstable. Storms and lightning are moving through the Alps and Pyrenees. Temperatures are unseasonably low." The news from the national weather report was unsettling, but no one at the sign-in area at the Café des Allées seemed to pay it much attention. Forecasting the weather has always been challenging, and the summer of 1948 seemed a particularly difficult subject for divination. Reports in Paris spoke about freak summer weather patterns that brought snowfall to the Black Forest, but in Cannes nothing seemed out of the ordinary. Summers in the Riviera tend to vary only between hot and blistering, and the last two days had been no different. On July 13, they had suffered through temperatures of over 100 degrees Fahrenheit, though the sea had become turbulent by the evening, with "menacing waves and white foam like fangs that wanted to bite." The rest day on July 14 had brought relief from the sun with some light cloud cover. Given all of this, it was no surprise that anybody who did pay attention to the weather reports might have greeted them with skepticism. Sympathetic souls might have chalked up this seeming mistake to the difficulty of interpreting regional weather patterns; more cynical hearts saw just another instance of the big-city bluster that has won Paris the eternal enmity of the provinces.

In any event, the press was much too distracted by a new arrival in their midst to bother about the weather. Maurice Chevalier, a famous vaudeville singer and an Academy Award–nominated actor, had been coaxed from his villa in nearby Bocca to serve as a guest columnist for two days. He had worked for Hollywood heavyweights like MGM and Paramount, but had no experience as a sports journalist, and it was unclear whether he had ever even seen a cycling race before. Yet he would receive 100,000 francs for his labors—the same amount that in Paris awaited the winner of the Tour's King of the Mountains contest.

There was little to indicate that the racers begrudged Chevalier all the attention or money that he was receiving. Most were too busy with more important things, such as filling the pockets of their jerseys with food to eat while they raced. Few, if any, noticed that Gino had arrived at the starting line with "smiling eyes" as one journalist put it, even if he was accompanied by a paltry honor guard of only four fans. Gino was just happy to be racing one of his favorite stages. As he had told a journalist a few days earlier, he wouldn't find it so hard to lose the Tour if he could just hear it announced that he was the first over the Izoard mountain pass one last time.

No doubt thinking about his own prospects, Ronconi was seen smiling widely at the starting line. Bobet looked visibly uneasy, like a star Thoroughbred that gets restless waiting in the gate. Robic, however, gleamed with happiness and confidence. "The three cols today are my lucky ones," he said. "I cannot lose."

✦

At ten after six, a pistol was fired and the race began. Gino pressed forward and his wheels began to glide easily over the road beneath them. Fans cheered and the whole Tour cavalcade rolled forward. Fueled by an inordinate quantity of diesel, the publicity caravan sped ahead and left a sizable cloud of exhaust fumes. The riders, many wearing bandages after falls in earlier stages, rode after them with the grim determination of injured cavalrymen riding into battle. Over the next several hours they would traverse a gradual ascent, a gentle valley descent, and then a climb up and down three mountain passes. A ride up one of them alone was a formidable journey. The smallest rose some 6,900 feet, which was even more impressive and unusual since the racers would start at close to sea level that day.

They had barely crossed through the city's gates when the Italians began their attack. One of Gino's teammates sprinted forward. In a telltale sign of nerves, Bobet parried, even though he should have had a whole team to rely on for support. Several other riders chased after him. Gino stayed back, with Robic watching his every move from just a few inches away. Within a few minutes, Bobet and the front group had caught the breakaway rider. The first attack had ended. The sky clouded over as the peloton regrouped beneath it.

There was an eerie lull as the cyclists made a slow climb out of the Riviera. After riding past endless rows of olive groves and fields of grapevines, they began a descent through a valley into a small village. The riders slowed down shortly before eleven as race officials handed over the first of two yellow food bags they would get to fuel them for the next eighty miles of hard climbing: some cold chicken, a chocolate bar, five cubes of sugar, and a few bananas. They transferred these meager rations to the pockets of their jerseys and flung the bags to the side of the road. Ahead stood the first mountain pass, the Col d'Allos, its top half invisible under the heavy fog that had begun to cover the valley in cold rain. The mood of the riders and the caravan changed as quickly as the weather. "Gone were the gay crowds, the villages, the flags. The little group of men in their gaily colored sweaters seemed forlorn in the vastness of this magnificent landscape," wrote one American journalist.

Remembering his surroundings from the last time he had raced there in 1938, Gino felt his heart squeeze as he was overwhelmed by emotion. "I could hear the shouts of the Italians who ten years earlier had deafened me on those same ascents," he said. But there wasn't much time for nostalgia. While changing his gear for the mountains, which required him to pedal backward and then lean over and pull a lever, he left himself vulnerable, if only for a brief moment.

Robic saw his moment and attacked. He broke away from the pack and rushed up the mountainside, where some lavender and a few small fir trees broke through the unending wall of gray. Gino, who was trying to conserve energy by drafting in the wind stream behind a teammate, weighed his next move. Robic kept sprinting, and soon took the lead. Within minutes he passed the red flag marking the final kilometer of the climb, and just as quickly he rolled over the top. Gino was already a minute behind, and the distance was growing.

Though he was steering through little more than mud and gravel, Robic sprinted skillfully through the descent. French journalists who had arrived earlier abandoned any pretense at objectivity as they stood on their cars and cheered him on. One newspaper car that was following him through the mud lost control and slid into a ravine. The driver was thrown from the car, but escaped any major injury. A passenger fractured his clavicle. Miraculously, no one died.

The temperature kept dropping, so much so that the cold rain turned into a wet snow. Yet the idea of snow in the middle of July seemed so otherworldly that journalists reached for literary allusions to describe it. One saw something of a biblical apocalypse, another Dante's vision of hell. Listeners across France heard all of this as they were tuning in to the noontime radio updates. Even if the change in weather seemed rather worrisome to some, everyone could sit down to lunch with the comfort of the facts. Robic was in the lead, and the yellow jersey remained safely in French hands.

✦

Lazarus awoke on the Vars mountain pass. Gino charged up this second and penultimate climb, his gaze blank and emotionless. His jersey and shorts were now completely stiffened by freezing mud, but underneath them his body moved fluidly from side to side. An icy wind blew as he pedaled, forcing the stunted firs that had taken root among the mountain's rocks to bend as though in deference to him. Seeing Robic in front of him on the road, Gino contemplated his final attack. The only thing left to do was to pick the right moment.

Ahead, crowds wrapped in drenched blankets and improvised jackets watched as the road leading up to the Vars summit capitulated to the onslaught of snow and freezing rain. The buses that had carried them there rested among the rocks, metallic behemoths in a lunar landscape. Robic still held the lead, but he periodically looked back and tried to gauge the strength of the familiar green figure behind him.

What he saw could not have been comforting. Pumping relentlessly on his pedals, Gino was gaining on him. On the roadside beside them, the French fans watched nervously as the Italian shortened the Frenchman's lead to a few hundred yards. Some, still furious that Italy had allied with Germany against France during the war, jeered him and later his teammates as Fascists. But these were just angry aberrations. The rest of the crowd was more passive, transfixed by the morbid suspense of watching a lion stalk his prey. "My heart was going boom-boom in my chest," said one middle-aged French journalist. "I wouldn't have traded my seat for the hair I had in my twenties."

Robic held out until the top of the Vars. Gino, however, had now whittled his lead down to thirty seconds. Panicked, Robic leaned sharply into the descent down the mountain. Gino followed after him, pedaling as aggressively in the descent as he had during his climb. Farther behind him, Louis Bobet was faltering. His vision had started to cloud, one of the first signs of bonking—the condition when a rider's body shuts down because he has consumed all the energy stores in his muscles. Bobet would soon suffer a further setback when his hollow pedal axle cracked in the mud. Even farther back, the rest of the peloton struggled. Between the roads and the elements, they were going to have a hard time finishing one climb, let alone three.

Robic raced madly through abrupt turns. The cold wind battered his tired body and made him ever more liable to take a nasty fall. During a fast glide, he yelled something incomprehensible to a passenger in a nearby official's car. Someone passed him a newspaper. He shoved it under his sweater, a haphazard shield against the cold, and he tried to stay ahead of Gino, who was slowly gaining ground in his wake.

As they came down the Vars, Gino caught him. Speeding over a road that had been ravaged by flooding, he rolled past Robic, who was now so forlorn that he couldn't even muster a rebuttal. Instead he looked up slowly at Gino, with the sadness of a man who knows his fate is sealed. Physical exhaustion, food deprivation, and the elements had taken their toll. Like Bobet behind him, Robic's body had crashed and other racers soon would overtake him. Many wondered whether he would even make it to the finish line.

Just minutes afterward, Gino realized that he was about to hit the same wall. He had missed the food satchel earlier in the race, and his body was threatening to shut down. "Heavens! What coldness! What absolute hunger!" he exclaimed later. "I was so hungry, I felt I would die of hunger." There was no doubt that he was starting to regret having refused the sausage and bread someone in a press car had offered him earlier, even if it was heavy fare to consume before a hard climb. Famished, Gino looked around to see if any spectator had something to eat. When nothing immediately materialized, he began to wonder whether he would have to walk his bike up the last mountain pass, the Col d'Izoard.

It was no small stroke of luck when someone reached out and handed him three bananas. To this day, the identity of this generous stranger remains unknown. It's possible that it was some anonymous Tour official with food to offer from an extra satchel. One of Gino's teammates believes it was a priest. Whoever it was, their gift could not have come at a more propitious moment. Gino made quick work of all three bananas. His body responded almost immediately.

At the foot of the Izoard, facing a twenty-mile climb steep enough to stall all but the most rugged cars, Gino felt his legs surge beneath him. "The cold blocked the fire of the muscles, but a numb and soaked Gino gunned his engine," observed the Tour director. The old wheelmen would chalk it up to the power of good fortune. It stood to reason that the man who won the 1938 Tour wearing the number thirteen jersey would rise again ten years later in the thirteenth stage. The *bartaliani,* the true believers, however, dismissed such musings as mere superstition. To them, this was nothing short of divine intervention. "The good Lord took a pair of wings from one of his angels to put them on the back of Bartali," wrote one.

Gino reveled in the clarity of one thought: *I feel like a giant.* Looking neither left nor right, he powered right past the crowds of stupefied onlookers. Covered in mud and remnants of grease applied earlier to ward off the cold, he was nearly unidentifiable. Man and bike had become one, a pulsing mass of muscle and chrome that shimmered in the light rain. Moving rhythmically from pedal to pedal, Gino was completely at ease as he worked his way up the slope. With a six-minute lead over the next racer, he rode to the top alone. At the summit, Maurice Chevalier yelled out to him from a French press car, "Bartali! You're immortal!" And for one fleeting moment when Gino crossed the finish line, he was right.

✦

The news traveled back over the Alps into Italy as fast as the radio signals could carry it. Italian radio had started broadcasting again at 1:00 p.m., and a good number of Italians, particularly in the north, were able to pick up the French channels, too. In Rome, a young representative ran into the Chamber of Deputies and made a loud announcement to the gathered officials:

"*Attenzione!* Great news. Bartali has won the stage and maybe the yellow jersey. Long live Italy."

The clapping that started on all sides of the room built into a loud and thunderous applause.

From the hospital where Togliatti lay, word traveled that he was slowly recuperating. The one-two punch of good news knocked Italy into a state of total euphoria. Outside, people rushed out of cafés and bars into the capital's great squares in a spontaneous and spectacular celebration.

Giorgina Rietti, an Italian Jew who had spent the war years hidden in Assisi and Perugia, was outside walking in the outskirts of Padua, passing through an alley, when she overheard a radio announcer declaring that Gino had won the mountain stage. Instead of protesting and fighting, people around her started cheering and toasting each other. Gino's victory changed their mood completely, Rietti recalls. "Italians who thought they were going to hurt each other ended up drinking together."

Similar scenes unfolded in cities and towns across the country, leaving citizens and journalists alike astounded by the speed of the change in the country's mood. The *Le Monde* correspondent stationed in Italy captured the sentiment of many Italians as he wrote, "No event in the world could have been as important as Bartali's victory. This was clearly apparent on July 15 when the news of his exploits transformed the highly dramatic atmosphere into which Italy had been plunged following the attack on Togliatti."

As had been the case ten years earlier, Gino's performance quickly took on a political value that was much larger than one man. To the cheering crowds across postwar Italy, he soon personified the whole country and all its emotions—angry, bruised, indomitable, and triumphant. No athletic victory had ever tasted as sweet for so many.

✦

In Briançon, the organizers at the finish line feted Gino's victory by playing an operatic aria from Puccini's *Tosca:* "I lived for art, I lived for love" floated out from the loudspeakers. Yet after ten hours, nine minutes, and twenty-eight seconds in the saddle, Gino was too tired to acknowledge the music or even just to lift his hand. Caked from head to toe in mud, he was shivering until Binda wrapped him in a trench coat. As he started to walk toward the team car, a few reporters swarmed him and asked him how he felt. Anyone expecting a florid victory speech, however, was left disappointed. Gino, his face slightly green and distorted from the day's exertions, barked out only one sentence: *"Ho fame"*—"I'm hungry." As was the custom after each stage, the Tour hostess, typically a pretty young girl from the local area, presented the victor with a bouquet of flowers. Gino, however, pushed them right back into her arms and told her to take them to the nearest church. With that, he got into the team car with Binda and left.

Eighteen minutes after Gino, Louis Bobet crossed the finish line. Utterly defeated, his face was covered in mud, except for the tiny furrows where tears had fallen down his cheeks. When he got off his bike, he had to be held up by a second person to keep from falling to the ground. Although immediate rest would have been most sensible, the cheering of the crowds clouded Bobet's judgment, and he soon allowed himself to be talked into a victory lap that was entirely unearned. Robic made it across the finish line six minutes after Bobet. Dangerously fatigued, he had fallen off his bike on the Izoard and might not have finished the race at all had several spectators not hoisted him back on so that a supporting rider could help push him to Briançon. At the finish line, he grabbed the rider and begged not to be left alone. Ronconi was the last of the great stars to cross the finish line, after a humiliating final climb that had seen him literally pushed up the Izoard by his teammates. In three days he would drop out of the Tour altogether.

At the hotel, the excitement among the Italians was palpable. Teammates, who earlier in the day had been preparing themselves for a premature return to Italy, now dared to imagine the final victory in Paris. Gino, however, peeled off his muddy jersey and lit a cigarette. The next day he would have to do it all again, except this time he would have to climb five mountain passes instead of three. Fearing the onset of a chill, he collapsed into a hot bath.

✦

In Rome, the man at the center of the political tempest in Italy lay unconscious as he recovered from his operation. By all accounts, his room in the hospital was spartan. There was nothing more to it than an iron bed painted white, and a little cupboard on which were placed several bottles of mineral water, along with a small basket of fruit and some sweets. It was only outside the room, where a security team kept a close eye over any visitors who appeared to gaze upon Togliatti through the window, that one could understand the importance of the patient who lay within.

When his eyes finally fluttered open, his family and friends must have wondered what he would ask. Italy had changed so dramatically in the last few days, and Togliatti, whose last memory was hearing Pallante's gunshots, was still completely oblivious to it all. As it turned out, however, it wasn't the country he wanted to focus on, or the whereabouts of the gunman. It wasn't even his own health that worried him. Instead, he whispered but two simple questions:

"What happened at the Tour? How did Bartali do?"

14

The Road Home

Gino Bartali rides his victory lap after winning the 1948 Tour de France.

DURING THE EVENING THAT followed Gino's resounding triumph, Italian journalists filed long, adoring articles. Gino had gone from a twenty-one-and-a-half-minute deficit to just sixty-six seconds away from the lead, thanks to his stage victory and the time bonus earned for summiting the Izoard first. Several French journalists, however, were more incredulous and speculated that Bobet might still keep the yellow jersey. Most of these skeptics were acting out of little more than economic self-interest. If they suggested that the Tour's winner had been definitively identified, readers might be less inclined to purchase newspapers and follow its progress. Yet a few of them, like so many other Frenchmen, genuinely believed in Bobet's prospects. Charmed by his earlier performances and his dashing persona, they clung to the prospect of a French victory in Paris. Bobet, soaring after his undeserved victory lap in Briançon, embraced this feeling in post-race interviews. He belittled Gino's success and offered a few defiant words that would soon haunt him. "Bartali doesn't have *my* yellow jersey yet!"

A little more than twelve hours after they had crossed the finish line, the men gathered again at the starting line and prepared to leave Briançon and its charming town walls behind. After the poor weather, the waterlogged roads, and the various mechanical and physical breakdowns, most riders probably wished to forget the previous day's stage. On this day, the weather at the start line was clear, with even a rainbow visible, giving credence to the hope that everything that had happened the day before was just a freak of nature. It would take but two hours to snuff out that illusion.

The first mountain pass of the day, the Galibier, was the Tour's highest, at 8,386 feet. As they began the ascent, the sky turned gray, the air started to get much colder, and flakes of snow began to fall. "It was horribly cold," said Gino. "The intense cold cut through your muscles, and I hadn't brought my raincoat." The racers climbed farther and were enveloped by a snowstorm. They were shrouded in darkness, save for the light that shone out from the headlights of the cars that followed them. In a telling sign of their fierce national loyalty, the French fans who had gathered in the mountains offered warm drinks to the French riders, leaving all the other competitors to shiver in the chill. Luckily, Gino got a few sips of coffee from one of the French racers who admired him. It was better than nothing, but he would have been happier with a glass of cognac, as he said later.

The pace of the snowfall slowed down but the weather remained miserable for the rest of the day as the cyclists pedaled toward Aix-les-Bains. The roads quickly became almost impossible to traverse. At least one press car saw its transmission break down completely under the pressure of a tough climb over ice and impenetrable mud. Riders who had gone blue in the cold found themselves with the unenviable task of trying to navigate 150 miles of climbing. Some invented wild hallucinations to survive the struggle, like one rider who imagined that his young son was starving on a distant mountain peak, just so he could muster the energy to ride up it. Another lost his saddle and was forced to ride many miles without a seat until his coach brought him a replacement bicycle. Others got off their bikes altogether, flapping their arms like hapless birds in a desperate attempt to regain feeling in their extremities. Still other racers had given up even on that, and so, like one Belgian racer, they were left to change their punctured tires with their teeth because their hands had frozen and their cramped fingers were completely unresponsive. The unluckiest of all had to be literally carried out by their teammates. A photographer captured this impossible feat. With an injured teammate draped over his shoulder, a racer pedals precariously, one hand on his own bike and the other hand holding his teammate's handlebars.

Robic crumpled under the weight of the pitiless weather, already utterly defeated by the previous day's stage. In a cruel twist, he discovered that many of the French spectators had turned on him. Barely a day after fans had crowded on the mountain passes to cheer him on, they now loudly second-guessed his every move. Some even mocked him with the kind of cowardice that only a spectator in a warm jacket or a heated trailer could know. At one point, Robic was so overcome by fury that he got off his bicycle and chased after an obnoxious fan who was sitting in a car. Ultimately he grew too weary to fight even these petty battles. Numb from the cold, Robic could do nothing as an angry fan screamed out at him, "What are you doing, you lazy bum?" Unable to muster a rebuttal, he simply broke down and started crying.

Bobet fared better at first, attacking aggressively early on in the race. Perhaps he thought Gino would struggle on the first mountains, mistakenly thinking, as one journalist humorously put it, that Gino, "like all elderly people, isn't very quick to throw his legs out of bed." Or perhaps he was just trying to emulate the success of the Italian team's attack on the previous day. Whatever his motives, Bobet's strategy failed. Like Robic before him, he would soon watch helplessly as Gino sped by him.

In this stage, as in the Cannes-to-Briançon stage, Gino rode like a man possessed. As Goddet noted, "A world of difference was created between the Florentine and the men who, for a moment, still passed as his adversaries." Gino endured all the usual insults from the French fans and even an occasional snowball, barreling up muddy mountain ascents at speeds that were often double those of his competitors. "He was," Goddet continued, "overheated by an interior flame that has consumed him for ten years, and nothing could extinguish the fire that had set his heart ablaze." Goddet was right. Gino's burning determination had only increased in the past decade, fueled in ways not even he fully understood by all the tumult and suffering he had witnessed as war tore apart his homeland.

As Gino crossed the finish line first, the crowds that had gathered in Aix-les-Bains booed him. He was undaunted, and reveled in the strength he had shown in the mountains. *I feel like a lion,* he thought. His victory in this stage had confirmed the precedent set by his previous day's performance. Henceforth, the yellow jersey was his to lose. As time would soon show, it would never leave his shoulders again.

It took a little while for the spectators who had gathered at the finish line to absorb the impact of what Gino already knew. For some, that moment arrived after just sixty-six seconds—the remaining gap of time between Gino and Bobet in the general classification. For everyone else, it arrived in the eerily quiet minutes that followed. With every passing second that other riders failed to appear, Gino's lead grew. For Bobet, it took a little longer to accept. And yet when he finally acknowledged it, the truth of Gino's victory was impossible to deny. Bobet's dream of winning the Tour was over. It had died, as he would later acknowledge, on the road from Cannes to Briançon.

✦

At the hotel in Aix-les-Bains, Gino received a surprise visitor, a Christian Democrat deputy who brought with him the good wishes of Prime Minister De Gasperi. In the two days that had passed since the phone call, Gino had far exceeded his promise to the prime minister. He had "defeated everyone and everything, nature and man," as one journalist declared, and emerged as a near shoo-in to win the Tour. By the next stage, it became apparent that the prime minister was not the only leader who wanted to pass on good wishes. An emissary from the Pope also appeared and gave Gino a special medal, telling him that "His Holiness wishes that you win the Tour, as a loyal and athletic champion."

Sitting with Gino in his room, surrounded by various floral bouquets and congratulatory telegrams, Coach Binda was stunned into silence by it all. Finally he managed to stammer a few words.

"My God, you nearly killed me, my champion."

"You did not always call me that. You, as well, did not have faith in me," said Gino with a smile.

"You're right, who would have thought . . . at your age," Binda replied, embarrassed.

Gino laughed it off and announced that he would write a telegram to his six-year-old son, Andrea. His message was but one sentence long: "Your father is a champion again."

In Italy, the celebrations that had started the previous night continued, gathering steam as Gino moved closer to Paris. There was a "feeling of resurrection," said one former Italian president who was in Rome at the time. In another part of the capital, it was reported that a union meeting ended abruptly when a car with loudspeakers drove by to inform the crowds of Gino's victory. The crowd dispersed to seek out a full update and a celebratory drink at nearby cafés. Near Gino's home in Florence, people cheered "Long Live Bartali" in the streets. Several even rang the doorbell of his home in celebration. Farther north, a young priest put a radio on the altar, its speaker barely audible, as his congregation gathered for evening prayers. When he heard the familiar timbre of Gino's voice, he interrupted the service and turned up the volume so that the whole church could listen to the cyclist being interviewed.

Elsewhere in Europe, Italian migrant workers and emigrants were enthralled by their countryman's performance. On a stage that crossed into Belgium, seven spectators wearing bright yellow shirts each held up signs with letters that spelled out Bartali's name. In Liège, the Belgian city where the Tour stopped overnight, ten thousand Italians gathered in the town square where Gino's hotel was located at 10:00 p.m. and cheered loudly until nearly 2:00 a.m. Some danced and threw their hats in the air; others embraced each other and cried tears of happiness. The celebrations only ended when the police cleared the square so that Gino and the other people living nearby could rest. The local Belgian newspapers, reflecting the sentiment in many countries where Italian workers lived, arrogantly dismissed it all as an example of "southern temperament." A French reporter, however, was more sympathetic to the Italians' enthusiasm. "Their unbridled praise does not make us laugh. We would also like to have our own Bartali and acclaim him like a god, express our admiration and cover him with flowers."

Other members of the press were similarly fervent when it came to their coverage of Gino's victories. Although at least one journalist tried to pretend that he had not written an article doubting the Italian's chances, most were more honest. One Italian journalist described the scope of Gino's triumph, "Bartali wrote in these last two days—if one can write with pedal strokes and drops of sweat—perhaps the most beautiful page of his career. . . . Today it is enough to remember that forty-eight hours ago in Cannes, Bartali was marked as a man already largely beaten and perhaps on the eve of his withdrawal."

The Tour director, who had also doubted Gino, offered his own poetic account of all that had passed. "From snowstorm, water, and ice, Bartali arose like a mud-covered angel, wearing under his soaked tunic the precious soul of an exceptional champion."

✦

In New York, the bomb threat at St. Patrick's Cathedral never materialized. In Italy, the incendiary political situation was slowly being extinguished. After the strike ended at noon on July 16, businesses and private citizens set themselves to the task of repairs and cleaning up. Taxis began running again, and buses and trains resumed their regular schedules of operation. Gino called home to his parents and asked them about the mood in Florence and its reaction to his victory. His parents responded with typical brevity: "Calm and enthusiastic."

Nevertheless, several aftershocks of angry protest continued to reverberate throughout the country. There were still outbursts of violence in several cities, even though 55,000 members of the navy and air force were mobilized alongside the 250,000 members of the army and police that had already been engaged. A skirmish in a remote region of Tuscany between the army and a renegade group of partisans continued for several days. In the Chamber of Deputies, angry recriminations were hurled about as politicians debated who was most to blame for everything that had unfolded.

All told, the human and financial costs of the riots were significant. Over the course of a few days, fourteen people were killed and another two hundred were seriously injured, many of them police. It was further estimated that the country had suffered some seventy billion lire of damages from the strike, which amounted to over ten percent of the country's GDP in 1948. Those costs were added to the enormous expense that the nation already faced with its rebuilding efforts after the war.

At the hospital, Togliatti continued to recover. He had a brief brush with pneumonia, but the infection was contained with a heavy dose of penicillin that had been manufactured in the United States. (Some critics noted the irony, given the acrimony between Communists and Americans.) At one point he asked his son to read him the newspapers to learn what had happened since he was shot. His doctors, however, advised against it. They were concerned that the news might adversely affect his health, given his weakened state. As a compromise, it was decided that his son should read only the sports news. Togliatti was very pleased by all of Gino's successes.

Across the city at Regina Coeli prison, Antonio Pallante, who was being held in isolation in a makeshift cell that the guards had crafted by outfitting the prison chaplain's office with bars, only learned about Gino's victory several days later. Listening to the guards' account of what had happened in France, he was overwhelmed by what he described as a "great national pride" that united him for a brief instant with his countrymen.

✦

As the Tour neared its final stage, the organizers had much to celebrate. While they would have no doubt preferred a Frenchman to carry the yellow jersey into Paris, if only for the greater number of newspapers that could be sold, Gino's dramatic comeback made for great newspaper copy. Underdogs and sports upsets always create headlines, and Gino's performance had injected a palpable sense of suspense into a race that had only a few days earlier been criticized as lacking the excitement of earlier years.

Spectators embraced the 1948 Tour to an extent that now seems extraordinary. In part, it was the dramatic tension of the race. More important, however, was that the Tour provided a welcome distraction from the struggles of postwar life. Fifteen million people in France, or nearly thirty-eight percent of the country's population, had stood on roadsides to see the race in person. If an event were to boast a similar national turnout in the United States today, it would require more than 115 million to appear. As it stands, the most popular multiday sporting event, in terms of attendance, in American history was the 1984 Los Angeles Olympics. With an estimated attendance of just 5.8 million, or 2.5 percent of the U.S. population, it paled in comparison.

These live attendance figures, large as they were, represented just a fraction of the audience that followed the Tour. Millions among the rest of the population read coverage in their newspapers, heard Tour radio broadcasts, or watched the newsreel updates at cinemas. Millions more followed the Tour in other European countries and around the world.

The 1948 Tour was more popular than anyone could have expected, but lucrative it was not. Gino would win a little over a million francs in prize money from the Tour, and had commitments for short races that would take place after the Tour, worth nearly 3.5 million francs. The total winnings would today be worth about $187,000, and Gino had agreed to split it all with his ten teammates. The other famous racers earned less. Bobet earned 486,400 francs, or what would be just over $20,000 today, and Robic earned 261,700 francs, or the modern equivalent of about $11,000. Compared to current earnings for Tour victors or even sports stars in general, these figures seem terribly small. Still, after years of reduced or totally diminished income, the racers were happy to get whatever they could. And in postwar Italy, the money could be stretched. One of Gino's youngest teammates got enough money from the Tour to marry his sweetheart, make a down payment on a house, and furnish it with all the latest appliances.

Every prize and even the mere chance to compete for one, however, came at a high price. After three weeks of hard racing that exposed them to the extremes of weather and terrain, no one could deny that the Tour wreaked a terrible toll on its participants. Of the 120 men who started the race, just forty-four completed it. The rate of attrition for the old guard—those like Gino who had raced before the war—was equally sobering. Only four of ten would cross the finish line in Paris, though three of those four placed in the top ten. This was an obvious testament to their abilities as racers, but also to the nature of the race. Between the elements and the great distances covered, the Tour demanded the kind of endurance and "capacity for suffering," as Gino called it, that many younger riders still hadn't yet cultivated.

The Tour had even transformed Gino, the one man who had endured its tests better than anyone else. The change wasn't immediately discernible in his physique or his general manner. On the surface, Gino was in excellent physical shape and he remained as irascible as ever, even punching an admiring armed French police officer who inexplicably tried to pat his face at a stage finish line. And yet there was an indelible sadness that began to mount during the final stages that Gino would only fully understand when he reached Paris.

✦

The last day of the Tour opened with a light drizzle, curiously appropriate for an odyssey that had been forged by the ravages of the elements. The rain would make the roads that led to Paris more slippery, but it could do little to douse the enthusiasm of the crowds who had turned out this day to see the crowning of the Tour champion. Officially, the final stage of the Tour is still a race, but its results have only ever mattered where the standings in the general classification are close, something that could not have been further from the case in 1948. With a twenty-six-minute lead over the next racer, there was no question that this was anything less than an extended victory parade for Gino.

The celebrations started early as the Tour riders snaked lazily through the streets of Roubaix as part of a pre-race show that lasted some forty-five minutes. By 10:00 a.m., they had begun the 178-mile journey into Paris. It was not long before they saw one of the first Italian flags that would be waved that day. It stood outside of an industrial workshop on the outskirts of Paris, where it had been placed by one of the many Italian workers now cheering on the Italian team from the side of the road. A simple but heartfelt message had been written across its green, white, and red fabric: *Viva Gino Bartali!*

As the crowds grew larger, it was obvious from the words of support shouted in French that many of the French fans had thawed in their attitudes toward Gino and the Italians. They had pelted him with snowballs, booed him at finish lines, and one spectator had even sent an anonymous death threat (Binda chose not to tell Gino about this letter). By Paris, however, Gino had finally earned a modicum of their respect. The French press had come around much more quickly. Though their own government was in a state of flux with the role of prime minister changing hands, they would dedicate front cover pages to long, baroque tributes to Gino's triumph. As one journalist wryly noted, "Gino Bartali, after having beaten his adversaries, defeated the prime minister."

By the time the Tour caravan reached the outskirts of Paris, the weather had improved and the cyclists began to enjoy some of the scenes of spontaneous ebullience that had greeted their arrival throughout so much of France. A pilot brought his plane down from the sky and flew it right beside them, its wings so close to the ground that they might have clipped a tree. Happy, screaming crowds of people lined up ten and twenty deep on the roadside to see the riders race by. And for the first time ever in Tour history, there were a few television cameras filming the race's finish. Few could appreciate their significance at the time, but with their help the Tour would grow into a truly global event.

Elsewhere, automobile traffic came to a complete standstill when cheering fans filled the streets as they made their way to the Parc des Princes velodrome where forty thousand of them would watch the end of the race. Still, in this sea of streamers and tanned faces that engulfed the Tour cyclists as they made their way into Paris, no one ever lost sight of the man of the hour. "Bartali stood out in his yellow jersey in the clear and overheated sky like the legionnaire's bugle call in the solitary desert," wrote one French journalist.

As Gino focused on safeguarding his overall victory, the Tour's lesser luminaries fought over the final stage. It was a feat of poetic beauty, then, when Giovanni Corrieri, Gino's roommate and lieutenant, rocketed through the tunnel and was the first to appear on the track of the velodrome to win the day's race. After riding for three weeks in Gino's service and in his shadow, the "Sicilian Arrow" could enjoy a triumph of his own.

Forty thousand voices roared as one when Gino burst through the tunnel into the velodrome a couple of minutes later. His dark tan glistened from beneath his yellow woolen jersey, and every ounce of him pulsed with swashbuckling vigor as he sped along the faded pink concrete track. His victory assured, he raced to the finish line where his teammates awaited him.

Just like that, it was all over. After almost 150 hours in the saddle, the race ended. Ten years after his first triumph, Gino Bartali had won the Tour de France once again and set a new record—the longest time span between victories—that remains undefeated to this day.

✦

After he had dismounted from his bike, Gino headed for the lawn in the middle of the track. As he stood there chatting with Corrieri and the others who had finished, waiting for the rest of the racers to arrive, he caught sight of a French rider, the other thirty-four-year-old member of the old guard, crying by himself. Gino walked over and embraced him, recognizing that he was contemplating the diminishing prospects of his own career, one that had seen him come maddeningly close to winning the Tour three times. Putting a hand on his shoulder as he held him, Gino tried to console him. "The war ruined us old men. It made us lose our best years and many victories that we will never recover." The French rider, with red eyes and a bristly, unshaved face, could only nod in agreement.

While the sting of the lost years would never completely disappear for Gino, as he spoke with the press that day, he showed the first signs that he had stopped fighting the weight of history. By any measure, he had defied the odds (only three winners in over a hundred years of Tour history have been older than Gino). When he thanked his teammates and his fans, he exuded gratitude for his improbable journey, a sentiment that he would most eloquently articulate only later: "Everyone in their life has his own particular way of expressing life's purpose—the lawyer his eloquence, the painter his palette, and the man of letters his pen from which the quick words of his story flow. I have my bicycle."

After some twenty minutes had passed, the last racer crossed the finish line and the awards ceremony began. Photographs and newsreels provided generations to come with an enduring record of those final moments of the 1948 Tour. In those images, Gino walks up to the podium where several officials congratulate him and hang a large sash bearing the title "Tour de France 1948" across his chest. The Tour hostess, a beautiful blond actress named Line Renaud, gives him a large bouquet of flowers and kisses him on the cheek. Gino smiles bashfully and wipes her red lipstick off his face. The crowd jumps to its feet in a standing ovation, and for a moment Gino is overcome. "I have won the most beautiful race in the world. With this, I will enter into history," he would later say. In the newsreels, he just smiles widely and waves back to his fans. Then he slowly makes his way down from the podium and mounts his bike.

As Gino begins his victory lap, it is a scene of bitter triumph as only the ancients could have written it. Winning the Tour fulfills a quest that motivated Gino for the better part of ten years. Yet by scaling the largest summit cycling had to offer, he is finally forced to accept the superiority of the one rival he could never hope to defeat: time. Riding in the yellow jersey at the age of thirty-four, he is coming to the end of a journey that he would never again repeat.

Alone on the track, a flicker of sadness crosses Gino's face. But it passes quickly and only heightens his ability to savor this one perfect moment. For as he heads into the home stretch, the happiness he radiates is as clear as day—it is the carefree pleasure of a boy on a bike, gliding effortlessly through the air, resplendent in the afternoon sun.

Epilogue

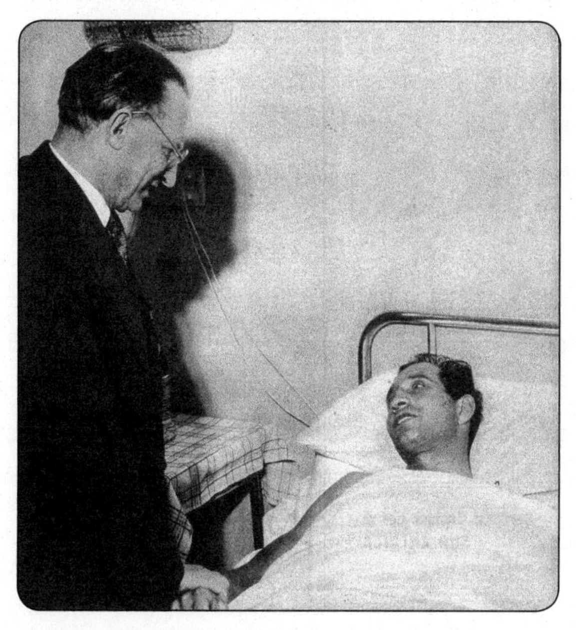

Alcide De Gasperi visits Gino Bartali in the hospital in 1953.

ON AN OVERCAST AFTERNOON in January 2011, we met with Giorgio Goldenberg in his home near Tel Aviv. With wavy silver hair and a jovial manner, Giorgio is now a seventy-nine-year-old grandfather. He speaks English confidently and with only a slight accent, a remarkable feat for a man who has never lived for an extended time in an English-speaking country. As we sipped espressos in his living room, he told us about how he arrived in Israel. In the months following the liberation of Florence in 1944, his parents made plans to evacuate him from Europe, fearful of a German counterattack. They secured a place for him on a British boat taking Jewish children to what was then Palestine. When he arrived, a Jewish relief group arranged for Giorgio and other children without family nearby to live on different *kibbutzim,* the large agricultural collectives that were being established around the country. Giorgio was sent to a kibbutz near Hadera. It was there that he first began to learn Hebrew and use his Hebrew name, Shlomo Pas. His parents and sister migrated to Israel three years later, in 1948. None of the Goldenbergs would ever see Gino Bartali again.

We had originally started talking with Giorgio by phone in the fall of 2010, after tracking him down through various Italian Jews who had all gone to elementary school together in Florence a half century earlier, and were now located in Italy, Israel, and the United Kingdom. After our first conversations with Giorgio, an Italian Jewish journalist found him as well, which spurred a whirlwind tour of interviews. Several Italian newspapers carried articles about his story, and they were quickly cross-linked and translated into other languages in various forums around the web. RAI, the national Italian broadcaster, filmed an interview segment that was aired as part of the Italian commemoration of International Holocaust Remembrance Day on January 27, 2011.

Nearly seven decades later, Giorgio's memory of his wartime experience still felt close and raw. Giorgio admitted as much himself, noting how for nearly half a century he had never spoken with anyone about Gino Bartali or anything else that had happened to him or his family during the war. Like many Holocaust survivors, he had felt the memories of relatives and friends who had perished were too painful, the darkness of the era too difficult to speak about with anyone, even his own children. It was only in recent years, on the suggestion of his wife, that he had begun to unburden himself and tell his story.

We talked for several hours and the conversation slowly drifted to the present. Giorgio grew more lighthearted again, beaming as he spoke proudly about being a father and grandfather. As we neared the end of our time together, Giorgio became reflective once more and took the measure of his wartime experience and how his family was saved. Time and geography may have kept him from meeting Gino again while he still lived, but Giorgio insisted on acknowledging his family's debt to the cyclist. "There is no doubt whatsoever for me that he saved our lives. He not only saved our lives but he helped save the lives of hundreds of people. He put his own life and his family's in danger in order to do so," Giorgio said, his voice cracking with emotion. "In my opinion, he was a hero and he is entitled to be called a hero of the Italian people during the Second World War."

✦

Like Giorgio, Gino avoided discussing what had happened during the war for much of his life. Although word about his involvement in Cardinal Dalla Costa's secret network spread through pockets of the Jewish community in Florence soon after the war ended, it would be decades before the nation learned the details about it. Many of Gino's countrymen were also reticent to speak about their wartime experiences and this silence was not unique to Italy. After years of occupation and war, citizens of several countries in Western Europe opted to willfully ignore the difficulties of the recent past, choosing to focus entirely in those first years on rebuilding for the future.

In 1978, a Polish Jewish journalist and filmmaker named Alexander Ramati published a book he had written with Father Rufino Niccacci about the work of the religious clergy in Assisi during the German occupation. (Ramati, an Allied war correspondent during the war, had first met Niccacci and Luigi Brizi on the day the Allied soldiers liberated Assisi in June 1944.) Seven years later, he followed up with a feature film based on the book. Although both were framed around Niccacci's first-person perspective of events, they revealed a good amount about Cardinal Dalla Costa, the Brizis, and Gino. The Italian press covered this story with great interest, and lavished praise on all the protagonists named in the counterfeiting network.

Gino reacted to the coverage with anger, and privately threatened to sue an Italian television channel when it announced that it would air Ramati's film. His son Andrea, however, argued against such measures, noting how closely Ramati had worked with Niccacci, Trento Brizi, and others. Gino slowly calmed down and came around to agreeing with his son, but he would remain tight-lipped with the press about his wartime activities for most of his life. The root of his reticence was a deeply felt concern that his celebrity as a cyclist would aggrandize his role in the network and overshadow the other participants' contributions, ordinary Italians and Catholic clergy who took extraordinary risks to save others. Speaking in an Italian documentary made later in his life, Gino justified his silence as a matter of respect for those who had suffered more than he had during the war: "I don't want to appear to be a hero. Heroes are those who died, who were injured, who spent many months in prison."

Gino's modesty, coupled with the broader need for absolute secrecy about the clandestine network during the war, has left only a thin paper trail about his wartime activities. In recent years it has come to light that Gino may have helped ferry documents to an even wider area in Tuscany and Umbria than was previously known. In 2006, the president of Italy, Carlo Ciampi, posthumously awarded Gino and four priests a gold medal for civil merit for their efforts in an underground network that helped Jewish refugees hidden in Lucca, in northern Tuscany. Very little is known about Gino's work for this particular network. Despite repeated calls, the government ministry responsible for the award would not share the file they compiled for Gino because, they said, the selection process for this award was not public. The two surviving members of this network in Lucca who also received awards told us that they did not meet with Gino during the war. They were quick to suggest that their deceased colleagues might have interacted with the cyclist, but that any record of such contact was lost. As they explained, it was most common *not* to know with whom their fellow priests were working. It was each member's commitment to secrecy and willful ignorance about his fellow members' dealings that protected these networks from detection and allowed them to save so many lives. Unfortunately, this same secrecy has also rendered these networks much more impenetrable to the light of historical investigation.

Other factors have only made the research about Gino's wartime work more challenging. As the safety of the network required that Gino minimize his interactions with the recipients of the false identity documents that he was ferrying, or avoid them altogether by working with other trusted intermediaries, he does not appear frequently in the growing body of survivor testimonies gathered by various Holocaust remembrance organizations. Likewise, many of those who did work with him, particularly in the Florence-Umbria network, died without giving a full account of their wartime experiences or what they knew about Gino's involvement. Gino himself was no help to the cause of research, refusing comment and steadfastly downplaying his role, even in the face of compelling testimony to the contrary from his fellow members.

One exception was Father Pier Damiano at the San Damiano monastery, whom we discovered early on, who had witnessed Gino dropping off documents to Father Niccacci on one occasion during the war. Overwhelmingly, however, after nearly ten years of research, it became clear that we will likely never know the full scope of everything Gino did or the risks he endured to help Cardinal Dalla Costa. But perhaps that is what Gino intended all along. For a man who had lived almost all of his adult life in the unrelenting scrutiny of the public eye, there is something fitting in the fact that he was able to keep some element of his greatest achievement private. As he would tell his son Andrea, "If you're good at a sport, they attach the medals to your shirts and then they shine in some museum. That which is earned by doing good deeds is attached to the soul and shines elsewhere."

✦

In the hours following Gino's critical stage win in the 1948 Tour, there was "an explosion of joy" all over the country, said Oscar Luigi Scalfaro, a former judge and Italian president who was a young politician in Rome at the time. "It was like a wind that swipes away the clouds," the ninety-one-year-old added, as he waved his hand energetically through the air to illustrate the effect of Gino's win on Italy after the attempted assassination of Palmiro Togliatti.

To this day Italians debate the question of how close the nation came to a wide-scale uprising at that tense moment in July 1948. Many ordinary Italians who saw the riots and destruction firsthand insist that they had witnessed the early signs of revolution and civil war. It is a characterization that historian Patrick McCarthy partly echoes when he describes an Italy where "Milan, Turin, and Genoa appeared on the brink of insurrection." Others are more skeptical. The historian Paul Ginsborg surveyed the protests in the north and the relatively muted response in the rural south and argued that the possibility of nationwide revolution was unlikely. He did, however, note that one prominent Communist politician had suggested to him that "insurrection was feasible in the North, but that Italy would have been cut in two."

The perception of the impact of Gino's victory in the aftermath of the riots would also evolve over the years. In the immediate days following the victory, the fact that Togliatti had survived the assassination attempt played a critical role in the nation's enthusiastic response to Gino's triumph. Had he died, the country would doubtless have been in a very different mood, regardless of how Gino fared at the Tour. In coming months and years, however, overeager *bartaliani* and hard-line right-wing Italians, looking to score points in the ongoing battle between Communists and Christian Democrats, inflated the importance of Gino's victory and dropped Togliatti's recovery out of the story. Gino became the "savior of the Fatherland" who singlehandedly stopped the outbreak of a civil war.

In recent years, national leaders and Italian cultural historians have advanced a more nuanced view of the victory's significance. Giulio Andreotti, a parliamentary deputy and prime minister, who witnessed the celebrations in the Chamber of Deputies at the news of Gino's victory, offered his assessment. "To say that civil war was averted by a Tour de France victory is surely excessive," but it was "undeniable," he insisted, that Gino "contributed to ease the tensions." Former president Oscar Scalfaro fleshed out this idea further when we met with him, describing Gino's triumph as an entertaining distraction, offering a hard-fought success that resonated deeply when the nation was trying to rebuild. At least two Italian historians have echoed this point. For his part, Gino steadfastly downplayed his accomplishment, saying, "I don't know if I saved the country, but I gave it back its smile."

✦

Although Gino had spoken seriously about retirement after his 1948 Tour victory, only a few weeks later, he set off for Holland with Fausto Coppi to the World Track Cycling Championships in Valkenburg. With the two of them racing together on one national team, Italy should have had no trouble winning. Tragically, neither star was in any mood to work cooperatively. Jealous of all the radio discussion about Gino's Tour victory, Coppi only agreed to race so that he might defeat his Tuscan rival. Gino proved himself no better when the race began, refusing to make any significant attacks lest he inadvertently help Coppi. Instead, the two men spent their time pacing each other, oblivious to the other competitors who were pulling out in front of them. Eventually, when both had fallen far behind the pack, they got off their bikes and quit the race while the spectators hissed angrily at them.

In Italy, this disgraceful performance was shocking enough to prompt the Italian Cycling Federation to suspend both men temporarily, adding more fuel to the fire of their rivalry. For several years already, the story of their match-ups had dominated the headlines. A hungry press, looking to sell newspapers, only ratcheted up the antagonism. But there was also some real substance in their battles. Neither man was afraid to speak dismissively about the other's prospects in public, and both had long since given up referring to the other by name, each preferring instead to call the other "that one." The fans followed suit, with whole neighborhoods taking sides as *coppiani* or *bartaliani*. Those who dared challenge these local allegiances risked confrontation. Men got into fights over whom they supported, and at least one woman was chased across her rural village by screaming young Bartali fans when she admitted she supported Coppi. Ultimately these divisions would even take on a political dimension, when the Communists rallied behind an apolitical Coppi to combat Gino's allegiance to the Christian Democrats.

The battle reached its zenith in the spring of 1949, when the time came to choose the Italian team for the Tour de France. Coppi had just defeated Gino at the Giro d'Italia, and his professional team, Bianchi, demanded that Gino be held back while Coppi led the effort in France. Gino, however, was the returning Tour champion, and his supporters felt it unconscionable that he be prevented from defending his title just so that Coppi could make his Tour debut. Both arguments had merit, and the debate quickly became a popular one in public circles. A satisfying resolution, however, seemed unlikely. At one point, Prime Minister Alcide De Gasperi even weighed in publicly and insisted that Gino and Coppi race together for Italy. In an unusual show of political unity, Palmiro Togliatti, his long-standing opponent, agreed.

As consensus mounted for a unified team, coach Alfredo Binda engineered an alliance between the stars whereby both men agreed to race cooperatively for the first part of the race. When they reached the Alps, each was allowed to race more freely. To the eternal disappointment of the *bartaliani,* Coppi outshone his rival and carried the yellow jersey into Paris. Though Gino came in second, Coppi overshadowed him by becoming the first cyclist to do what had long been considered impossible: winning the Giro and the Tour in the same year. The symbolic importance of the moment could not be understated. In head-to-head battle through some of Western Europe's most challenging terrain, Coppi had realized the dream that Gino had held since his earliest years as a cyclist.

Coppi went on to win a second Tour title, and by the end of his career his distinctions included five Giro victories as well. Compared to Gino's two Tour titles and three Giro wins, some felt the debate about who was the best Italian racer was now over. Others argued that it wasn't a fair comparison since Gino would likely have won more Tour and Giro titles if his career hadn't been interrupted by the war, which impacted Coppi less because he wasn't yet in his prime years. To buttress this argument, the *bartaliani* point to Gino's enduring Tour record—the ten-year time span between victories. Even as advances in general health and training have allowed current cyclists to extend their careers and win races like the Tour de France at a later age in life, no other racer has stayed at the very top of the sport for that length of time.

To this day, outside of Italy, Coppi remains better known, partly because his victories were more recent and partly because he helped pioneer the modern, scientifically based way of training, in contrast to Gino's defiantly old-fashioned approach to cycling. Within Italy, however, most contemporary Italians of all ages, when asked about this duo, will feel a multigenerational loyalty to either Bartali or Coppi. With time the bitter edges of the rivalry have worn down and transformed into celebrations of the legacy of each cyclist.

Among the *bartaliani*, the remembrances have taken many forms. In 2006, a Gino Bartali museum opened in his hometown of Ponte a Ema, showcasing old bikes, photographs, and other Bartali paraphernalia. In 2009, Ivo Faltoni, one of Gino's former bike mechanics and a lifelong friend, launched an annual *ciclopelegrinaggio,* or cycling pilgrimage, retracing part of Gino's routes between Florence and Assisi when he was shuttling documents. For the inaugural year, more than a hundred riders, including young boys, a couple on a tandem bicycle, and several white-haired cyclists, pedaled from Terontola to the main square in Assisi, where they were treated to one of Gino's favorite training snacks, prosciutto panini. The winners of the first pilgrimage came from a Roman Catholic cycling society in the north of Italy, which had pledged to live according to the values of Gino Bartali.

✦

On October 18, 1953, Gino and a few friends made their way to what would be one of the last races of his career. Thirty-nine years old, he had raced eighty times that season and won only twice, giving the press yet more fodder to poke fun at his age. In the years since his Tour victory, he had gone from being known as *Il Vecchio* to *Il Vecchiaccio*—"the Old Geezer" and even Methuselah, the oldest man in the Bible. Gino grudgingly accepted the jibes, and even enjoyed such moments as when he was parodied in an Italian comedy revue by an actor wearing a yellow jersey "and a beard so long it reached his navel." Gino took it all in stride. "We athletes are not like beautiful women who can hide their years, and what's more, I have no desire to hide them. If the affectionate mirth that my 'venerable' age provokes can be a distraction for the spectators from the chores and annoyances of daily life which aren't enjoyable for anyone, all the better."

As they drove that morning to Switzerland, where the race was being held, Gino dozed in the passenger seat. He was ripped from his slumber, however, when he felt the car lurch and heard the thunderous crash of metal. When he opened his eyes, he saw that the "car was turning over and over, as if in a vortex." The door flew open and he was catapulted out of the vehicle. He hit the ground on the side of the road, and the car continued to flip several times before it finally came to a standstill a few feet from where he lay.

He could see warm blood pouring out of his leg where he had made impact with the pavement, and as he attempted to move, he felt a stab of pain in his back and winced. Soon he became aware of hands stretching out to him, strangers gathered around him, leaning over to help him up.

"Don't touch me! Don't touch me!" Gino groaned, worried that his back would be damaged by further movement. "If you want, cover me, but do not touch me!" Gino tried to yell. "You will lift me only when the ambulance arrives."

An ambulance soon appeared, and as Gino traveled to the hospital, he kept his eyes closed, murmuring the names of his sons to keep calm. At the hospital, he was surrounded by a great commotion of doctors and nurses. When he was finally settled in a room, he was able to focus his thoughts. He needed to call Adriana. He picked up the phone and dialed.

"Adriana . . . Adriana!" Gino said feebly when she picked up. "I'm here in Milan," he said, telling her the name of the hospital.

"What happened to you, Gino?" Adriana asked anxiously.

"I was in a car accident. Come here right away."

"Is it serious? Tell me, Gino, is it serious?" she continued.

"I don't know yet. Come to Milan right away. Don't say anything to the kids. Tell my mom."

Overcome by the effort of the call, Gino fainted.

Adriana rushed to Milan and found Gino in a terrible state. He had been cut badly, fractured two vertebrae, and damaged his bowels. In the following days, he was operated on, and part of his intestine was removed. Slowly he began to heal.

As he recuperated at the hospital, Alcide De Gasperi, the former prime minister who had called him during the 1948 Tour, visited him. No record of their conversation remains, but a photograph taken of the moment speaks volumes. The soft-spoken, gray-haired politician, now politically past his prime, leans over and tenderly holds the forearm of the aging athlete lying in bed, rendered immobile by his injuries. It is a warm moment between old friends, and a poignant end to an era during which the great characters in sports and politics performed together on the same stage.

De Gasperi would die within a year from a heart attack. Gino recovered enough to briefly race again, but retired formally from the sport in February 1955.

✦

In his retirement, Gino focused full-time on several business ventures that he had started on the side during his final years of cycling. As early as 1949, after years of racing for Legnano, a professional cycling team owned by the second-largest bike brand in Italy, Gino convinced himself that he could earn more money by launching a professional team and his own line of bicycles. It was a decision that he would regret almost from the get-go. The early Bartali bikes were of poor quality, and the cyclist quickly realized how unprepared he was to help run a bicycle factory and business. "It's one thing to ride on [a bicycle] and push it at high or impossible average speeds in storms and in the battles of a race, it's another thing to administer its production and sales," he said. His professional team fared no better. They lacked the money to compete with established teams like Legnano and Bianchi when it came to signing good cyclists, leaving them with a group of third-string racers whom most saw as a joke. Even Gino could find nothing redeeming about the experience, and later regretted it deeply. "If I had remained with the Legnano team, I would have won more races which were lost because of our inferior bikes."

For all the money and effort wasted, Gino kept trying. He continued to dabble in business, pitching Bartali razor blades and even his own brand of Chianti wine that dubiously promised "eternal youth" to whoever drank it. A few years after his disappointment with Bartali bikes, he started a small department store that sold everything from Bartali-branded motorcycles to Bartali sewing machines and Bartali shaving cream. It was another area of business that Gino knew little about, and though his intentions were good, it wasn't long before it, too, ran into trouble. "It was the era of paying by installments," his son Andrea explained. "Papà sold, but then was embarrassed to ask for the missing payments from those who couldn't or wouldn't pay. And so in time that venture didn't go so well."

✦

While Gino struggled with his businesses in the 1950s, a powerful economic boom unfolded across Western Europe as the continent rebuilt and restored its industrial base. Rising consumer incomes enriched manufacturers, and their enduring need to secure effective advertising helped transform cycling into a potent money-maker. Race prizes and appearance fees for winners soon reflected this growing prosperity. In 1952, just four years after Gino's victory, the Tour winner landed twenty million francs in contracts, or the modern equivalent of approximately $517,000 (nearly three times what Gino took home from the 1948 Tour). In subsequent decades, corporate endorsement deals linked to expanded television coverage would make a victory at the Tour exponentially more lucrative.

Paradoxically, however, this same prosperity would slowly push the sport from its central place in European life. From 1950 onward, bicycle sales in France and Italy began to decline, eclipsed first by mopeds and then later by small cars. As they did so, the connection between everyday cyclists and the professionals slowly withered, and the popular experience and understanding of cycling dissipated. Subsequent technological innovations have only further eroded that connection. Today it is difficult for newcomers to the sport to fully appreciate the majestic endurance of a cyclist riding up the Alps at fifteen miles per hour, when a mass-market car can easily manage the task at twice or even three times the speed. Likewise, the audacity of riding around France in three weeks feels diminished in an era when anyone could do it sleeping on a discount flight in a matter of hours. None of this, of course, can take away from a great cyclist's achievement, but since bikes have ceased to be a part of daily life for so many, spectators no longer instantly understand the stamina and sheer will required to complete races as grueling as the Tour.

In this changing world, a newly retired Gino struggled to find his place. After his businesses failed and his savings were gutted, Gino worked for a period of time as a sportscaster for RAI, the Italian state channel, and generated some controversy by refusing to follow his producers' guidelines for his commentary. In later years, he covered the races as a reporter for other media outlets. He also made appearances and signed autographs during promotional events set up by Coca-Cola.

Various figures in the cycling world remember Gino in this era for the sharpness of his tongue, a trait that was memorialized in his most enduring public nickname, *Ginettaccio*—"Gino the Terrible." Two-time world champion Gianni Bugno described Gino covering the races "in order to tell us every day what we had done wrong." Others remember his willingness to be baited into a loud argument. For his part, Gino defended his cantankerous tone as proof of his honesty, and regularly even played it up. He agreed to write a racing column for Italy's largest sports newspaper during the Giro d'Italia that was called "A Mistake a Day"; he titled one of his autobiographies *It's All Wrong, It All Has to Be Redone,* in reference to an infamous episode from his racing days when he had shouted at the mechanics who made a mistake when assembling his bike. There was a certain element of humor in all of this, and yet Gino was also occasionally pigeonholed in this part. Where other retired athletes had segued gracefully to roles as benevolent elder statesmen, he was at times depicted as a caricature of a national curmudgeon.

In his late seventies, Gino agreed to co-host a news-satire program where he helped parody the daily news while scantily clad showgirls danced provocatively in the background. It was a controversial decision and, in the eyes of many, a hypocritical and tawdry lapse for a man who had been one of Catholic Action's most prominent members. Although financial considerations were probably one of his primary motivations for doing the show, Gino defended his decision in the name of his fierce sense of independence. "At my age," he said, "I think I know what's good for me." In the recordings of the show, however, his discomfort occasionally betrays him through forced smiles and a few poorly concealed grimaces.

✦

Despite all the career changes and frustrations, Gino's family would be a refuge and a source of lasting happiness. To this day, Adriana lives in the home that Gino bought after his 1938 Tour win, where she invited us to talk about her husband. Now a graceful, eloquent, and generous ninety-one-year-old woman, Adriana grew animated as she spoke about Gino and the life they shared together. At one point she paused to catch her breath, and we asked whether she needed a break. Nearby, Andrea, now a seventy-year-old man, piped up, "Yes, tell them when you're tired, that way we'll throw a bucket of water on you!"

"Don't you dare," said Adriana, laughing, with a flash of mischief in her eyes. "I'm not in a race here!"

Through his family's anecdotes, Gino emerges as a playful, affectionate, and loyal father and husband. Family photos reveal a relaxed Gino, freed of the burden of the heavy scowl that he wears in so many of his public photos. Spending time with Adriana Bartali, one also realizes what a wide array of people befriended her husband—everyone from Juan and Evita Perón to Pope Pius XII to the opera singer Maria Callas. When Callas met Gino and Adriana one night at the Florence opera, she told Gino, "Signor Bartali, we're the same, you and I. We're tenacious, combative, generous, nothing stops us, we always give the maximum." Was Adriana excited to meet so many legends? Certainly, but it is also clear that she has grown accustomed to living with her husband's fame after more than seventy years.

"Let's put it this way," she explained. "These were all normal events that were a part of our lives, that happened from time to time."

After Andrea and Luigi, Adriana and Gino went on to have a daughter, Bianca Maria. All three children live nearby with their families. For Gino's children, at least in their early years, their father's celebrity could be double-edged. Andrea, who was six years old when his father won the Tour in 1948, understood firsthand the commitments of a national champion. His father was away from home for long stretches of time during the racing season, and when he returned, friends and well-wishing strangers were constantly looking to spend time with him. Andrea would spend much of his formative years at a Catholic boardingschool, and even there the rivalry between the *coppiani* and *bartaliani* was bitterly felt. With time, however, he would come to accept his father's unique place in the national imagination. As he matured and his father retired from life as a racer, the two found more time for each other, enjoying road trips together around the country or just quiet games of cards at home.

Gino's parents, Torello and Giulia, would continue to be pillars of strength in his life for the rest of their days. Both played an active role in their grandchildren's lives, with Torello sharing stories from the old life in Ponte a Ema around the family hearth while Giulia prepared culinary delights, including a popular rabbit stew. Both had lived to see Gino enjoy international success, though they were relieved when he stopped cycling. As Gino put it when he retired, "For a quarter of a century my mother has been waiting for me to stop racing. I know her and her anxieties well. I have always felt her prayers in my heart. Now she will finally have a bit of peace."

✦

In his early eighties, Gino's health began to fail him. The heart that had powered him through a staggering lifetime tally of 370,000 miles of cycling became more capricious and soon required a pacemaker to regulate its beat. His voice became so gravelly that it was almost incomprehensible, hardened by the cumulative toll of a throat operation and decades of heavy smoking. His skin yellowed and his hair receded. His body grew heavier, slowed by a propensity to get out of breath and tire easily.

Sensing that his life was drawing to a close, Gino grew increasingly reflective. Interviews with the press in those final years reveal a man at peace with himself. In one interview, Gino offered a heartfelt description of his vision of life: "Life is like a Giro D'Italia, which seems neverending, but at a certain point you reach the final stage. And perhaps you don't expect it. Now I'm beginning to expect it. Yes, I'll soon be called and I'll go up there. . . . Heaven should be a happy place, like those green summits of the Dolomite Mountains, after you've rounded a hundred curves, pedaling all the way."

Privately, he shared his wishes for his final arrangements with his family members. He requested a traditional Roman Catholic funeral mass and asked to be buried in the brown robes of the Carmelites, a Catholic religious order of which he was a lay member. Finally, he confessed to his family that he had been praying that he would die peacefully at home, and be spared the difficulty of a drawn-out terminal decline in the hospital.

True to his wishes, an eighty-five-year-old Gino spent his last days at home in bed. On the afternoon of May 5, 2000, with his wife and children gathered around him, his breathing grew weaker until he quietly passed away.

News of his death was broadcast on Italian television. Pope John Paul II hailed him as a "great sportsman," and newspapers across Europe and North America published obituaries about him. In Italy, the *Corriere Dello Sport* dedicated its front page to a reflection on his career with the headline "Good-bye, *Ginettaccio.*"

The funeral was held three days later. Friends and family gathered inside a local church while a group of aging *bartaliani,* many wearing their old cycling jerseys, stood outside. Speaking to a journalist, one of those fans offered a simple tribute to the cyclist's legacy: "When we were poor and weary, he gave us back our honor."

After the mass was completed, Gino's former teammates carried his casket out of the church. They brought it to the Ponte a Ema cemetery and laid it to rest near his parents; his stillborn son, Giorgio; and his beloved brother, Giulio.

Where They Are Now

Louis Bobet would go on to win the Tour de France in 1953, 1954, and 1955. During the 1959 Tour de France, he quit midrace after climbing the Col de l'Iseran. He retired in 1960 and died of cancer in 1983.

Luigi and Trento Brizi continued to work in their Assisi print shop for the rest of their lives. Luigi died in 1969; Trento died in 1992. Both were recognized by Yad Vashem as Righteous Among the Nations in 1997.

Mario Carità fled Florence before the liberation and traveled to the north of Italy. He was killed in May 1945 in a skirmish with Allied soldiers trying to apprehend him.

Fausto Coppi, like Gino, would lose his brother, Serse, to a biking accident in 1951. In the fall of 1959, he joined the San Pellegrino racing team, coached for a period by Gino. Tragically, however, their reunion was cut short when Coppi contracted malaria while racing in Africa and died in January 1960.

Giovanni "the Sicilian Arrow" Corrieri would continue to race professionally until 1956. He lives to this day in Tuscany.

Cardinal Elia Dalla Costa would continue to serve as the archbishop of Florence until his death in 1961.

Giorgio Goldenberg arrived in Palestine in the spring of 1945. His parents and sister Tea followed after the creation of the state of Israel. Tea died in 2009. Giorgio currently lives near Tel Aviv and remains in contact with friends and family in Italy.

Father Rufino Niccacci would continue to live in Umbria for the rest of his life. He was recognized by Yad Vashem as Righteous Among the Nations in 1974 and died in 1976.

Antonio Pallante was convicted and sentenced to ten years and eight months in prison for his attack on Palmiro Togliatti. His sentence was later reduced as part of a national amnesty program. Upon his release, he returned to Sicily, where he worked with his father for a branch of the police that deals with national forests. He married and had children, and would continue to follow cycling even after Bartali's retirement. He is currently a pensioner and lives in Sicily.

Jean Robic, although he never won the Tour again, would continue to race professionally until 1961. He died in a car accident in 1980.

Aldo Ronconi would spend the remaining years of his professional career racing separately from Gino Bartali and Fausto Coppi. He placed third in the 1950 Tour of Switzerland and retired from racing in 1952. He currently lives in Faenza, Italy.

Palmiro Togliatti would remain the leader of the Italian Communist Party until his death in 1964.

Notes

PROLOGUE

1 **Bartali lost his temper** Dante Gianello, "Bartali m'a dit: 'Je croyais mourir de faim,'" *L'Équipe,* July 16, 1948: 4.

1 **muddy road . . . stunted fir trees** H. W. Heinsheimer, "Le Tour de France," *Holiday,* July 1949: 85 (although this article was published in 1949, it is exclusively about the author's experience attending the 1948 Tour); Jacques Goddet, "Bartali avait rendez-vous avec L'Izoard," *L'Équipe,* July 16, 1948.

1 **July 15, 1948 . . . the Queen Stage** "Aujourd'hui repos à Cannes. Demain treizième étape," *L'Équipe,* July 14, 1948: 2.

1 **heavy clouds . . . mud beneath his wheels** Heinsheimer, "Le Tour de France," 87; Goddet, "Bartali avait rendez-vous avec L'Izoard," 1.

1 **Gino's sensations and emotions during this critical stage** These are drawn from Gino's autobiographies and author interviews with Gino's supporting rider Giovanni Corrieri. See full discussion in the chapter 12 and 13 notes.

2 ***Il Vecchio* . . . "the Old Man"** Pier Lietto Chiapponi, *Il Tirreno,* April 12, 1948: 1.

2 ***Ginettaccio*—"Gino the Terrible"** Gino Bartali with Mario Pancera, *La mia storia* (Milano: Stampa Sportiva, 1958), 65.

2 **Reports of large-scale protests** Carlo Maria Lomartire, *Insurrezione: 14 luglio 1948* (Milano: Mondadori, 2006), 145–54.

2 **Prime minister's phone call** See full discussion of this telephone call in chapter 12 notes.

2 **stood up out of his saddle** Benjo Maso, *Wir Alle Waren Götter: Die berühmte Tour de France von 1948* (Bielefeld: Covadonga Verlag, 2006), 181.

2 **the French cyclist cast a worried look** Heinsheimer, "Le Tour de France," 88.

3 **Gino stood to attack** Maso, *Wir Alle Waren Götter,* 181.

3 **French rider exhausted at summit** Gino Bartali, *Tutto sbagliato, tutto da rifare* (Milano: Mondadori, 1979), 145.

3 **Gino trembled with excitement** "Dans L'Izoard, Bartali fit le vide autour de lui," *L'Équipe,* July 16, 1948: 2. Bartali was thirty-two seconds behind.

3 ***I am at one with the mountain*** Bartali, *La mia storia,* 85.

3 **Gino's lips curled into a knowing smile** André Costes from *France Soir*

wrote, "His red lips, which the mud dripped over, began to curl up," as cited in Maso, *Wir Alle Waren Götter*, 181.

PART I

CHAPTER 1. ACROSS THE ARNO

To describe Gino Bartali's childhood, we drew from several published interviews with Gino, including Gino Bartali, "La mia vita," *Tempo*, November 29, 1952:13–15; our conversations with his son Andrea and wife, Adriana (author interviews July 17, 2009; August 3, 2009, and September 14, 2009), and his three autobiographies: Gino Bartali with Mario Pancera, *La mia storia* (Milano: Stampa Sportiva, 1958); Gino Bartali, *Tutto sbagliato, tutto da rifare* (Milano: Mondadori, 1979); and Gino Bartali with Romano Beghelli and Marcello Lazzerini, *La leggenda di Bartali* (Firenze: Ponte Alle Grazie Editori, 1992). In order to bring to life Gino's hometown of Ponte a Ema and nearby Florence in the early twentieth century, two historians and librarians at the local Bagno a Ripoli library near Florence were invaluable: Raffaele Marconi and Maria Pagnini, whom we interviewed at length on August 12, 2009, and September 11, 2009. Longtime residents of Ponte a Ema Gabriella Nardi (author interview September 11, 2009) and Cesare and Tullia Grifoni (author interview July 31, 2009) also provided helpful details on the industries and daily life in this small town from the time Gino was born through World War II. Another Ponte a Ema native, Fosco Gallori (author interview July 31, 2009), attended the same elementary school as Gino Bartali and helped flesh out his childhood personality.

7 **"When we race together, let's each win a little!"** Bartali, *La mia storia*, 30.
8 **Bartalis lived on Via Chiantigiana** Bartali, *La leggenda*, 197–98.
8 **Apartment had a room** Jean-Paul Ollivier, *Le Lion de Toscane: La Véridique Histoire de Gino Bartali* (Grenoble: Editions de l'Aurore, 1991), 12–13.
8 **Home reminded** Gino Bartali, "La mia vita," 13–15.
8 **"The furniture"** Carlo Callodi, *Pinnochio*, translated by Carol Della Chiese (Public Domain Books, 2006), ch. 3.
9 **"Little as Geppetto's house was, it was neat"** Ibid.
9 **"I would have liked to have friends"** Bartali, "La mia vita," 13–15.
9 **"I was an unlucky marbles player"** Ibid.

10 **"As children we had fun with little"** Marco Pastonesi interview with Gino Bartali in Paolo Costa, *Gino Bartali: la vita, le imprese, le polemiche* (Portogruaro: Ediciclo Editore, 2001), 173–80.
10 **The Arno River and the cookie factory nearby** Alberto Marcolin, *Firenze in Camicia Nera* (Florence: Edizioni Medicea, 1993), 191; author interview with Fosco Gallori, July 31, 2009.
10 **Giulia stole Gino's clothes when swimming** Author interview with Adriana Bartali.
10 **father's leather belt** Costa, *Gino Bartali,* 173–80.
10 **he hatched a plan** Bartali, *La leggenda,* 14.
11 **"I had little will to study"** Bartali, "La mia vita," 13–15.
11 **"I don't like school"** Carlo Maria Lomartire, *Insurrezione: 14 luglio 1948* (Milan: Mondadori, 2006), 133. Author interview with Adriana Bartali.
11 **Gino failed the first grade** Bartali, "La mia vita," 13–15.
11 **charitable remark** Claudio Gregori, "La pagella di Bartali pedalava in salita," *La Gazzetta Dello Sport,* May 17, 2005.
11 **"To go to Florence you need a bicycle"** Bartali, "La mia vita," 13–15.
11 **Torello and Giulia Bartali** In addition to Gino's interviews and autobiographies and our conversations with Andrea and Adriana Bartali, we used the following sources: Ollivier, *Le Lion;* Marc Dewinter, "Gino the Pious," *Cycle Sport,* July 1999: 40.
12 **bluish shale** *The Quarterly Journal of the Geological Society of London* 1 (1845): 275.
12 **Daily wages for day laborers** Gaetano Salvemini, *Under the Axe of Fascism* (London: V. Gollancz, 1936), 161–62.
12 **U.S. dollar exchange rate during this period** Michele Fratianni and Franco Spinelli, *A Monetary History of Italy* (New York: Cambridge University Pess, 1997), 135. The exchange rate fluctuated in the first decades of the twentieth century, so the USD equivalent of what Torello would have likely earned is by necessity an approximation.
12 **Story of Gino's birth** Author interview with Andrea Bartali.
12 **Peasants' work schedule in Tuscany** Frank M. Snowden, *The Fascist Revolution in Tuscany,* 1919–1922 (New York: Cambridge University Press, 1989), 26–27; Kate Carlisle, *Working and Living: Italy* (London: Cadogan Guides, 2007), 103.
13 **"Money is necessary for food"** Bartali, "La mia vita," 13–15.
13 **many without pedals** Bartali, *La leggenda,* 14.
13 **"A lot of time was still to pass"** Ibid.
14 **Early bike history** Geoffrey Wheatcroft, *Le Tour: A History of the Tour de France, 1903–2003* (London: Simon and Schuster, 2005), 2–3.
14 **"some of the Harvard College students"** Wheatcroft, *Le Tour,* 2–3.
14 **"boneshaker"** Todd Balf, *Major: A Black Athlete, a White Era, and the Fight to Be the World's Fastest Human Being* (New York: Three Rivers Press, 2008), 8.
14 **"The rider was a stratospheric"** Balf, *Major,* 9.
14 **Bianchi** David Forgacs and Stephen Gundle, *Mass Culture and Italian*

Society from Fascism to the Cold War (Bloomington: Indiana University Press, 2008), 13.

14 **Cost of bike in labor hours in 1893** Wheatcroft, *Le Tour,* 7.

15 **Catholic and Socialist organizations** Forgacs and Gundle, *Mass Culture,* 13.

15 **"A memory of motion"** H. G. Wells, *The Wheels of Chance: A Bicycling Idyll* (New York: Breakaway Books, 1997), 71.

15 **"genital satisfactions," "sportive masturbations"** Wheatcroft, *Le Tour,* 9.

15 **"stimulate criminal and aggressive tendencies"** Benjo Maso, *The Sweat of the Gods: Myths and Legends of Bicycle Racing* (Norwich, England: Mousehold Press, 2005), 3.

15 **bicycle taxes** Marcolin, *Firenze in Camicia Nera,* 194–95; Forgacs and Gundle, *Mass Culture,* 13.

16 **desperate sons who stole their mothers' bicycles** Balf, *Major,* 55–56.

16 **notable figures assassinated while cycling** "Assassinato in bicicletta un ragionere a Putignano," *Il Tirreno,* January 6, 1948: 1.

16 **Gino spent the summer** Bartali, "La mia vita," 13–15.

16 **"From that pile of raffia"** Ibid.

16 **"I certainly wouldn't"** Ibid.

16 **"You can imagine my joy"** Bartali, *La mia storia,* 16.

16 **"The roads that led to us"** Bartali as quoted in Leo Turrini, *Bartali: L'uomo che salvo' l'Italia pedalando* (Milano: Mondadori, 2004): 7.

16 **"like a bunch of ripe apples"** Bartali, "La mia vita," 13–15.

16 **sneak up on a member** Author interview with Fosco Gallori, July 31, 2009.

16 **The Moccoli** *Moccoli* technically means "snot" in Italian. Oscar Casamonti, video interview by the Instituto Luce, *Coppi e Bartali: Gli eterni rivali,* 2004.

17 **"balcony"of Florence** D. Medina Lasansky, *The Renaissance Perfected: Architecture, Spectacle, and Tourism in Fascist Italy* (University Park: Pennsylvania State University Press, 1988 and 2005), 30, 92.

17 **View from Piazzale** D. H. Lawrence, *Sketches of Etruscan Places and Other Italian Essays* (Cambridge, England: Cambridge University Press, 2002), 324.

17 **"When I descended into Florence"** Interview with Gino Bartali in Augusto De Luca, *Firenze: Frammenti d'anima* (Roma: Gangemi Editore, 1998).

17 **Rag men, umbrella men, rod men, and cricket men** Marcolin, *Firenze in Camicia Nera,* 195–97.

17 **"I was killed for you"** Ibid.

18 **Information about Armando Sizzi's bike shop** Interview with Andrea Bartali by Adam Smulevich in "Sono vivo perché Bartali ci nascose in cantina," *Pagine Ebraiche,* February 2011; author interviews with Gino's teammates.

18 **Giacomo Goldenberg's appearance, background, and arrival in Italy** Author interviews with Giorgio Goldenberg, December 20, 2010; January 25, April 4; and November 14, 2011; photos of Goldenbergs shared during interviews.

19 **Friendship with Armando Sizzi and Gino Bartali** Smulevich, *Pagine Ebraiche,* February 2011. Author interviews with Giorgio Goldenberg and An-

drea Bartali. Although it's unknown where they first met, it is most likely that the three men would have interacted in Sizzi's shop, where Sizzi and Gino spent so much time.

19 **Appeal of Italy to Jewish refugees** Susan Zuccotti, *The Italians and the Holocaust: Persecution, Rescue, and Survival* (New York: Basic Books, 1987), 8.

20 **"Politics is a trap"** Turrini, *Bartali,* 27. Author interview with Andrea Bartali.

20 **issued various decrees** Frank Rosengarten, *The Italian Anti-Fascist Press* (1919–1945) (Cleveland: The Press of Case Western University, 1968), 64.

20 **Torello's Socialist activities** Lomartire, *Insurrezione,* 131–32; Turrini, *Bartali,* 27; author interview with Andrea Bartali.

20 **Italia Libera circle, Gaetano Pilati attack** Rosengarten, *The Italian Anti-Fascist Press,* 64–65; Pietro Nenni, *Ten Years of Tyranny in Italy,* translated by Anne Steele (London: G. Allen & Unwin, 1932), 185–87.

20 **Details about Torello periodically working for Pilati** Lomartire, *Insurrezione,* 131–32; author interview with Andrea Bartali.

21 **"You see, I defended an ideal"** Turrini, *Bartali,* 27; author interview with Andrea Bartali.

CHAPTER 2. IN THE SADDLE

In addition to the sources provided below, a number of details about cycling and the racing culture in Italy during the first half of the twentieth century came from author interviews with several Italian cyclists who trained and raced with Gino Bartali, or worked for him as his bike mechanic, at different points in his long career. These include Giovanni Corrieri (July 15, 2009; September 10, 2010; October 2, 2011; November 27, 2011), Ivo Faltoni (July 18, 2009; September 12–13, 2009; October 2, 2009; September 18–19, 2010; October 2, 2011), Alfredo Martini (July 16, 2009; September 10, 2009; October 2, 2011), Renzo Soldani (July 27, 2009; September 14, 2009), Fiorenzo Magni (September 17, 2009), Aldo Ronconi (August 27, 2009), and Vittorio Seghezzi (August 13, 2009).

22 **"I felt like one of those foals"** Gino Bartali, "Qui giace il campione fra la polvere," *Tempo,* December 20, 1952: 17.

23 **"Let's see who can reach the top of that hill"** Gino Bartali with Mario Pancera, *La mia storia* (Milano: Stampa Sportiva, 1958), 17.

23 **"Heavens, how they struggled!"** Ibid.

23 **"Annoyed by our presence on their wheels"** Gino Bartali, *Tutto sbagliato, tutto da rifare* (Milano: Mondadori, 1979), 16.

23 **"Everyone had a racing one"** Bartali, *La mia storia,* 18.

23 **"I didn't want to disrespect him"** Gino Bartali with Romano Beghelli and Marcello Lazzerini, *La leggenda di Bartali* (Firenze: Ponte Alle Grazie Editori, 1992), 16.
24 **cycling was the symbol of summer** Cycling's popularity in rural areas is explored by Carlo Levi in *Christ Stopped in Eboli* (New York: Farrar Strauss, 1947) and by Orio Vergani, who covered the sport for *Corriere della Sera,* and later other news outlets.
24 **"For many houses lost in the mountains"** Orio Vergani, "Quando la Corsa è Passata," *Corriere delle Sera,* June 8, 1936.
24 **Backgrounds of racers** Author interview with Giovanni Corrieri; cyclist Jef Janssen in *Tour des Légendes,* a documentary about the 1948 Tour de France, directed by Erik Van Empel.
25 **"Back then, racers were personalities"** Author interview with Renzo Soldani.
25 **"These racers were once similar"** Vergani, "Quando la Corsa è Passata."
26 **Charles Terront attire** Todd Balf, *Major: A Black Athlete, a White Era, and the Fight to Be the World's Fastest Human Being* (New York: Three Rivers Press, 2008), 11.
26 **Terront celebrations** Graham Robb, *The Discovery of France: A Historical Geography from the Revolution to the First World War* (New York: W.W. Norton & Company), 340.
26 **Paris opera seat of honor and opera box** Eugen Weber, *France: Fin de Siècle* (Cambridge, MA: The Belknap Press of Harvard University Press, 1986), 197; Benjo Maso, *The Sweat of the Gods: Myths and Legends of Bicycle Racing* (Norwich, England: Mousehold Press, 2005), 10.
26 **Paul D'Ivoi novel** Maso, *The Sweat of the Gods,* 10.
26 **Details about "wheeling" in the USA** Balf, *Major,* 55–57.
26 **electric tricycle** "Planning an Electric Tricycle," *New York Times,* January 5, 1896.
26 **personal information for some five hundred women:** "Ils sont pendant un mois les fiancés de la France," *Match,* August 4, 1938: 9.
27 **"pretty little lecherous souls"** Henri Desgrange as quoted in Christopher Thompson, *The Tour de France: A Cultural History* (Los Angeles: University of California Press, 2006), 109.
27 **Riders' familiarity with Rome's prostitutes** Livio Trapè, a gold and silver Olympic medalist in cycling, shared this story about a teammate (author interview September 18, 2010).
27 **Pélissier's marriage proposals** Maso, *The Sweat of the Gods,* 58.
27 **Pélissier's wife's suicide and his own death** Bill and Carol McGann, *The Story of the Tour de France* (Indianapolis: Dog Ear Publishing, 2006), 79–80; Serge Laget and Luke Edwardes-Evans, *The Official Treasures: Le Tour de France* (London: Carlton Books, 2008), 18.
27 **"We were all gods"** Benjo Maso, *Wir Alle Waren Götter: Die berühmte Tour de France von 1948* (Bielefeld: Covadonga Verlag, 2006),19.

28 **"There I was, enchanted"** Bartali, *La mia storia,* 17.
28 **"*Babbo* didn't want me to bicycle race"** Ibid., 16.
28 **Torello and Giulia's fear of bicycle racing** Bartali, *La mia storia,* 16; Paolo Costa, *Gino Bartali: la vita, le imprese, le polemiche* (Portogruaro: Ediciclo Editore, 2001), 173–80.
28 **violence wreaked by bicyclists** Many newspapers printed the equivalent of a crime blotter recording bicycle accidents and crimes, e.g., *Il Telegrafo,* June 23, 1938: 6.
29 **"When Torello returned home"** Bartali, *La mia storia,* 19.
29 **Sickness in winter of 1929** Bartali, *La leggenda,* 16; author interview with Andrea Bartali.
30 **"One day you will bring him back in pieces"** Jean-Paul Ollivier, *Le Lion de Toscane: La Véridique Histoire de Gino Bartali* (Grenoble: Editions de l'Aurore, 1991),17.
30 **"If need be, you do it"** Bartali, *La mia storia,* 19; Gino Bartali, *Tutto sbagliato, tutto da rifare* (Milano: Mondadori, 1979), 16.
30 **"My heart leapt"** Bartali, *La mia storia,* 19.
30 **Gino is disqualified** Bartali, *La mia storia,* 19; Bartali, *Tutto sbagliato,* 16.

CHAPTER 3. THE FIRST TEST

To illuminate Gino's early training and racing habits and his quick rise through the professional ranks, we mined details from his three autobiographies, from various interviews with him, and from our interviews with his son Andrea; wife, Adriana; and various former teammates.

32 **"Listen, Gino, if we arrive"** Gino Bartali with Mario Pancera, *La mia storia* (Milano: Stampa Sportiva, 1958), 20; author interview with Andrea Bartali.
32 **"Up until this point"** Gino Bartali with Romano Beghelli and Marcello Lazzerini, *La leggenda di Bartali* (Firenze: Ponte Alle Grazie Editori, 1992),17.
32 **"Often my classmates jeered"** Bartali, *La mia storia,* 16.
32 **Morning routine** Bartali, "Qui giace il campione fra la polvere," *Tempo,* December 20, 1952.
32 **chest size** Bartali, *La leggenda,* 57.
32 **training bible:** Bartali, *La mia storia,* 124.
33 **"the Accountant"** Gino Bartali, *Tutto sbagliato, tutto da rifare* (Milano: Mondadori, 1979), 29.
33 **"capacity for suffering"** Gino Bartali, *Match,* August 4, 1938: 8.
33 **Plain pasta and bananas** Paolo Costa, *Gino Bartali: la vita, le imprese, le polemiche* (Portogruaro: Ediciclo Editore, 2001), 176–77.
33 **Sports nutrition in the 1920s and 1930s in the light of current scientific thinking** Author interviews with Dr. Helen Iams, sports medicine physician, March 29, 2010; Leslie Bonci, director of Sports Nutrition at the University of

Pittsburgh Medical Center, March 29, 2010; Dr. Massimo Testa, a physician and exercise physiologist who has helped train cyclists including Levi Leipheimer, April 15, 2010; and Chris Carmichael, a coach of contemporary Tour cyclists including Lance Armstrong, April 27, 2010.

33 **French physician's advice for cyclists** Benjo Maso, *The Sweat of the Gods: Myths and Legends of Bicycle Racing* (Norwich, England: Mousehold Press, 2005), 4.

34 **"Bartali did a climb in bursts"** Author interview with Renzo Soldani, July 27, 2009.

34 **"He looked"** Racer Jean Robic as quoted in Jean-Paul Ollivier, *Le Lion de Toscane: La Véridique Histoire de Gino Bartali* (Grenoble: Editions de l'Aurore, 1991), 34.

35 **"He would burst forward"** Author interview with Renzo Soldani.

35 **"To respond to his attacks"** Robic as quoted in Ollivier, *Le Lion,* 33.

35 **"dancing behind the knee"** Author interview with Giovanni Corrieri.

36 **"dynamite"** One of the first discussions of drug use in the Tour was a 1924 exposé by Albert Londres in *Le Petit Parisien* (Christopher Thompson, *The Tour de France: A Cultural History* [Los Angeles: University of California Press, 2006],190). During the 1930s and 1940s, the products used by cyclists were not "performance-enhancing" as it is understood today, but rather these medications were used to extend the "the pain threshold and the tolerance for exhaustion," as Benjo Maso explains. He notes that the "the most popular were amphetamines, which because of their supposedly explosive effects were called '*La Bombe*' in France, '*La Bomba*' in Italy, and '*Atoom*' in the Netherlands" (*Wir Alle Waren Götter: Die berühmte Tour de France von 1948* [Bielefeld: Covadonga Verlag, 2006],156). Though Gino enjoyed cigarettes and coffee, he was a vocal critic of *la bomba* and other performance-enhancing substances in cycling because he believed they shortened a cyclist's career and were "degrading not only for the sport, but above all for man," Bartali, *La mia storia,* 74.

36 **"like Sherlock Holmes"** Bartali, *La leggenda,* 145–46.

36 **"No one could tell me anything"** Ibid., 31.

36 **"I finished with a bare foot"** Bartali, *La mia storia,* 32.

36 **"Among the many little misadventures"** Ibid., 32.

36 **"I felt degraded"** Ibid.

36 **"You could be like Binda"** Ollivier, *Le Lion,* 29.

37 **Gino misidentified as 'Lino'** "Lino Bartali, Vencedor En La VIII Vuelta Al Pais Vasco," *As,* August 12, 1935: 1, 6–7.

37 **team contract** Costa, *Gino Bartali,* 36.

37 **five times as much as the average factory worker** The average daily wage of an industrial worker in Italy was 14.3 lire per day, according to Antonio Fossati, *Lavoro e produzione in Italia dalla metà del secolo XVIII alla seconda guerra mondiale* (Torino: G. Giappichelli, 1951), 630–34.

37 **new house for his parents** Author interview with Adriana and Andrea Bartali.

38 **already won six races** Bartali, *La leggenda,* 12.

38 "I tried to give him advice" Bartali, *La mia storia,* 35.
38 "I was barely of age" Ibid., 34.
38 press secretary Ibid.; Bartali, *Tutto sbagliato,* 32.
38 "You're the salt" Bonheur,"Ils sont pendant un mois les fiancés de la France," 8.
39 "Here in the dust " Bartali, "Qui giace il campione fra la polvere."
39 "It's better that you don't read them" Ibid.
39 "I was in seventh heaven" Bartali, *Tutto sbagliato,* 31–32.
39 "Giulio was physically more gifted" Ibid., 32.
39 Details of Giulio's bike accident Bartali, *Tutto sbagliato,* 32; Bartali, *La mia storia,* 37; Bartali, *La leggenda,* 9.
40 "Has something happened to Giulio?" Bartali, *La leggenda,* 8
40 "These things happen" Ibid.
40 He died squeezing his older brother's hand Bartali, *La leggenda,* 9.
40 "The deepest sadness fell" Bartali, *Tutto sbagliato,* 33.
40 "You see now that my fears were justified?" Ibid.
40 Increased dedication to the Church: Ollivier, *Le Lion,* 48.
41 Catholic Action history Gianfranco Poggi, *Catholic Action in Italy: The Sociology of a Sponsored Organization* (Palo Alto: Stanford University Press, 1967), 15; Paul Ginsborg, *A History of Contemporary Italy: Society and Politics, 1943–1988* (New York: Palgrave Macmillan, 2003), 169; R. J. B. Bosworth, *Mussolini's Italy: Life Under the Fascist Dictatorship* (New York: Penguin, 2005), 261.
41 small chapel Adriana Bartali showed the family chapel and discussed its history with Aili McConnon on August 3, 2009.
42 "Giulio is gone. My Giulio, my brother" Bartali, *La mia storia,* 36.
42 visits to his brother's tomb Gino's son Andrea spoke of this ritual; Gino also frequently stopped when training in the place where Giulio was killed, according to Gino's teammate Renzo Soldani.
42 Adriana's advice about Giulio's death Author interview with Adriana Bartali, July 17, 2009.
42 Gino's romance with Adriana Bani Author interviews with Adriana Bartali; Bartali; *La mia storia,* 35–36; Bartali, *Tutto sbagliato,* 32; Bartali, *La leggenda,* 48–51.
43 "With these looks" Author interview with Adriana Bartali.
43 "Shouldn't you say something" Bartali, *La leggenda,* 50.
43 "He was so embarrassed" Adriana Bartali as quoted in Paolo Alberati, *Gino Bartali: Mille diavoli in corpo* (Firenze: Giunti, 2006), 48–49.
43 Brother-in-law escort and details of first kiss Costa, *Gino Bartali,* 176–77.
44 "A racer?" Author interview with Adriana Bartali.
44 "Let's wait a little" Ibid.
44 "Too familiar" Ibid.
44 "Sometimes we would go to the movies" Ibid.
45 "We would have kids" Bartali, *La mia storia,* 36.
46 Winning both Tour and Giro "Il toscano riprenderà a correre soltanto in autumno," *Il Popolo d'Italia,* July 15, 1937: 4; Bartali, *La mia storia,* 46–47;

"Le decisioni federali per il Giro d'Italia e il 'Tour,'" *Il Popolo d'Italia,* April 6, 1938: 4; "Precisazioni del Presidente della F.C.I.," *Il Popolo d'Italia,* April 9,1938: 6.

CHAPTER 4. "ITALY'S NUMBER ONE SPORTSMAN"

To depict the growing importance of sports in Italy from the turn of the twentieth century through World War II, we relied on the following sources: Patrizia Dogliani, "Sport and Fascism," *Journal of Modern Italian Studies* 5, no. 3 (October 2001); Gigliola Gori, "Model of Masculinity: Mussolini, the 'New Italian' of the Fascist Era," in J. A. Mangan's *Superman Supreme: Fascist Body as Political Icon—Global Fascism* (London: Frank Cass, 2000), 45; David Forgacs and Stephen Gundle, *Mass Culture and Italian Society from Fascism to the Cold War* (Bloomington: Indiana University Press, 2008); George Baer, *Test Case: Italy, Ethiopia, and the League of Nations* (Stanford, California: Hoover Institution Press, 1976); Gigliola Gori, *Italian Fascism and the Female Body: Sport, Submissive Women and Strong Mothers* (London: Routledge, 2004).

48 **"warrior people"** Forgacs and Gundle, *Mass Culture,* 242.
48 **"biological engineers"** Dogliani, "Sport and Fascism," 327.
48 **controlling children's athletic training** Gori, *Italian Fascism and the Female Body,* 97.
48 **"grotesque foreign imitation"** Angela Teja, "Italian sport and international relations under fascism," in *Sport and International Politics,* edited by P.Arnaud and J.Riordan (New York: Routledge, 1998), 153.
48 **"I don't want a population"** Alberto Marcolin, *Firenze in Camicia Nera* (Florence: Edizioni Medicea, 1993), 183.
49 **"Cigarette of Great Athletes"** The brand that used this catchphrase was Macedonia Extra. *Lo Sport Fascista,* June 1936: 74.
49 **"skepticism, sloth and pessimism"** Elizabeth David, *Italian Food* (Harmondsworth: Penguin, 1963), 93, as quoted in Forgacs and Gundle, *Mass Culture,* 242.
49 **dive from a springboard** Gori, "Model of Masculinity," 45.
49 **bayoneted rifles** "Mussolini alle prove atletiche dei Gerarchi del Partito" and accompanying photo, *Il Popolo d'Italia,* July 2, 1938: 1.
49 **Mussolini's sports** D. Medina Lasansky, *The Renaissance Perfected: Architecture, Spectacle, and Tourism in Fascist Italy* (University Park: Pennsylvania State University Press, 1988 and 2005), 172; Gori, "Model of Masculinity," 43.
49 **ascetic diet** Carol Helstosky, *Garlic and Oil: Politics and Food in Italy* (New York: Oxford International Publishers, 2004), 99.

49 **Mussolini, Hitler, and Franco's lack of interest in sports in earlier life** Forgacs and Gundle, *Mass Culture,* 240; John Pollard, "Sport," in *World Fascism: A Historical Encyclopedia,* vol. 1 (Santa Barbara, CA: ABC-Clio, 2006), 630.
49 **low angle** Gori, "Model of Masculinity," 37.
49 **"big bald head, a pockmarked face"** Ibid., 45.
49 **"Italy's Number One Sportsman"** This was a popularly used title for Mussolini. Forgacs and Gundle, *Mass Culture,* 240.
50 **Importance of appearance fees** Benjo Maso, *The Sweat of the Gods: Myths and Legends of Bicycle Racing* (Norwich, England: Mousehold Press, 2005), 63, 79.
50 **"calling card for the nation abroad"** Forgacs and Gundle, *Mass Culture,* 241.
50 **"blue ambassadors"** Teja, "Italian sport," 156.
51 **"a gold medal"** Ibid.
51 **Athletic governing bodies** General Antonelli was the head of the Italian Cycling Federation; Paolo Costa, *Gino Bartali: la vita, le imprese, le polemiche* (Portogruaro: Ediciclo Editore, 2001), 50. Lando Ferretti, a Fascist journalist, became head of the Italian Olympic Committee (CONI); Dogliani, "Sport and Fascism," 329.
51 **answered to the regime** Gori, "Model of Masculinity," 38.
51 **pneumonia** James Le Fanu, *The Rise and Fall of Modern Medicine* (New York: Carroll & Graf, 2000), 5–6. The first patient to receive penicillin, the antibiotic most commonly used to treat pneumonia, was treated in 1941.
51 **"You can imagine"** Gino Bartali with Mario Pancera, *La mia storia* (Milano: Stampa Sportiva, 1958), 40.
52 **"There is no point"** Giorgio Boriani, "Dal 'Giro' al 'Tour,'" *Lo Sport Fascista,* June 26, 1937.
52 ***Il Popolo d'Italia*** Marco Palla, *Mussolini and Fascism* (New York: Interlink Illustrated Histories, 2000) 20; Gori, "Model of Masculinity," 34.
52 **"to understand"** Nino Nutrizio, "Gino Bartali andrà al 'Tour' al commando della squadra italiana" *Il Popolo d'Italia,* June 2, 1937: 6.
52 **200,000-lire payoff and "a soldier who defends his flag"** Nino Nutrizio, "Se lo sport è milizia Gino Bartali debe andare al 'Tour,'" *Il Popolo d'Italia,* June 17, 1937: 4.
53 **Schmeling** For details on Max Schmeling's 1936 victory over Louis, and Schmeling's contacts, see David Margolick's *Beyond Glory: Joe Louis vs. Max Schmeling, and a World on the Brink* (New York: Knopf, 2005), 146–78; see also David Clay Large, *Nazi Games: The Olympics of 1936* (New York: W.W. Norton, 2007), 173.
53 **Kristallnacht** Margolick, *Beyond Glory,* 350.
53 **Schmeling meeting with Hitler** Large, *Nazi Games,* 173.
53 **Joseph Goebbels** Margolick, *Beyond Glory,* 151, 339.
54 **leading investigative journalists** Paolo Facchinetti, *Bottecchia: Il forzato della strada* (Portogruaro: Ediciclo Editore, 2005), 186–89.
54 **Details about Bottecchia's death and theories** Les Woodland, "Cycling's

murder mysteries," *cyclingnews.com*, March 10, 2007; Facchinetti, *Bottecchia*, 185–88.

55 **Friendship with Cardinal Elia Dalla Costa** Author interviews with Andrea and Adriana Bartali; see chapter 6 notes.

55 **"It gave me the push to try again"** Gino Bartali, *Tutto sbagliato, tutto da rifare* (Milano: Mondadori, 1979), 78.

55 **"magnificent Christian athlete"** C. Trabucco, "Gino Bartali di Azione cattolica," *Gioventù nova*, June 14, 1936, cited by Stefano Pivato, "Italian Cycling and the Creation of a Catholic Hero: The Bartali Myth," in *European Heroes: Myth, Identity, Sport*, edited by Richard Holt, J. A. Mangan, and Pierre Lanfranchi (London: Frank Cass, 1996), 130.

55 **a three-engined aircraft** Marco da Faenza, "Asso pigliatutto," *Credere*, June 13, 1937, in Pivato, *Sia Lodato Bartali* (Rome: Edizioni Lavoro, 1985), 187–89.

55 **criticizing a regime** Pivato, "Italian Cycling," 132.

56 **"the Little Monk"** Pivato, *Sia lodato*, 39. The sports newspaper that defended Bartali's Catholicism was the *Guerin Sportivo*.

56 **"for Italy and for Il Duce" and "Mussolini's boys"** Robert S. C. Gordon and John London, "Italy 1934: Football and Fascism," in *National identity and global sports events: culture, politics, and spectacle in the Olympics and the World Cup*, edited by Alan Tomlinson and Christopher Young (Albany: State University of New York Press, 2006), 42.

56 **Fascist formation** Dogliani, "Sport and Fascism," 331–32.

56 **"Four years"** Mussolini quoted in Large, *Nazi Games*, 167.

57 **character assassination** On the Fascist regime's control of the press, see Gigliola Gori, "Mussolini's Boys at Hitler's Olympics," in *The Nazi Olympics: Sports, Politics and Appeasement in the 1930s*, edited by Arnd Kruger and William Murray (Urbana and Chicago: University of Illinois Press), 115.

57 **intention to compete** "Bartali si è deciso," *Il Popolo d'Italia*, June 18, 1937: 4.

57 **"truly radical change"** Geoffrey Wheatcroft, *Le Tour: A History of the Tour de France, 1903–2003* (London: Simon and Schuster, 2005), 123.

57 **Gear changes in previous Tours** Bill and Carol McGann, *The Story of the Tour de France* (Indianapolis: Dog Ear Publishing, 2006), 132.

58 **favorite to win** McGann, *The Story of the Tour de France*, 133.

58 **2,740 miles in 1937 Tour de France** Wheatcroft, *Le Tour*, 360.

58 **tailored suits** Benjo Maso, *Wir Alle Waren Götter: Die berühmte Tour de France von 1948* (Bielefeld: Covadonga Verlag, 2006), 219.

58 **"Bartali will never be caught"** Jacques Goddet, "Dans le Tour, un trop grand effort se paie toujours," *L'Auto*, July 8, 1937: 2.

59 **Fall in Colau River** Robert Perrier, "Le Miracle!" *L'Auto*, July 9, 1937: 2; Henri Desgrange, "Nous l'avons échappé belle!" *L'Auto*, July 9, 1937: 1; photo of Gino being brought to bike, *L'Auto*, July 9, 1937: 2; "Suivez Le Guide," *L'Auto*, July 9, 1937: 2; Bartali, *La mia storia*, 42–46; Bartali, *Tutto sbagliato*, 36–43.

59 **"like a ball into space"** Perrier, "Le Miracle!" 2.

59 **"Get on the bike, Bartali"** Ibid.

59 **"like bloody steaks"** Nino Nutrizio, "Bartali resta maglia gialla nonostante una drammatica caduta con Camusso, Simonini e Giulio Rossi," *Il Popolo d'Italia,* June 9, 1937: 4.
60 **"I was mute"** Bartali, *Tutto sbagliato,* 41.
60 **"full health and form"** Henri Desgrange, "Le fait majeur," *L'Auto,* July 12, 1937: 1.
60 **Another Tour organizer** Jacques Goddet, "Un temps qui paraît être pour rien," *L'Auto,* July 12, 1937: 2.
60 **health reasons** Gino Bartali with Romano Beghelli and Marcello Lazzerini, *La leggenda di Bartali* (Firenze: Ponte Alle Grazie Editori, 1992), 72–73; Paolo Alberati, *Gino Bartali: Mille diavoli in corpo* (Firenze: Giunti, 2006), 53.
60 **card-carrying Fascist** Bartali, *La leggenda,* 73.
60 **"I was crying"** Bartali, *La mia storia,* 46.
60 **"When the doctor"** Bartali, *Tutto sbagliato,* 37.
60 **"greatest injustice suffered"** Bartali, *La leggenda,* 73.
61 **train ticket** Ibid.
61 **onlookers who spotted him** "Il toscano riprenderà a correre soltanto in autumno," *Il Popolo d'Italia,* July 15, 1937: 4; Bartali, *La mia storia,* 46.
61 **time off to recuperate** "Il toscano riprenderà a correre soltanto in autumno," 4.
61 **following year's cycling season** Ibid.
61 **Bartali sidelined from the 1938 Giro** "Le decisioni federali per il Giro d'Italia e il 'Tour,' *Il Popolo d'Italia,* April 6, 1938: 4; "Precisazioni del Presidente della F.C.I.," *Il Popolo d'Italia,* April 9, 1938: 6.
61 **"had as much to do with cycling"** Bartali, *La mia storia,* 47.
61 **Dialogue between Gino and I.C.F.** Ibid.
62 **Mussolini eager to improve relations with Hitler** Gori, "Model of Masculinity," 53; John Gooch, *Mussolini and His Generals: The Armed Forces and Fascist Foreign Policy, 1922–1940* (Cambridge, UK: Cambridge University Press, 2007), 384.
62 **failed artist** Ian Kershaw, *Hitler: 1889–1936 Hubris* (New York: W.W. Norton, 2000), 82.
62 **"Operation Florence beautiful"** Lasansky, *The Renaissance Perfected,* 85.
63 **Details of Hitler's arrival, greeting ceremony, and visit** Ibid., 73–75.
63 **rouge** *Diary 1937–1943: The complete unabridged diaries of Count Galeazzo Ciano, Italian Minister for Foreign Affairs, 1936–1943* (London: Phoenix, 2002), 88.
63 **motorcade of convertibles** Lasansky, *The Renaissance Perfected,* 85.
63 **Donati family experience of Hitler's visit** Author interview with Giulia Donati.
64 **Elia Dalla Costa's protest and secret report written by Fascist political police** Cardinal Elia Dalla Costa File, Ministero dell' Interno, Divisione di Pubblica Sicurezza, Divisione Polizia Politica 13 157, 2 Pacco #378, Fascicoli #70, 378, #9. Letter titled *Rome, 18 February 1939*; Marcolin, *Firenze in Camicia Nera,* 74.

64 **cardinal's office aflame** Author interview with Attilio Piccini, October 20, 2009. Piccini worked with Cardinal Dalla Costa at the Sparugoru Murbis convent and in later years, helped Dalla Costa's secretary Meneghello.
64 **full satisfaction** *Diary 1937–1943,* 88; Marcolin, *Firenze in Camicia Nera,* 75.
64 **nineteen million lire** Lasansky, *The Renaissance Perfected,* 98.
65 **"pavement had been temporarily relandscaped"** Ibid., 91.
65 **"Now no force" and Hitler's eyes moistening** *Diary 1937–1943,* 89.
65 **precursor to Berlin's infamous 1936 Olympics** Gordon and London, "Italy 1934," 42.
65 **players saluted Mussolini** Richard Witzig, *The Global Art of Soccer* (New Orleans: Cusiboy Publishing, 2006), 349.
65 **Italians playing in black shirts, and anti-Fascist fans' response** Teja, "Italian sport," 163; John London, "Football/Soccer," in *World Fascism,* 239.
65 **broken bottles** Ulrich Hesse-Lichtenberger, *Tor! The Story of German Football* (London: WSC Books, 2002), 84–85.
65 **"city, a prejudice"** Lando Ferretti, "Uno, due. . . (e tre?)," *Lo Sport Fascista,* July 1938: 13.
65 **lavish event** "Il Duce riceve oggi a Palazzo Venezia i calciatori campioni del mondo," *Il Popolo d'Italia,* June 29, 1938: 4; "Il Duce riceve i calciatori azzurri," *Il Popolo d'Italia,* June 30, 1938: 1.
66 **army and navy uniforms** Photo of Mussolini and 1938 Italian World Cup soccer team in military outfits, *Il Popolo d'Italia,* June 30, 1938: 1
66 **soccer players' jerseys** Ferretti, "Uno, due. . . (e tre?)," 14.
66 **sleeper carriage** "Gli azzurri per il 'Tour' partono stasera per Parigi," *Il Popolo d'Italia,* June 29, 1938: 4; "L'équipe italienne du Tour arrivera ce matin a Paris," *L'Auto,* June 30, 1938: 1.
66 **Voltaggio** Jean Leuillot, "Italie, Belgique, France trois méthodes pour le Tour," *L'Auto,* June 30, 1938: 1, Al; Baker d'Issy,"Vicini et son 'double' Cottur," *Paris-Soir,* July 2, 1938: 10.
67 **"It was my most intense period"** Bartali, *Tutto sbagliato,* 44.
67 **"Dear Giulio, you see what condition"** Bartali, *La mia storia,* 12.

CHAPTER 5. STORM AT THE SUMMIT

68 **crowds cheered** "Gli azzurri del Giro di Francia sone partiti ieri sera per Parigi con la ferma volontà di puntare alla vittoria," *Il Popolo d'Italia,* June 30, 1938: 4.
68 **shortly after nine** "L'équipe italienne du Tour arrivera ce matin a Paris," *L'Auto,* June 30, 1938: 1.
69 ***The past is set,* he thought** Gino Bartali with Mario Pancera, *La mia storia* (Milano: Stampa Sportiva, 1958), 13.
69 **lounging around** Claude Tillet, "Les Italiens du Tour ont rallié Saint-Germain," *L'Auto,* July 1, 1938: 1; R. de LaTour, "Les Italiens du 'Tour' sont arrivés à Paris," *Paris-Soir,* July 1, 1938: 6.
70 **"superhuman task"** LaTour, "Les Italiens du 'Tour,'" 6.

70 **first phone call** Tillet, "Les Italiens du Tour," 4.
70 **charming a pair of women** Géo Villetan, "Gagner le Tour de France," *Paris-Soir,* July 10,1938: 6A.
70 **Gino's nose injury** On May 24, 1934, during a competition in Grosseto, Italy, Gino fell on a stone-covered road that left him with a permanent "scar in the form of the sun," on his nose. Paolo Costa, *Gino Bartali: la vita, le imprese, le polemiche* (Portogruaro: Ediciclo Editore, 2001), 173–80; Bartali, *La leggenda,* 30.
71 **"delicate, nervous"** Raymond Huttier, *Le Miroir des Sports,* July 26,1938: 1.
71 **"remind you of ivy"** Georges Vigarello, "The Tour de France," *Realms of Memory: The Construction of the French Past,* vol. 2; *Traditions,* edited by Pierre Nora and Lawrence Kritzman (New York: Columbia University Press, 1998), 496.
71 **149 pounds** Costa, *Bartali,* 183.
71 **"like the olive trees"** Gino Bartali, "Qui giace il campione fra la polvere," *Tempo,* December 20, 1952.
71 **French rider accident** "La chute de Paul Maye est à retenir," *L'Intransigeant,* July 6, 1938: 4.
71 **private airplanes** In an advertisement on July 5,1938, on p. 1 of *Paris-Soir,* the paper mentions they will have a team of ten vehicles, eight motorcycles, and one airplane.
72 **twenty different newscasts** "La radiodiffusion," *L'Auto,* July 13, 1938: 4, 19.
72 **Origin of the Tour de France** For the discussion of the origin of the Tour de France we drew on the following sources: Christopher Thompson, *The Tour de France: A Cultural History* (Los Angeles: University of California Press, 2006), 17; Bill and Carol McGann, *The Story of the Tour de France* (Indianapolis: Dog Ear Publishing, 2006); Serge Laget and Luke Edwardes-Evans, *The Official Treasures: Le Tour de France* (London: Carlton Books, 2008), 14; Hugh Dauncey and Geoff Hare, *The Tour de France, 1903–2003: A Century of Sporting Structures, Meanings and Values* (Taylor and Francis eLibrary, 2005), 55; Geoffrey Wheatcroft, *Le Tour: A History of the Tour de France, 1903–2003* (London: Simon and Schuster, 2005); Les Woodland, *The Yellow Jersey Companion to the Tour de France* (London: Random House, 2007).
73 **"If I understand you"** McGann, *The Story of the Tour de France,* 7.
73 **"If I'm not murdered"** Wheatcroft, *Le Tour,* 21.
74 **Desgrange famously said** Dauncey and Hare, *The Tour,* 7.
74 **"Murderers!"** Laget and Edwardes-Evans, *Official Treasures,* 16.
75 **Cyclist with sepsis** Daniel Coyle, *Lance Armstrong's War* (New York: HarperCollins, 2005), 101.
76 **Girardengo's strategy of saving attacks** Gino Bartali, "Mon Beau Maillot," as told to Robert Perrier, *L'Auto,* August 9, 1938: 1, 4; Jacques Goddet, "Gino, tu es un héros ," *L'Auto,* July 23, 1938: 2.
76 **"most important of the Tour"** Henri Desgrange, "Entre eux et moi," *L'Auto,* July 16, 1938: 1.

77 **"leave meat on the road"** Coyle, *Lance Armstrong's War,* 16.
77 ***à tombeau ouvert*** Henri Desgrange, "Je ne suis pas très content de Bartali," *L'Auto,* July 15, 1938: 3.
77 **"It's unimaginable"** Gaston Bénac, "Le Tour n'est pas fini!" *Paris-Soir,* July 15, 1938: 9.
77 **"This stage is one of the worst"** Gino Bartali, "Mon Beau Maillot," 4.
77 **"Suddenly, from the small group"** Raymond Huttier, *Le Miroir des Sports,* July 16, 1938: 11.
78 **"Do Not Push!"** Ibid., 6.
78 **"launched by an invisible catapult"** Ibid., 11.
78 **"eat some tender little pigeons"** Gino Bartali, *Tutto sbagliato, tutto da rifare* (Milano: Mondadori, 1979), 45–46.
78 ***Am I not going to be able to get rid of this leech?*** Bartali, "Mon Beau Maillot," 4.
78 **"I felt my heart"** Bartali, *Tutto sbagliato,* 45–46.
78 **"I can't go on"** Ibid., 46.
79 **"difficult, mean and made of rock"** Ibid.
79 **"Go, go, go!"** Ibid.
79 **His arms and back, hunched now** Ibid.
79 **the yellow jersey was virtually his** Ibid.
79 **"I flew off my bike"** Robert Perrier, "Les Pensées de l'homme du jour: 'Quel dommage cette chute . . . nous dit Gino Bartali," *L'Auto,* July 15, 1938: 4.
80 **seven hours and sixteen minutes on his bike** Bartali's time was seven hours, sixteen minutes, fourteen seconds. "Classement de la 8e Etape," *L'Auto,* July 15, 1938: 1.
80 ***Manifesto of the Racial Scientists*** Susan Zuccotti, *Under His Very Windows: The Vatican and the Holocaust in Italy* (New Haven: Yale University Press, 2000), 27; Susan Zuccotti, *The Italians and the Holocaust: Persecution, Rescue, and Survival* (New York: Basic Books, 1987), 35; *Antisemitism: A Historical Encyclopedia of Prejudice and Persecution,* ed. by Richard S. Levy (Santa Barbara, CA: ABC-Clio, 2005), 442.
80 **"practically wrote it himself"** *Diary 1937–1943: The complete unabridged diaries of Count Galeazzo Ciano, Italian Minister for Foreign Affairs, 1936–1943* (London: Phoenix, 2002), 109.
80 **"Aryan, Nordic and heroic"** Otto D. Tolischus, "Nazi Press Hails Italian 'Aryanism'" *New York Times,* July 15, 1938: 6.
80 **"Jews do not belong to the Italian race,"** Zuccotti, *The Italians,* 35; Patrick J. Gallo, *For Love and Country: The Italian Resistance* (Lanham, Maryland: University Press of America, 2003), 19.
80 **"The time has come for Italians"** Stanislao G. Pugliese, ed., *Fascism, anti-fascism, and the resistance in Italy: 1919 to the present* (Oxford, UK: Roman & Littlefield, 2004), 194–95.
80 **Jewish community in Italy** Gallo, *For Love and Country,* 19.
81 **Fascist conflict with Catholic Church over Manifesto** Tolischus, "Nazi Press hails Italian 'Aryanism,'" 6; Zuccotti, *The Italians,* 36–38.

81 **publicly criticized the Manifesto** Zuccotti, *Under His Very Windows,* 33–34.
81 **"in the name of Mussolini"** Lando Ferretti, "Uno, due . . . (e tre?)," *Lo Sport Fascista,* July 1938: 14.
81 **"uses his bicycle as a weapon"** Bruno Roghi, "L'alto valore e la nera disdetta di un grande atleta italiano," *La Gazzetta Dello Sport,* July 15, 1938: 2.
81 **heralding his performance** Bruno Roghi, "Da un traguardo all'altro, nell ritmo incessante dei trionfi dello sport fascista—Gino Bartali Ha Vinto Il 32° Giro de Francia," *La Gazzetta Dello Sport,* August 1,1938: 1.
81 **former winner of the Tour de France** " 'Cet arrêt à Luchon marquera peut-être la fin de ma carrière cycliste,' nous déclare Georges Speicher," *Paris-Soir,* July 16, 1938: 8.
82 **"The king of the mountains"** *Le Miroir des Sports,* July 16, 1938.
82 **"He is the great and real champion"** Ibid., 5.
82 **Torello visits Gino** Jean Leuillot, "Papa Bartali est venu embrasser son fils 'Gino' à Cannes," *L'Auto,* July 21, 1938: 3.
82 **hear his heart pounding** Bartali, *La mia storia,* 49.
82 **"It was an uproar"** Ibid., 50.
82 **"It's true"** Félix Lévitan, "Bartali, un être de légende," *L'Intransigeant,* July 24, 1938: 4.
83 **"Think about destiny"** Bartali, *Tutto sbagliato,* 47.
83 **"Sir, my faith"** Robert Bré, "Il ne faut pas confondre Bartali coureur avec Bartali 'civil,' " *L'Auto,* August 1, 1938: 5.
83 *"Niente"*—**"No!"** Géo Villetan, "Le Tour continue," *Paris-Soir,* July 27, 1938: 9.
84 **Bartali wearing a muddy jersey and a dusty cap** Géo Villetan, "Le 'Parc' est plein . . . c'est jour de fête!" *Paris-Soir,* August 1, 1938: 8.
84 **"I have realized one of the dreams "** *L'Intransigeant,* August 1, 1938: 6A.
84 **"Seeing you pedal, Gino,"** Ibid.
84 **"During a moment when my legs"** Ibid.
84 **medal for "athletic valor"** Roghi, "Da un traguardo all'altro," 1.
85 **Mussolini's sports ambassador to Italy** Ibid.
85 **"democracy and international pigswill"** Sisto Favre, "Il valore e lo spirito della vittoria azzurra," *Lo Sport Fascista,* August 1938: 14.
85 **"The ovations"** Roghi, "Da un traguardo all'altro," 1.
85 **address to French radio listeners:** "Radio-Arrivée du 32ème Tour de France au Parc des Princes—Radio Actualités Françaises," Radio and Newsreel Archives from Inatheque de France, at the Bibliothèque Nationale de France.
85 **"In 1938, everyone knew"** Author interview with Italian historian Mauro Canali, August 10, 2009.
86 **"holding high the colors"** "Da Lilla a Parigi," *Il Popolo d'Italia,* August 1, 1938: 1.
86 **"mumbled"** Gino Bartali file, Ministero dell' Interno, Divisione di Pubblica Sicurezza, Divisione Polizia Politica 13 157, 1 Pacco #82, Fascicoli #70, 82 #66.
86 **"I present to you"** André Bourdonnay, "Le premier acte de Bartali ce matin

fut d'aller déposer des fleurs à Notre-Dame des Victoires," *Paris-Soir,* August 2, 1938: 6.

86 **"An Italian wins the Tour de France"** Robert Perrier, "Nul est prophète dans son pays," *L'Auto,* August 5, 1938: 1, 3.

87 **first appearance as a Tour champion** "Au Velodrome de Turin" *L'Auto,* August 5, 1938: 4.

87 **she cried softly** Ibid.

87 **Details on the Ufficio Stampa** Arnd Krüger and William Murray, eds., *The Nazi Olympics: Sports, Politics and Appeasement in the 1930s* (Urbana and Chicago: University of Illinois Press, 2003), 115.

87 **"The newspapers should cover Bartali exclusively as a sportsman"** Report from August 9,1938, F. Flora, *Stampa dell'era fascista: Le note di servizio* (Rome: Mondadori, 1945), 79.

PART II

CHAPTER 6. FROM THE STARS TO THE STABLES

We based our discussion of the Racial Laws in Italy, and their impact, on the following sources: Susan Zuccotti, *The Italians and the Holocaust: Persecution, Rescue, and Survival* (New York: Basic Books, 1987), 5–6; Susan Zuccotti, *Under His Very Windows: The Vatican and the Holocaust in Italy* (New Haven: Yale University Press, 2000); Michele Sarfatti, *The Jews in Mussolini's Italy: From Equality to Persecution,* trans. by John and Anne C. Tedeschi (Madison: University of Wisconsin Press, 2006); Patrick J.Gallo, *For Love and Country: The Italian Resistance* (Lanham, MD: University Press of America, 2003), 16; Mirjam Viterbi Ben Horin, *Con gli occhi di allora: Una bambina ebrea e le leggi razziali* (Brescia: Editrice Morcelliana, 2008), 15; *Racial Policies in Fascist Italy: New Documents and Perspectives,* a conference and exhibit organized in New York by the Center for Contemporary Jewish Documentation (CDEC) in Milan and several American organizations, fall 2010.

To illuminate the day-to-day experience of living in Italy during the Racial Laws, we spoke with the following survivors of the Holocaust in Italy: Giorgio Goldenberg (December 20, 2010; January 25, 2011; April 4, 2011; and November 14, 2011); Giulia Donati (January 26 and 28, 2011); Giorgina Rietti (August 5, 2009; November 6, 2009; and September 11, 2010); Graziella Viterbi (July 14, 2009, and August 31, 2009);

Gianna Maionica (November 22, 2007; August 4, 2009); Hella Kropf (January 15, 2008, and August 4, 2009); Cesare Sacerdoti (October 19, 2010); Claudia Maria Amati (February 1, 2011); Lya Haberman Quitt (October 20, 2011); and Renzo Ventura, a son of survivors (July 27, 2009). We also consulted video and audio testimonies from the following individuals: Enrico Maionica (University of Southern California Shoah Foundation interview by Susanna Segrè, April 30, 1998); Emanuele Pacifici (USC Shoah Foundation interview by Silvia Antonucci, March 10, 1998); Louis Goldman (USC Shoah Foundation interview by James Bond, February 3, 1995).

91 **bad team strategy** Gino Bartali with Romano Beghelli and Marcello Lazzerini, *La leggenda di Bartali* (Firenze: Ponte Alle Grazie Editori, 1992), 86.
92 **spy report speculated** Gino Bartali file, Ministero dell' Interno, Divisione di Pubblica Sicurezza, Divisione Polizia Politica 13 157, 1 Pacco #82, Fascicoli #70, 82 #66.
92 **"But the noise of them en masse"** Gino Bartali with Mario Pancera, *La mia storia* (Milano: Stampa Sportiva, 1958), 52.
92 **"Milanese, you are not sportsmen!"** Bartali, *La leggenda,* 52.
92 **"The pedestal of fame is neither very comfortable"** Bartali, *La mia storia,* 51.
92 **"bronzed faces bent over handlebars"** Orio Vergani, *Corriere delle Sera,* June 7, 1936.
93 **Giorgio's experience of the Racial Laws** Author interviews with Giorgio Goldenberg.
94 **Jewish children banned from state schools** Zuccotti, *Under His Very Windows,* 42; Sarfatti, *The Jews in Mussolini's Italy,* 155.
94 **Even in Nazi Germany** Michele Sarfatti, director of the Center for Contemporary Jewish Documentation, in a roundtable discussion, "Beyond the Racial Laws, Fascist Anti-Semitism Revisited," Museum for Jewish Heritage, November 3, 2010.
94 **Jewish job loss in Italy** "Italy's 'Race' Laws Take 15, 000 Jobs," *New York Times,* November 20, 1938.
94 **"No Entry to Jews and Dogs"** USC interview with Enrico Maionica.
94 **Jewish obituaries** Author interview with Giulia Donati.
95 **"We went from the stars to the stables"** Author interview with Graziella Viterbi, July 14, 2009.
95 **with fierce determination** Bartali, *La leggenda,* 87.
95 **"reed-thin lad"** Fausto's coach, Biagio Cavanna, as quoted in William Fotheringham, *Fallen Angel: The Passion of Fausto Coppi* (London: Yellow Jersey Press, 2009), 20.

95 "more like a thin, starving goat than a cyclist" Ibid.

95 Coppi's background and early training Ibid, 9, 20, 24.

96 Early interactions between Gino and Coppi Jean-Paul Ollivier, *Fausto Coppi* (Paris: Éditions PAC, 1985), 14; Bartali, *La leggenda,* 100.

96 newest reconnaissance strategy Gian Paolo Ormezzano with Marina Coppi and Andrea Bartali, *Coppi & Bartali* (Milano: Edizioni San Paolo, 2009), 137.

96 throbbing pain Bartali, *Tutto sbagliato,* 62; Bartali, *La mia storia,* 54.

97 "A great tragedy was to befall us all" Bartali, *La leggenda,* 109.

97 Arrest of the Kleins in Fiume Author interviews with Giorgio Goldenberg.

97 Experience of foreign nationals Mary Felstiner, *Refuge and Persecution in Italy, 1933–1945,* translated by Martha Humphreys and Sybil Milton (Simon Wiesenthal Center Annual, vol. 4); Zuccotti, *Under His Very Windows,* 83.

98 Villa La Selva Nissim Labi was an Italian Jew who was imprisoned in Villa La Selva during World War II. Labi's testimony was consulted at the Yad Vashem library, Jerusalem, Israel. Researchers at the Bagno a Ripoli library helped uncover details about this camp (author interviews with Raffaele Marconi and Maria Pagnini, August 12 and September 11, 2009).

98 allowance of 6.5 lire for food At different camps throughout Italy, 6.5 lire was the daily allowance given to prisoners. Felstiner, *Refuge and Persecution.*

98 a bowl of watery soup Testimony of Nissim Labi.

99 The Goldenbergs' life in Fiesole and Gino Bartali's visit Author interviews with Giorgio Goldenberg.

100 "Bartali was a kind of demigod" Author interview with Giorgio Goldenberg, December 20, 2010.

101 "Don't worry, I won't end up beneath the bombs" Bartali as quoted in Leo Turrini, *Bartali: L'uomo che salvo' l'Italia pedalando* (Milano: Mondadori, 2004), 20.

101 Adriana's older brother Author interview with Adriana Bartali.

101 check up Bartali, *La mia storia,* 54; Jean-Paul Ollivier, *Le Lion de Toscane: La Véridique Histoire de Gino Bartali* (Grenoble: Editions de l'Aurore, 1991), 97–98.

102 didn't like carrying a gun Bartali, *La leggenda,* 115.

102 Olesindo Salmi Bartali, *La mia storia,* 56; Ollivier, *Le Lion,* 98.

102 "I plunged myself into reading" Bartali quoted in Ollivier, *Le Lion,* 99.

102 "Gino, the chatterbox" Bartali quoted in Ollivier, *Le Lion,* 99.

102 *No one knows what will happen* Bartali, *La leggenda,* 110.

102 "Better a widow than a girlfriend" Ibid.

103 "My dream from boyhood, for my future" Bartali quoted in Paolo Alberati, *Gino Bartali: Mille diavoli in corpo* (Firenze: Giunti, 2006), 46.

104 "the moment was a bit peculiar" Author interview with Adriana Bartali, July 17, 2009.

104 Gino and Adriana's wedding, honeymoon, and reception Author interviews with Andrea and Adriana Bartali.

104 "It was all racing around" Author interview with Adriana Bartali, July 17, 2009.

104 **Food shortages** Carole Counihan, *Around the Tuscan Table* (New York: Routledge, 2004), 24, 52; Alberto Marcolin, *Firenze 1943–'45: Anni di terrore e di fame, fascisti e antifascisti* (Firenze: Edizioni Medicea, 1994), 36–37.
105 **"gray as ash"** Coppi quoted in Fotheringham, *Fallen Angel*, chapter 4.
105 **"surrounded by people who are thinking only about races"** Bartali quoted in Alberati, *Mille diavoli*, 70.
106 **giant holding cell for seven thousand Jews** Sarah Fishman, *The Battle for Children: World War II, Youth Crime and Juvenile Justice in Twentieth Century France* (Cambridge, MA: Harvard Historical Studies, 2002), 72.
106 **Coppi would spend the rest of World War II** Coppi arrived in Africa in March 1943. For a detailed account of his time there, see chapter 4 of Fotheringham's *Fallen Angel*.
106 **"It was beautiful"** Author interview with Giulia Donati.
107 **Ubaldo Pugnaloni's race** Fotheringham, *Fallen Angel*, 55–56.
107 **prominent anti-Semitic newspaper editor** Zuccotti, *The Italians*, 71.
107 **Killer of Matteoti arrested** Marcolin, *Firenze 1943–'45*, 24.
107 **many (though not all) prisoners in internment camps** Author interview with Dr. Iael Nidam-Orvieto, editor-in-chief of Yad Vashem publications, January 24, 2011.
107 **submitted the paperwork to be discharged** Bartali, *La mia storia*, 56.
108 **others were less inclined to follow any procedures** Zuccotti, *The Italians*, 6–7.
108 **Figures on captured and imprisoned soldiers** Zuccotti, *The Italians*, 7.
108 **Gino gathered up his family** Bartali, *La leggenda*, 120.
109 **"In this little lost corner"** Ollivier, *Le Lion*, 99.
109 **long, restless hours in bed** Ibid.
109 **"Are you Gino Bartali?"** Bartali, *La leggenda*, 120,122.

CHAPTER 7. AN IMPOSSIBLE CHOICE

We know of Gino Bartali's participation in Dalla Costa's rescue effort in Tuscany and Umbria because of accounts left by people involved in the network (Fr. Rufino Niccacci and Trento Brizi), and the testimonies of people who personally saw him or interacted with him when he was picking up documents or dropping them off (Fr. Pier Damiano, Sister Alfonsina, and Sister Eleonora Bifarini). Giulia Donati, a Jewish survivor, has testified that Bartali delivered false identity documents to the house where she and her family were hiding, but was turned away by the Gentile woman who was sheltering them (who panicked). Renzo Ventura, the son of Jewish survivors, has testified that his mother and grandparents found out soon after the war ended that Gino was the one who brought their identity documents to Florence.

We know of Gino's close relationship with Dalla Costa from interviews with two of Dalla Costa's colleagues (Fr. Attilio Piccini and Fr. Giulio Villani) and interviews with Adriana and Andrea Bartali. Unfortunately, Gino left no detailed firsthand account of how Cardinal Dalla Costa asked him to join the network, or on what exact date this happened in the fall of 1943. Interviews with Gino's wife, Adriana, and son Andrea confirmed the meeting occurred and that it was likely late November or early December 1943.

We used the testimony of another individual, a priest named Don Leto Casini, recruited by Dalla Costa to work in the same network, to construct the scene of Dalla Costa asking Gino to join the network. Marcolin's *Firenze 1943–'45: Anni di terrore e di fame, fascisti e antifascisti*— (Firenze: Edizioni Medicea, 1994), illuminated the day-to-day life in Florence at that time. We also relied on extensive interviews with Gino's family and his closest friends, as well as interviews with Dalla Costa's colleagues and Italian Jews whom Dalla Costa helped, to characterize how each man would have likely behaved during this meeting.

111 **Dalla Costa had never been one to call just to chat** Author interview with Attilio Piccini, October 20, 2009. Piccini worked with Cardinal Dalla Costa at the Sparugoru Murbis convent and, in later years, helped Dalla Costa's secretary, Monsignor Giacomo Meneghello.

112 **"Old things, old places"** Henry James, *Collected Travel Writings: The Continent* (New York: Penguin, 1993), 533.

112 **first war damages** Marcolin, *Firenze 1943–'45,* 52.

112 **stagings of Shakespeare and Chekhov** Ibid., 39.

112 **Florentines traded their valuables** Ibid., 51.

112 **Scavenging garbage at market for food and hunting stray cats** Carole Counihan, *Around the Tuscan Table* (New York: Routledge, 2004), 52.

113 **Description of cardinal's secretary, Giacomo Meneghello** Author interview with Lya Quitt Haberman, October 20, 2011. Haberman was saved by Monsignor Meneghello.

113 **Cardinal's study** As described by Father Ruffino Niccacci in Alexander Ramati, *The Assisi Underground: Assisi and the Nazi Occupation as told by Padre Rufino Niccacci* (London: Unwin, 1978), 47.

113 **Elia Dalla Costa's appearance** Photograph of Dalla Costa at Gino Bartali's wedding, November 14, 1940, Fotocronache Olympia, Milano.

113 **Seventy-one years old** "Milestones," *Time,* December 29, 1961.

113 **Dalla Costa as a rumored papal candidate** Elia Dalla Costa file, Ministero

dell' Interno, Divisione di Pubblica Sicurezza, Divisione Polizia Politica 13 157, 2 Pacco #378, Fascicoli #70, 378, #9. Already in 1933 (on March 19 and April 25), secret reports by Fascist spies discuss Dalla Costa as one of the probable successors to the Pope.

113 **a quick judge of character** Author interview with Attilio Piccini, October 20, 2009.

113 **"like a father does on his own sons"** Ibid.

114 **Dalla Costa's involvement in rescue effort** For discussion of how and when Cardinal Elia Dalla Costa started helping, see Susan Zuccotti, *The Italians and the Holocaust: Persecution, Rescue, and Survival* (New York: Basic Books, 1987), 211; Susan Zuccotti, *Holocaust Odysseys: The Jews of Saint-Martin-Vésubie and Their Flight through France and Italy* (New Haven: Yale University Press, 2007), 161; Susan Zuccotti, "The Rescue of Jews in Italy and the Existence of a Papal Directive," in *Nazi Europe and the Final Solution,* edited by David Bankier and Israel Gutman (Israel: Yad Vashem, 2003), 532; Louis Goldman, *Amici per la vita* (Florence: Coppini, 1999), 59–60.

114 **Meneghello received Jewish refugees** Zuccotti, "The Rescue of Jews in Italy," 532; Susan Zuccotti, *Under His Very Windows: The Vatican and the Holocaust in Italy* (New Haven: Yale University Press, 2000), 252.

114 **Another priest recruited to reach out to various convents** Zuccotti, *Holocaust Odysseys,* 161; Zuccotti, *Under His Very Windows,* 253.

114 **"He told us to peremptorily"** Interview with Monsignor Giulio Villani at the Archivio della Curia Fiorentina, as quoted in Alberati, *Mille diavoli,* 86–90.

115 **Cardinal houses and feeds several Jews** Author interview with Lya Haberman Quitt, October 20, 2011.

115 **Cardinal's speaking manner** Author interview with Attilio Piccini, October 20, 2009.

115 **refugees needed food, shelter, and false identity documents** Zuccotti, *Holocaust Odysseys,* 160.

115 **Threat of imprisonment, execution, or deportation** Casini, *Ricordi,* 49–50. After the Carta di Verona, which identified Jews as enemies of the state, it was widely understood that helping an enemy of the state was dangerous and punishable. Author interview with Dr. Iael Nidam-Orvieto, editor-in-chief of Yad Vashem Publications, January 24, 2011.

115 **Danger of Italian Fascists** David Tutaev, *The Consul of Florence* (London: Secker & Warburg, 1966), 142.

116 **Importance of secrecy** Casini discusses the importance of secrecy, as Fascist spies were everywhere. On November 26, 1943, several members of the network including Casini and the Rabbi of Florence were arrested after a Fascist spy had infiltrated their group. The Rabbi of Florence ultimately perished in Auschwitz. Casini, *Ricordi,* 52–53.

116 **an alarming piece of news** Author interview with Dr. Iael Nidam-Orvieto, editor-in-chief of Yad Vashem Publications, January 24, 2011.

117 **Giorgio Goldenberg taken to live at the Santa Marta Institute** Author interview with Giorgio Goldenberg. For additional details on how Dalla Costa

approached local convents to house Jewish refugees, see Zuccotti, *Under His Very Windows,* 253.

117 **a reward of anywhere from one thousand to nine thousand lire per person** Zuccotti, *The Italians,* 156.

117 **Average factory worker earnings** Ibid.

117 **Allied prisoners worth just 1,800 lire in reward** Marcolin, *Firenze 1943–'45,* 28.

117 ***Carta di Verona,* "Those belonging to the Jewish race are foreigners"** Zuccotti, *Under His Very Windows,* 215–16.

118 **Arrest danger for all Jews on Italian soil** Zuccotti, *The Italians,* 159–60; Alexander Stille, *Benevolence and Betrayal: Five Italian Jewish Families Under Fascism* (New York: Picador, 1991), 259; Zuccotti, *Under His Very Windows,* 254–57.

118 **Goldenberg and Sizzi's meeting** Author interview with Giorgio Goldenberg.

118 **Sizzi's background** Adam Smulevich, interview with Andrea Bartali, *Pagine Ebraiche,* February 2011, discussing Andrea Bartali's reaction to Giorgio Goldenberg's testimony; Alberati, *Mille diavoli,* 13 and 75.

118 **Gino's real estate investments** Author interviews with Andrea and Adriana Bartali, July 17, 2009; Sepember 14, 2009; August 3, 2009. In that era, real estate was a popular investment for cyclists with money. Giorgio Goldenberg and Andrea Bartali believed that Gino owned the apartment, but it's also possible that Gino leased the apartment under his own name and let the Goldenbergs live in it secretly.

118 **Change in Gino's demeanor** Author interview with Adriana Bartali, July 17, 2009.

119 **"It was something that we all had to do"** Author interview with Father Arturo Paoli, a participant in a Lucca-based Jewish refugee rescue network, February 17, 2007.

120 **November raid described by Niccacci** Ramati, *The Assisi Underground,* 45–47.

120 **"I saw a whole family lined up against a wall"** Ibid.

121 **Niccacci's appearance** Author's review of Rufino Niccacci photos at the Franciscan historical archive in Assisi in February 2007.

121 **Niccacci's family background** Author interview with Rufino Niccacci's nephew, Alviero Niccacci, October 26, 2009. While some sources identify Niccacci as "Nicacci," we consulted Niccacci's family and have used their preferred spelling for their surname.

121 **certain earthly pleasures** Ramati, *The Assisi Underground,* 2.

121 **Niccacci's work with first group of Jewish refugees in Assisi** Ibid., 10–17.

121 **Description of Dalla Costa in his study** Ibid., 47, and Casini, *Ricordi,* 79–80.

121 **Scene and dialogue between Niccacci and Dalla Costa** As described by Niccacci in Ramati, *The Assisi Underground,* 44–50.

122 **Gino prepares Goldenberg apartment** Gino left no written record about

how he first prepared the Goldenberg apartment. We constructed this scene on the basis that we know Gino regularly gathered foods from farmers he knew to help several people displaced by the war (Paolo Alberati, *Gino Bartali: Mille diavoli in corpo* [Firenze: Giunti, 2006], 75; Gino Bartali with Mario Pancera, *La mia storia* (Milano: Stampa Sportiva, 1958), 58. We also drew on Giorgio Goldenberg's memories of his parents' time in the apartment (*La Vita in Diretta* [*Rai Uno*] segment featuring Giorgio Goldenberg, which aired Thursday, January 27, 2011) and our interviews with Eldad Doron (December 20, 2010, and February 1, 2011), husband of the late Tea Goldenberg, who confirmed that Tea had shared these details.

CHAPTER 8. THE COUNTERFEITERS' RING

Gino never wrote a detailed account of what happened during his bike trips from Florence to Assisi, and spoke about it only in passing with his family and closest friends. Consequently, to create these scenes we relied on the accounts of various other people who either interacted with Gino during this time or witnessed his work in the network.

In our account of Gino's time in Assisi, one important source was Alexander Ramati's *The Assisi Underground*. As noted earlier, Ramati was a Polish Jewish war journalist who first met Niccacci and Luigi Brizi when he arrived with the Allied soldiers liberating Assisi in June 1944. Vowing to write about the story, he later returned to interview Niccacci in depth, as well as Trento Brizi and several Italian Jews who spent part of World War II hidden in Assisi. When Ramati's book was first published in 1978, it was generally well received, although some faulted it for focusing narrowly on Niccacci's perspective of life in wartime Assisi. Ramati, however, deliberately chose to make his book an "as told to" narrative, with all the benefits and limitations of that structure, and to reflect his close collaboration with Niccacci. He was also committed to his reporting. When one journalist raised questions about certain facts in the book, several of the key figures from the book provided written testimonies and notarized affidavits confirming them. These included people who had been saved (Enrico Maionica, Paolo Jozsa, and Paolo Gay), nuns who sheltered Jews in Assisi, and Trento Brizi. We reviewed these documents with Father Marino Bigaroni at the Franciscan historical archive in Assisi in 2007.

We used Ramati's book primarily for Niccacci's direct interactions with Gino and Cardinal Dalla Costa during the war, since Niccacci was the only eyewitness who left an account of these events. Niccacci's nephew, Alviero Niccacci, provided helpful details about the Niccacci family and his uncle's personality. We interviewed Padre Pier Damiano, a member of Niccacci's monastery who directly witnessed Gino's involvement in this network, who spoke with Niccacci about the network and provided a wealth of information to characterize Niccacci, given his years working closely with him. He also showed us key parts of the San Damiano monastery where Niccacci and Gino interacted. We interviewed Sister Eleonora Bifarini at the San Quirico monastery, who spoke with Gino when he arrived at the convent. The nuns were cloistered, so only one nun, Sister Alfonsina, met Gino face-to-face. Sister Alfonsina is now deceased, but discussed Gino's involvement with a journalist from the newspaper *La Nazione* and with an Italian writer, Paolo Alberati, as part of his research for his book *Gino Bartali: Mille diavoli in corpo* (Firenze: Giunti, 2006).

In order to further flesh out the Brizis, we drew on a detailed published interview Trento Brizi gave before he died. We also conducted several interviews with Ugo Sciamanna, the grandson of Luigi and the nephew of Trento Brizi. Ugo recalled Ramati interviewing his uncle Trento at length (Luigi was deceased by this point), and he was able to confirm the veracity of details regarding the Brizis. At the time of our interviews, Ugo worked out of his grandfather and uncle's print shop (now a souvenir store) where all the printing had occurred. Ugo graciously allowed us to inspect the printer that had been used to make the identity documents, and showed us the mechanics of its operation.

Andrea and Adriana Bartali described Gino's outlook on the war to us, sharing some of his stories, and what he had thought about some of the daily conditions. Friends and teammates also gave us a sense of him as a man at that moment. One other important source was the extremely detailed testimony given by Enrico Maionica, a key player in the document fabrication network in Assisi, before he died (University of Southern California Shoah Foundation interview with Enrico Maionica by Susanna Segrè, April 30, 1998).

123 **"Don't wait for me this evening"** Author interview with Adriana and Andrea Bartali; Alberati, *Mille diavoli,* 80–84.

124 **Description of photos** We reviewed the false IDs of Renzo Ventura's mother and grandparents, who learned soon after the war that Gino Bartali had brought documents to Florence through Dalla Costa's network (author interview, July 27, 2009); false identity documents of Graziella Viterbi made by the Brizi press (author interviews on July 14, 2009, and August 31, 2009).

125 **Pedestrians streamed across sidewalks** Alberto Marcolin, *Firenze 1943–'45: Anni di terrore e di fame, fascisti e antifascisti* (Firenze: Edizioni Medicea, 1994), 11–12, 20.

125 **Description of the German SS** Louis Goldman, *Friends for Life: The Story of a Holocaust Survivor and His Rescuers* (Mahwah, NJ: Paulist Press, 2008), 71.

125 **"He liked to say everything," "He never stopped talking"** Author interview with Alfredo Martini, July 16, 2009.

126 **"grandfather taken for walks"** Gino Bartali with Mario Pancera, *La mia storia* (Milano: Stampa Sportiva, 1958), 65.

126 **"most fertile years"** Ibid.

126 **Gino's stop at the train station in Terontola** Much less is known about this episode because only one direct eyewitness, Ivo Faltoni, is still alive and none of the deceased witnesses left written testimonies. When Faltoni was a young boy in Terontola during the war years, he witnessed Gino's visits (author interviews, July 18, 2009; September 12 and 13, 2009; September 19, 2010). The son of the tailor who made Gino sandwiches during these visits and the son of another resident, the town taxi driver, also confirmed that their fathers had talked of Gino Bartali's visits to the town during this period. (Author interview with Luigi Magari, November 5, 2009; author interview with Luciano Batani, November 5, 2009). In 2008, a memorial plaque was mounted in the Terontola train station to honor Gino's work during the war ferrying documents between Florence and Assisi.

127 **"That's where one was most likely to get cornered"** Goldman, *Friends for Life,* 116–17.

128 **Life at the Santa Marta boardinghouse** To describe Santa Marta and the boys' daily routine during the war, we drew on our interviews with Giorgio Goldenberg; the testimony of Emanuele Pacifici, who was also sheltered at Santa Marta (USC Shoah Foundation interview by Silvia Antonucci, March 10, 1998), and our interview with Suor Mariana, who was the headmistress in the years following the war. While she was not there during the war years, she had spoken extensively with her predecessors about this period and the role Santa Marta played sheltering Jews during the war.

129 **"hunger was almost a blessing"** Cesare Sacerdoti, 2007 speech given about his memories of being a Jewish child in the Madonna Del Grappa orphanage in Montecatini.

129 **Gino getting dressed in the morning in Perugia** Niccacci's account to Ramati of Gino's arrival at the monastery describes Gino's attire and Gino timing his trip to Assisi (Ramati, *The Assisi Underground,* 57–59). We based our scene on that information and our interviews with Gino's teammates Giovanni Corrieri and Renzo Soldani, who described how Gino typically started his training rides. In addition, we traveled these roads by car to get a better sense of the landscape.

130 **"warming up the engine"** Gino Bartali with Romano Beghelli and Marcello Lazzerini, *La leggenda di Bartali* (Firenze: Ponte Alle Grazie Editori, 1992), 143.

131 **"You'll catch a cold, Bartali!"** The dialogue between Gino and Niccacci in this scene is drawn from Ramati, *Assisi Underground,* 57–59.

131 **Description of Gino unscrewing his bike seat and removing photos** Ramati, *The Assisi Underground,* 57–59; author interviews with Padre Pier Damiano (July 29, 2009; December 2, 2009; and December 4, 2010); author interviews with Andrea and Adriana Bartali (July 17, 2009; August 4, 2009; and September 14, 2009).

131 **Niccacci hiding cache, and Niccaci and Gino dialogue in refectory** Ramati, *The Assisi Underground,* 57–59.

131 **Description of refectory** Author visit to monastery and refectory, July 29, 2009.

131 **"I'll be champion again one day"** Ramati, *Assisi Underground,* 57–59.

132 **Padre Pier Damiano sees Gino** Author interviews with Padre Pier Damiano, one of Father Niccacci's students, July 29, 2009; December 2, 2009; and December 4, 2010.

132 **Description of identity documents** Viterbi's false documents; Franchi's false documents; Giorgina Rietti's false documents.

132 **Necessity of IDs to everyday life** Susan Zuccotti, *Under His Very Windows: The Vatican and the Holocaust in Italy* (New Haven: Yale University Press, 2000), 175.

132 **"A man without identity documents"** Author interview with Giorgio Goldenberg, January 25, 2011.

132 **Punishment for false document fabrication** "Due falsificatori di tessere annonarie condannati a morte a Berlino," *Il Telegrafo,* July 7,1943: 4. Stories like this continued to appear in newspapers in the later months of the war.

133 **Luigi Brizi, his early life and family background** Author interview with Ugo Sciamanna, July 28 and August 31, 2009; photo of Luigi Brizi in the Assisi rescue effort file at the Franciscan Historical Archive.

133 **Brizi printing store** Author interview with Ugo Sciamanna, July 27, 2009.

134 **Brizi was an atheist** Ibid.

134 **"Luigi Brizi, are you going to help them?"** Ramati, *The Assisi Underground,* 35.

135 **"I will do it"** Ibid., 37.

135 **Brizi's request that his son not know about the counterfeit printing** *Ibid;* Andrea Biavardi, "La straordinaria storia di uno stampatore di Assisi," *Gente,* June 15, 1989.
135 **"I fought for three years on the front"** Trento Brizi as quoted in Biavardi, Ibid.
135 **Details of Brizis making documents** Ibid.
135 **"making prints was like making fritters"** Ibid.
136 **"What a scare" and Brizi's account of speaking with Niccacci** Ibid.
137 **Enrico Maionica's background and arrival in Assisi** USC interview with Maionica.
137 **The fabrication of the false identity documents** USC interview with Maionica; Biavardi, "La straordinaria storia di uno stampatore di Assisi;" Ramati, *The Assisi Underground,* 40–42.
138 **"I put three- or four-year-old tags"** USC interview with Maionica.
138 **"He would arrive with his bicycle"** Sister Alfonsina quoted in Maurizio Naldini, "Cosi Bartali salvo' gli ebrei, 1943–44," *La Nazione,* July 2, 2003.
138 **another nun, Sister Eleonora, also spoke with him** Author interview with Sister Eleonara Bifarini at the San Quirico Monastery, July 29, 2009.
139 **Punishment for curfew violation** In a tribunal of September 8, 1943, three Florentines were condemned to a year in prison for violating curfew. Marcolin, *Firenze 1943–'45,* 20.
139 **Episode in Bastia Umbra and "sacrilegious,"** Interview with Andrea Bartali in Gaspare di Sclafani, "La Sua Fuga Per I Giusti," *Novella Duemila,* October 20, 2005: 77.
139 **"If you are stopped"** Marcolin, *Firenze 1943–'45,* 10. Italics are our emphasis.
139 **dove into a ditch** Bartali, *La leggenda,* 123.
139 **"I was neither hot nor cold about politics"** Bartali, *La mia storia,* 35.
140 **Gino's checkpoint encounters** Although Gino left no written description of the minute details of going through a checkpoint, we know from Father Niccacci's account in *The Assisi Underground* that Gino's face was so well known to the Fascists and "the police at the German checkpoints that they simply waved him on, convinced that he was training"(57–59). We have constructed this scene on the basis of others facing similar experiences at checkpoints. Louis Goldman described seeing a German soldier demand to see his father's identity documents in occupied Italy in *Friends for Life* (32). Gino's friends shared various stories about his capacity to charm strangers. Photos from Gino's races in the 1940s also reveal how popular he was with soldiers.
141 **Documents handed over to one of the cardinal's assistants** From the Frankenthals, we know that while Gino brought their documents to Florence, a separate intermediary delivered them. This would have been the most effective way to maintain the security of the group, so it would likely have been the normal modus operandi. Some of these intermediaries likely worked for the cardinal, while others would have just been affiliated with the rescue initiative.
141 **Frankenthals who became the Franchis** Interview with Renzo Ventura on

July 27, 2009. Mr. Ventura's grandparents were the Frankenthals and became the Franchis.

141 **refugees received their documents** Giorgio Goldenberg believes his parents received their false identity documents directly from Gino. Author interview with Goldenberg, January 25, 2011.

141 **Donati story in Lido di Camaiore** Author interviews with Giulia Donati, October 24, 2010; January 26 and 28, 2011.

142 **Danger of life in Assisi** Author interview with Giorgina Rietti, September 11, 2010. Rietti spent time during this period in both Assisi and Perugia.

142 **The final scene and dialogue featuring Trento Brizi and Niccacci** Biavardi, "La straordinaria storia di uno stampatore di Assisi."

143 **"Yes, the idea of taking part"** Ibid.

CHAPTER 9. FREE FALL

144 **"Germany offers you work"** Alberto Marcolin, *Firenze 1943–'45: Anni di terrore e di fame, fascisti e antifascisti* (Firenze: Edizioni Medicea, 1994), 34–35.

144 **twelve thousand workers went on strike** Luciano Casella, *The European War of Liberation: Tuscany and the Gothic Line,* trans. by Jean M. Ellis D'Alessandro (Florence: La Nuova Europa, 1983), 92.

145 **were executed publicly** Ibid., 93–97.

145 **Adriana Bartali discovers she is pregnant** Gino Bartali with Mario Pancera, *La mia storia* (Milano: Stampa Sportiva, 1958), 58. Author interview with Andrea Bartali, September 14, 2009.

145 **Olive oil, soup bones, and bread rations** Casella, *The European War,* 93.

145 **"anxious personality"** Author interview with Adriana Bartali, July 17, 2009.

146 **Gino reports on the placement of German checkpoints** Ramati, *The Assisi Underground,* 68, 96.

146 **Gino met some of the human smugglers** Ibid., 76–77.

146 **When a German patrol killed one of these smugglers** Ibid., 99.

146 **Mamma Cornelia** Author interviews with Giorgio Goldenberg; USC Shoah Foundation interview with Emanuele Pacifici by Silvia Antonucci, March 10, 1998.

147 **more than 6,500 Jews** Susan Zuccotti, *The Italians and the Holocaust: Persecution, Rescue, and Survival* (New York: Basic Books, 1987), 190.

147 **Giorgio leaves Santa Marta and life in the cantina** Author interviews with Giorgio Goldenberg, December 20, 2010; January 25, 2011; and April 4, 2011. Author interviews with Eldad Doron (husband of the late Tea Goldenberg, who shared her war memories with Eldad), December 10, 2010; February 1, 2011.

147 **"What can you do if you are closed in a room"** Author interview with Giorgio Goldenberg, January 25, 2011.

148 **the shrill cry of an air-raid alarm** Author interviews with Giorgio Goldenberg.

148 **the sound of German jackboots** Author interviews with Eldad Doron.

148 **Air raids in Florence** Author interviews with Adriana Bartali. Louis Gold-

man was a young boy in Florence during World War II and described the experience of air raids at the end of the war in great detail in his memoir *Friends for Life: The Story of a Holocaust Survivor and His Rescuers* (Mahwah, NJ: Paulist Press, 2008), 84–85, 145–46.

148 **"The air reverberated"** Goldman, *Friends for Life,* 145.

149 **sporadic gunshots** Author interview with Adriana Bartali, August 3, 2009.

149 **shells could appear unannounced** Goldman, *Friends for Life,* 202.

149 **The shell that dropped near Adriana** Author interview with Adriana Bartali, August 3, 2009.

149 ***If it had exploded*** Ibid.

149 **"Try to line up, day after day"** Gino Bartali, *Tutto sbagliato, tutto da rifare* (Milano: Mondadori, 1979), 76.

150 **"war neurosis"** Interview with Dr. Peter Faux, psychiatrist, March 1, 2011.

150 **"Everywhere, I felt like I was being tracked"** Gino Bartali, "Mes Memoires," *Bibliotheque France-Soir* (Paris: Serie Sport, 1949), 42.

150 **Gino is summoned to Villa Triste** Bartali, *La mia storia,* 57–58; Paolo Alberati, *Gino Bartali: Mille diavoli in corpo* (Firenze: Giunti, 2006), 20; Leo Turrini, *Bartali: L'uomo che salvo l'Italia pedalando* (Milan: Arnaldo Mondadori Editore, 2004), 73–74; author interview with Andrea Bartali.

150 **"These were times when life"** Gino Bartali with Romano Beghelli and Marcello Lazzerini, *La leggenda di Bartali* (Firenze: Ponte Alle Grazie Editori, 1992), 125.

150 **"an insane Minotaur," "the Himmler of Italy"** David Tutaev consulted the private letters and papers of the consul of Florence during World War II for his account of Major Mario Carità in *The Consul of Florence* (London: Secker & Warburg), 67–68.

151 **"The close-carpeted corridors"** Tutaev, *The Consul of Florence,* 126–27.

151 **"a sinister place that aroused terror"** Bartali, *La leggenda,* 124.

151 ***How will I ever get out of here?*** Bartali, *La leggenda,* 124; Bartali as quoted in Turrini, *Bartali,* 72.

151 **Torture techniques used in Villa Triste** Tutaev, *The Consul of Florence,* 76–78, 126–128.

151 **he fired his revolver** Ibid., 76

151 **"Neapolitan songs and Schubert's Unfinished Symphony"** Ibid., 74–75.

152 **"thick whips, rods of steel, pincers, manacles"** Ibid., 127, 128.

152 **"froglike mouth," and "hooded eyelids"** Ibid., 68.

152 **Conversation between Carità and Gino** Bartali, *La mia storia,* 57–58; Bartali, *La leggenda,* 124; Paolo Alberati, *Mille diavoli,* 20.

154 **"If Bartali says"** Comments by Olesindo Salmi in Bartali, *La leggenda,* 124.

154 **Description of Olesindo Salmi** photo of Olesindo Salmi (also known as "Selmi") in Riccardo Caporale, *La "Banda Carità": Storia del Reparto Servizi Speciali (1943–1945)* (Lucca: Edizioni S. Marco Litotipo, 2005), 397.

154 **now living in downtown Florence** Bartali, *La leggenda,* 124.

155 **Destruction of Florence as the Germans withdrew** Tutaev, *The Consul of*

Florence, 203–4; Casella, *The European War,* 229; Carlo Francovich, *La Resistenza in Firenze, A cura di Carlo Francovich e Giovanni Verni* (Firenze: La nuova Italia, 1969), 253; Marcolin, *Firenze 1943–'45,* 72.

155 **ordered to evacuate their homes** Casella, *The European War,* 234.

155 **the famed Pitti Palace** Tutaev, *The Consul of Florence,* 225.

155 **"It is as if a cross-section of London's population"** Ibid., 255.

156 **"From this moment on"** Casella, *The European War,* 236–37.

156 **"The sky toward the Palazzo Pitti"** Diary entries of Miss Gladys Hutton as cited by David Tutaev, *The Consul of Florence,* 240.

156 **"What is it, Papà?"** Author interview with Andrea Bartali, July 17, 2009.

156 **A huge load of explosives** Marcolin, *Firenze 1943–'45,* 75.

156 **"the most artistic one"** Tutaev, *The Consul of Florence,* 245; Marcolin, *Firenze 1943–'45,* 50.

156 **"The spectacle of Florence was devastating"** Bartali, *La leggenda,* 124.

157 **The stillborn son** Bartali, *La mia storia,* 58; Bartali, *La leggenda,* 119; author interview with Andrea Bartali, September 14, 2009.

157 **The scene near Campo di Marte** Tutaev, *Consul of Florence,* 225.

157 **The houses in the neighborhood nearby** Marcolin, *Firenze 1943–'45,* 51.

158 **Gino and Adriana consoled** Author interview with Andrea Bartali, September 14, 2009.

158 **the first Allied tanks** Marcolin, *Firenze 1943–'45,* 74, 80.

158 ***"Gli inglesi son arrivati!"*** Author interview with Giorgio Goldenberg, January 25, 2011.

159 **"My heart seemed to want to burst"** Cassella, *The European War,* 249.

159 **"God Save the King"** Ramati, *The Assisi Underground,* 170.

160 **"The Jews of Italy have Italian blood"** Ibid., 171.

160 **an estimated 330 Jews had been saved** The 330 Jews saved in Florence by the efforts of Cardinal Dalla Costa and his associates included 110 Italian and 220 Foreign Jews. Susan Zuccotti, *Under His Very Windows: The Vatican and the Holocaust in Italy* (New Haven: Yale University Press, 2000), 253.

160 **three hundred Jews had been saved in Assisi and Perugia** Estimates vary for the number of Jews saved in Assisi. Of a range of 100, 200, and 300, we have chosen the middle ground of 200. One survivor, Graziella Viterbi, put the number at 100 (Zuccotti, *Under His Very Windows,* 386.) Father Brunacci, a member of the network, put the number at 200 (Zuccotti, *Under His Very Windows,* 386). Father Niccacci put the number at 300 (Ramati, *The Assisi Underground,* 173.) In Perugia, 100 Jews were saved (Susan Zuccotti, *The Italians and the Holocaust: Persecution, Rescue, and Survival* [New York: Basic Books, 1987] 215). While no final figures exist on how many Jews in other parts of Italy benefited from the blank false identity documents created on Brizi's press, it is worth noting that as a foot-powered printing press that could also be powered by electricity, it was capable of printing hundreds of documents in short order. Enrico Maionica, one of the key members in the networks, said many of the false identity documents he created went to additional cities including Genoa and Rome (USC interview with Maionica).

160 **In little more than eighteen months** Zuccotti, *Under His Very Windows,* 324; Zuccotti, *The Italians,* xvii.

160 **a record of how many identity documents Gino carried** The precise number of photos and false identity documents carried by Gino remains unknown. Sister Alfonisna (who is now deceased) told author Paolo Alberati that she estimated that Gino had come through her convent about forty times. Nevertheless, given the amorphous and secretive nature of the network, and the fact that there were other couriers, it's likely that we will never know the full extent of Gino's work.

161 **corpses of Mussolini and one of his lovers** Bartali, *La leggenda,* 129; Ray Mosely, *Mussolini: The last 600 days of il Duce* (Lanham, MD: Taylor, 2004), 312–19; Alberati, *Mille diavoli,* 97–98; Carlo Maria Lomartire, *Insurrezione: 14 luglio 1948* (Milano: Mondadori, 2006), 140–43.

161 **"It was an obscene spectacle"** Bartali as quoted in Turrini, *Bartali,* 78.

161 ***This is not the Italy I dreamed of for myself*** Ibid.

PART III

CHAPTER 10. GINETTACCIO

165 **"What we had earned"** Gino Bartali, *Tutto sbagliato, tutto da rifare* (Milano: Mondadori, 1979), 80.

166 **"I think that all that time"** Bartali, Ibid.,76.

166 **"He taught me that poverty"** Marc Dewinter, "Gino the Pious," *Cycle Sport,* July 1999: 40 .

166 **"like clowns in a traveling circus"** Bartali as quoted in Paolo Alberati, *Gino Bartali: Mille diavoli in corpo* (Firenze: Giunti, 2006), 97.

166 **"The triumphant years"** Bartali, *Tutto sbagliato,* 77.

167 **Haphazard races and unusual prizes** William Fotheringham, *Fallen Angel: The Passion of Fausto Coppi* (London: Yellow Jersey Press, 2009), chapter 4.

167 **"We were all really hard up"** Bartali, *Tutto sbagliato,* 79.

167 **"I ended up completely demoralized"** Gino Bartali with Mario Pancera, *La mia storia* (Milano: Stampa Sportiva, 1958), 62.

167 **"Then I found my strength again"** Ibid.

168 **"the inseparable companion of the peasant"** Bruno Roghi in a 1946 column in *La Gazzetta Dello Sport* as quoted in Forgacs and Gundle, *Mass Culture and Italian Society from Fascism to the Cold War* (Bloomington: Indiana University Press, 2008), 13–14.

168 **Car cost in 1948** Ibid., 13. Forgacs and Gundle note that the "cheapest car, the Fiat Topolino 500B, launched in 1948, when the average wage was 139,000 lire, cost 650,000 lire."

168 **3.5 million bikes and 184,000 cars in 1947** Ibid.

168 **Rita Hayworth's support for Gino** "Oggi il Tour parte da Parigi. Rita Hayworth e Tito Schipa, intervistati, danno favorito Bartali. Le ire de Hedy Lamarr," *Il Tirreno,* June 30, 1948: 1.

168 **Gino was also a Hayworth fan** Gino Bartali with Romano Beghelli and

Marcello Lazzerini, *La leggenda di Bartali* (Firenze: Ponte Alle Grazie Editori, 1992), 170.

169 **Severity of bike theft in Italy** Author interview with President Oscar Scalfaro, October 7, 2009.

169 **Six hundred thousand agricultural day laborers** Paul Ginsborg, *A History of Contemporary Italy: Society and Politics, 1943–1988* (New York: Palgrave Macmillan, 2003), 114.

169 **Italian gas shortages** "Benzina a 118 lire," *Il Tirreno,* June 16, 1948: 1.

169 **Unemployment rate of over sixty percent in 1948** "Due milioni e mezzo i disoccupati in Italia," *Il Tirreno,* June 24, 1948: 4.

170 **"half-naked children crowded together"** H. W. Heinsheimer, "Le Tour de France," *Holiday,* July 1949: 78.

170 **750,000 Italians working abroad** Benjo Maso, *Wir Alle Waren Götter: Die berühmte Tour de France von 1948* (Bielefeld: Covadonga Verlag, 2006), 275–76.

170 **"utterly honest and sincere" and "Italy's most brilliant politician"** Emmet Hughes, "Pre-election Report on Italy," *Life,* April 12, 1948: 31–32.

171 **De Gasperi friendship with Gino Bartali,** *La leggenda,* 198.

171 **"influence the course of European history"** Hughes, "Pre-election report on Italy," 29.

171 **"Now I didn't have the worry about the authorities"** Bartali, *La mia storia,* 63.

172 **"Yes, I had become *Ginettaccio*"** Ibid., 65.

172 **"I was slow to get in gear"** Ibid., 63.

173 **Espresso coffee consumption** Fotheringham, *Fallen Angel,* 102.

173 **"The cigarette that I had avoided"** Gino Bartali, "Qui giace il campione fra la polvere," *Tempo,* December 20, 1952: 17. Alfredo Martini, a teammate of Gino's who was often charged with fetching cigarettes for Gino from fans, put it bluntly, saying, "Gino smoked, and he smoked a lot, especially after the war when he was at his strongest."

173 **"more of a life of a normal person"** Giovanni Corrieri interview in Alberati, *Mille diavoli,* 120.

173 **Gino training at nighttime** Author interview with Adriana Bartali, August 3, 2009.

173 **Gino's training regimen** See Gino's autobiographies *La mia storia* and *Tutto sbagliato* for a wide-ranging discussion of his training methods. See also the interviews with Gino in the documentary *Fausto Coppi Story—'Il Campionissimo,' Part 1* (Bromley Video, 2000).

173 **Importance of rest days for older racers** Author interview with Dr. Massimo Testa, a physician and exercise physiologist, April 15, 2010.

173 **explosive, top-end, ability for hard accelerations** Author interview with Chris Carmichael, a coach of contemporary Tour cyclists, April 27, 2010; author interview with Dr. Massimo Testa.

173 **muscular endurance improves** Author interview with Dr. Massimo Testa.

174 **Effectiveness of shorter and more intensive rides** Author interview with Dr. Massimo Testa; author interview with Chris Carmichael.

174 **"total glory for the winner"** Gianni Granzotto, "Bartali vinse Marie," *L'Europeo,* August 2–8, 1948: 3.

174 **anti-Catholic slur** The heckler called Gino a "lying priest." Paolo Costa, *Gino Bartali: la vita, le imprese, le polemiche* (Portogruaro: Ediciclo Editore, 2001), 82.

174 **Gino used to mobilize support for Christian Democrats** Stefano Pivato, "Italian Cycling and the Creation of a Catholic Hero: The Bartali Myth," in *European Heroes: Myth, Identity, Sport,* edited by Richard Holt, J. A. Mangan, and Pierre Lanfranchi (London: Frank Cass, 1996), 135.

175 **"De Gasperi on a bike"** Indro Montanelli, "Il De Gasperi del ciclismo," *Corriere della Sera,* June 11, 1947.

175 **"With a crushed face and not at all handsome"** Ibid.

175 **Gino offered spot on the electoral list for deputies** John Foot, *Pedalare! Pedalare!* (London: Bloomsbury, 2011), 129.

175 **Pope Pius XII citing Bartali** *Discorsi e Radiomessaggi di Sua Santità Pio XII,* IX, Nono anno di Pontificato, 2 marzo 1947–1 marzo 1948, Tipografia Poliglotta Vaticana, 213–20, Translation from Foot, *Pedalare!* 128.

175 **"unmistakable" and "ready to struggle for their faith"** Pivato, "Italian Cycling and the Creation of a Catholic Hero," 134.

175 **Catholic Action outreach to voters** "The Nations: How to Hang On," *Time,* April 19, 1948: 6.

175 **moral suasion campaign** Interview with Father Lucio Migliaccio, a clergy leader of one of these campaigns, in CNN *Cold War* documentary series: Episode 3, "Marshall Plan (1947–1951)," released November 10, 1998.

176 **American involvement in Italian elections** Beyond general political histories of the era, we consulted the CNN *Cold War* documentary series, which features interviews with different key figures, and Tim Weiner's *Legacy of Ashes: The History of the Central Intelligence Agency* (New York: Doubleday, 2007).

176 **"covert psychological operations designed"** National Security Council Order as quoted in Weiner, *Legacy of Ashes,* 29.

177 **"illegal from the start"** CIA Agent F. Mark Wyatt as quoted in Weiner, *Legacy of Ashes,* 30.

177 **"into the bank accounts"** Ibid., 30–31.

177 **"Donors were instructed"** Ibid.

177 **10 million dollars of cash** Ibid.

177 **Money in black suitcases at Hassler Hotel** "F. Mark Wyatt, 86, C.I.A. Officer, Is Dead," *New York Times,* July 6, 2006.

177 **"We would have liked"** Weiner, *Legacy of Ashes,* 30–31.

178 **Reporter's estimate of Russian aid** Hughes, "Pre-election report on Italy," 32.

178 **"a sort of European Wisconsin"** Ibid., 29.

178 **"cloven foot of the devil"** Ginsborg, *A History of Contemporary Italy,* 118.

178 **smearing De Gasperi as a Fascist** "Togliatti profetizza per De Gasperi la fine di Mussolini e di Hitler," *Il Tirreno,* February 19, 1948: 1.
178 **death threat to De Gasperi** Ibid.
178 **Lloyd's of London offering odds on event** "De Gasperi a un terzo e Togliatti alla pari," *Il Tirreno,* March 16, 1948.
178 **"Italy Picks Uncles Today"** *New York Daily News* as quoted in "Italy: Victory," *Time,* April 26, 1948.
179 **"How do we feel?"** Hughes, "Pre-election report on Italy," 33.
179 **"With sincere thanks I underline"** The poster version of the telegram is photographed and reproduced in Bartali, *La leggenda,* 197.
179 **"bedroom strike" and details about parliamentary fight** "Italy: Yes, Petkoff," *Time,* June 21, 1948; Arnaldo Cortesi, "Italian Deputies Battered in Fight," *New York Times,* June 10, 1948: 13; "Fighting Stirs Rome Chamber," *Washington Post,* June 10, 1948: 2.
179 **"You Communists find your recruits"** Cortesi, "Italian Deputies Battered in Fight," 13.
179 **"the worst fight in parliamentary history"** Ibid.
180 **Plan to shorten deputies' summer holidays** "Il piano Fanfani abbrevia le vacanze agli onorevoli: Discussione immediata e gratifica in salvo," *Il Tirreno,* July 11, 1948; 1.
180 **Results of vote where Coppi gets 21 votes and Bartali, 1** "Fausto Coppi a apporté à l'U.V. Italienne le Trophée international Edmond Gentil!" *L'Équipe,* February 6, 1948: 1.
180 **"Italy's greatest cyclist"** "Ce succès es pour moi le plus beau . . . fait répondre Coppi à Guido Giardini," *L'Équipe,* February 6, 1948: 2.

CHAPTER 11. LES MACARONI

181 **"Lots of discussion"** Gino Bartali, *Tutto sbagliato, tutto da rifare* (Milano: Mondadori, 1979), 134.
181 **"I would really like to compete"** "'Je veux faire le Tour de France mais si je suis opposé et non allié à Bartali' declare Fausto Coppi," *L'Équipe,* May 4, 1948: 1.
181 **Coppi's refusal to race with Gino** Ibid.
182 **"Ten years have passed—that's a lot"** Carlo Maria Lomartire, *Insurrezione: 14 luglio 1948* (Milan: Mondadori, 2006), 145.
182 **"nothing but the Tour"** Guido Giardini, "Guido Giardini téléphone de Milan: L'Italie ne pense qu'au Tour 48 et . . . espère!" *L'Équipe,* June 19–20, 1948.
182 **Italian newspapers' pessimism and number of international reporters** Benjo Maso, *Wir Alle Waren Götter: Die berühmte Tour de France von 1948* (Bielefeld: Covadonga Verlag, 2006), 38.
183 ***les Macaroni*** Piero Monti, "Bartali ha vinto il Giro di Francia. Corrieri è primo sul traguardo di Parigi," *Il Tirreno,* July 26, 1948: 1.
183 **"Papà, what gave you the idea"** Paul Guitard, "Leçon des Hommes et L'Ecole des Femmes," *L'Équipe,* July 18, 1948: 4.
183 **Final training and trip to France** Albert de Wetter, "Pas de 'Tour de Suisse

Pour Gino,'" *L'Équipe,* May 20, 1948: 2–3; G.Bollini, "Bartali joue au modeste et affirme ne souhaiter que de . . . terminer," *L'Équipe,* June 26–27, 1948: 4; "Bartali n'avait pu fermer l'oeil de la nuit," *L'Équipe,* June 28, 1948: 4; Maso, *Wir Alle Waren Götter,* 38–39.

184 **Early postwar Tour planning and slate of international characters** Author interview with Aldo Ronconi and son, August 20, 2009; Geoffrey Wheatcroft, *Le Tour: A History of the Tour de France, 1903–2003* (London: Simon and Schuster, 2005), 141; Maso, *Wir Alle Waren Götter,* 13, 15, 18, 227.

186 **"These detractors"** Pierre Bourrillon, "Jean Robic vainqueur du Tour de France 1947 retenu pour le 'Tour,'" *L'Équipe,* April 9, 1948: 1.

186 **"the Emancipated Slave"** Claude Tillet, "Ronconi L'Esclave Affranchi," *L'Équipe,* June 23, 1948: 4.

186 **Ronconi's background** Author interview with Aldo Ronconi, August 20, 2009; Albert de Wetter, "Ronconi veut égaler Bartali et gagner . . ." *L'Équipe,* March 5, 1948: 1–2.

186 **"After the Tour"** Ibid.

187 **"without wine, the Tour"** Victor Peroni, "Le ventre du Tour," *Le Miroir Sprint:* Numéro Special, June 1948: 9.

187 **Tour provisions** "Le Tour . . . A L'Envers," *L'Équipe,* June 19–20, 1948: 4; R. Bastide, "Quelques chiffres sur le 'Tour,'" *L'Équipe,* June 11, 1948: 2.

187 **Caravan description** H. W. Heinsheimer, "Le Tour de France," *Holiday,* July 1949, 82 (Although this article was published in 1949, it is exclusively about the author's experience attending the 1948 Tour); "La caravane va passer," *L'Équipe,* June 22, 1948: 3.

188 **"After the Match" cologne** "Une Declaration de Fachleitner" (advertisement), *L'Équipe,* May 3, 1948: 6.

188 **"game for children"** DDT Advertisement, *Il Tirreno,* July 18, 1948: 4.

188 **Towns paying for privilege to host Tour** Christopher Thomson, *The Tour de France: A Cultural History* (Berkeley: University of California Press, 2006), 83–85.

188 **Hedy Lamarr** "Oggi il Tour parte da Parigi. Rita Hayworth e Tito Schipa, intervistati, danno favorito Bartali. Le ire de Hedy Lamarr," *Il Tirreno,* June 30, 1948: 1.

188 **Vichy regime defendant trial anecdote** Maso, *Wir Alle Waren Götter,* 127.

188 ***Pierrot Le Fou* and escape plan** Raymond Vanker, "Douze Policiers armés ont cherché hier 'Pierrot le Fou' au passage d'Auteuil," *L'Intransigeant,* July 13, 1948: 1.

189 **"Little Goat"** Pierre Bourrillon, "Jean Robic vainqueur du Tour de France 1947 retenu pour le 'Tour,'" *L'Équipe,* April 9, 1948: 1. In French, *Biquet* can be translated as both "little goat" or kid, or used as a term of endearment like "sweetheart" or "darling."

189 **"a very normal, second-class rider"** Journalist Wilhelm Van Wijnendaele as quoted in Maso, *Wir Alle Waren Götter,* 42.

189 ***le jump*** Jean Leuillot, "Bobet fait honneur a son maillot jaune," *L'Intransigeant,* July 9, 1948: 4.

189 **could pass for Gino's nephew** "Avant les Alpes, Robic leader du 'Meilleur Grimpeur,'" *L'Équipe,* July 13, 1948: 2.
189 ***"Le Pin-Up Boy"*** "Bobet, nouveau 'pin-up boy,'" *L'Intransigeant,* July 5, 1948: 3.
189 **Bobet's background** Maso, *Wir Alle Waren Götter,* 42.
190 **"We doubt that Bobet can"** Jacques Goddet, "Mi Temps," *L'Équipe,* July 13, 1948: 2.
190 **Race on July 13 and attack on Col de Turini** Claude Tillet, "Miracle! Louison Bobet ressucité double vainqueur de la montagne et du sprint," *L'Équipe,* July 14, 1948: 1; Jacques Goddet, "La glorification du beau maillot de Bobet," July 14, 1948: 2; Maso, *Wir Alle Waren Götter,* 160–61.
190 **"On that stage"** Bartali, *Tutto sbagliato,* 141.
190 **"Everyone would say"** Gino Bartali with Mario Pancera, *La mia storia* (Milano: Stampa Sportiva, 1958), 82.
190 **"I thought he was a wild card"** Gino Bartali with Romano Beghelli and Marcello Lazzerini, *La leggenda di Bartali* (Firenze: Ponte Alle Grazie Editori, 1992), 190.
191 **"Bobet didn't have anything"** Bartali, *La mia storia,* 82.
191 **"I was in a black mood"** Ibid., 83.
191 **"Of course, if I had known"** Bartali, *La leggenda,* 191.
191 **Bobet spotted by train conductor** Paul Guitard, "Quand le train bleu fait des galipettes," *L'Équipe,* July 14, 1948: 4.
192 **"Uncontested Hero"** Pierre le Marrec of *L'Humanité* as quoted in Roger Dutilh, "Petit Bonhomme vit encore," *L'Équipe,* July 15, 1948: 4.
192 **"For those who rode beside the racer"** Jacques Goddet, "Dans les Alpes, les grimpeurs resteront-ils des auxiliaires?" *L'Équipe,* July 15, 1948: 2.

CHAPTER 12. FOUR BULLETS

There is an expansive trove of primary source information about Bartali's progress at the 1948 Tour de France between Gino's accounts of the 1948 Tour de France in his autobiographies and other interviews, and our own interviews with the men who competed at the 1948 Tour with him, including Giovanni Corrieri (his roommate, *gregario,* and confidant), Vittorio Seghezzi, and Aldo Ronconi. The breadth of secondary sources was equally impressive. We reviewed French and Italian newsreel footage, and listened to French radio recordings from different stages at the National Library in Paris. In an era before television, the newspaper coverage of the Tour was all-encompassing. Sports photographers captured stirring images of every race's multitude of moments, and journalists wrote expansive profiles not just of the stars, but also of their supporting riders. Each stage race became the subject of countless broadsheets of coverage, interviews, and analysis. Taken together, they form a body of work that offers an exciting vision of the Tour of 1948 in all its minute detail, and a lasting tribute to a race that so fully captured the popular imagination.

For coverage of the Tour, including its rest days, we drew on several newspapers, with a particular focus on *L'Équipe, Le Parisien Libéré, L'Intransigeant, La Nazione,* and *Il Nuovo Corriere di Firenze*. Antonio Pallante, Togliatti's attempted assassination, and all the details of the unrest that followed were widely covered in the press. We focused most on accounts from the *New York Times, Time, Le Monde, Ce Soir, Il Corriere della Sera, La Nazione, Il Tirreno,* and the transcripts of the BBC radio broadcasts (the BBC collected and translated radio broadcasts from a variety of sources, including the Agenzia Nazionale Stampa Associata [Italian National Associated Press Agency]). Antonio Pallante answered a series of our questions in writing, with his son kindly facilitating the logistics of the interview. Alberto Custadero's article in *La Reppublica* on the occasion of Pallante's trial documents being made public was also very helpful, since it included details from various testimonies given to the police and also Pallante's personal letters that were seized by the state censor.

193 **Debate of proposed law to round up firearms** "A Madman's Act," *New York Times,* July 15, 1948: 22.

194 **Togliatti goes for ice cream** "Italy: Blood on the Cobblestones," *Time,* July 26, 1948.

194 **Togliatti's interest in Bartali and cycling** "Togliatti giubilante per le vittorie di Bartali," *Il Tirreno,* July 20, 1948: 1; "Blood on the Cobblestones," July 26, 1948.

194 **"warm-eyed," "full-bosomed"** "Blood on the Cobblestones," July 26, 1948.

194 **"Jotti! The bag!"** "Ritorno al lavoro dopo due giornate di sciopero e di sanguinosi episodi in molte città d'Italia," *Il Tirreno,* July 16, 1948: 1.

194 **Togliatti's question about whether gunman had been stopped** Ibid.

195 **"Arrest him! Arrest him!"** Jotti quoted in Alberto Custodero, "Attentato a Togliatti— Le lettere segrete," *La Repubblica,* April 29, 2007: 38–39.

195 **"incite riots"** "A Madman's Act," *New York Times,* July 15, 1948: 22.

195 **a charge Pallante would vehemently reject** Custodero, "Attentato a Togliatti," 38–39.

195 ***Mein Kampf*** "Il Pallante leggeva Hitler," *Il Tirreno,* July 17, 1948: 1.

195 **"dreamy"** "Chi è l'attentatore," *Il Tirreno,* July 16, 1948: 1.

195 **Pallante's background** Custodero, "Attentato a Togliatti," 38–39.

196 **Pallante discussion about the Tour de France** "Il Procuratore della Repubblica al Policlinico: 'Non vido nulla' ha dichiarato Togliatti," *La Nazione,* July 23, 1948: 1. In his written responses to the authors' questions, Pallante revealed why he enjoyed cycling so much: "I always told my son that the sport of cycling is the sport that best embodies the concept of sacrifice to achieve personal satisfaction and ambitious goals, and I would focus in particular on the tenacious Bartali."

197 **"I have always thought"** Custodero, "Attentato a Togliatti," 38–39.

198 **"Maharajahs and the blondes"** H. W. Heinsheimer, "Le Tour de France," *Holiday,* July 1949: 83.

198 **Italians staying in Carlton hotel** Luigi Chierci, *Bartali: Disastrosa partenza e avventuroso viaggio del vincitore del Tour de France 1948* (Roma: Compagnia Editoriale, 1977), 68–71.

198 **Inspiration for Carlton hotel's cupolas** Stephen Gundle, *Glamour: A History* (Oxford, UK: Oxford University Press, 2009), 108.

199 **Room 112** Albert De Wetter, "Le dernier espoir de Bartali: Cannes-Briançon," *L'Équipe,* July 15, 1948: 1.

199 **Telegrams from Monsignor Montini and Prime Minister De Gasperi** Benjo Maso, *Wir Alle Waren Götter: Die berühmte Tour de France von 1948* (Bielefeld: Covadonga Verlag, 2006),167; "De Gasperi avait incité Bartali à bien faire," *Le Parisien Libéré,* July 17, 1948: 6. The text of De Gasperi's telegram read: "I received today the greetings that you were kind enough to send me from Lourdes. I want my heartfelt thanks to reach you the day before the first stage of the Alps and that they inspire you to shine brilliantly there."

199 **"Always the same questions!" and ensuing dialogue** De Wetter, "Le dernier espoir de Bartali: Cannes-Briançon," 1.

200 **"While I felt really good"** Gino Bartali, *Tutto sbagliato, tutto da rifare* (Milano: Mondadori, 1979), 142.

200 **"Bartali is embraced"** Maso, *Wir Alle Waren Götter,* 166.

200 **Adriana and son spend night with Gino** Gianni Granzotto, *L'Europeo,* August 2–8, 1948: 3.

200 **Criticism for spending time with Adriana** Maso, *Wir Alle Waren Götter,* 166.

200 **"Bartali, the old king of the mountains"** Giardini, "Bartali et Ronconi battus dans le Turrini espèrent encore," *L'Équipe,* July 15, 1948: 4. Giardini's *Gazzetta Dello Sport* were often reprinted in *L'Équipe.*

200 **three major reasons for his poor performance** De Wetter, "Le dernier espoir de Bartali: Cannes-Briançon," 1, 4.

201 **"race with international impact"** Ibid.

202 **"Bartali has found his master"** Maso, *Wir Alle Waren Götter,* 121.

202 **female fishmongers** J. J. Povech, "Robic a été porté en triomphe par les poissonières toulossaines," *L'Équipe,* July 10, 1948: 4.
203 **"overtiring, too much eating, and perhaps abuse of performance-enhancing substances"** Maso, *Wir Alle Waren Götter,* 155.
203 **Bobet getting nervous** Jean Leuillot, "L'équipe de France adopte enfin Louison Bobet comme leader," *L'Intransigeant,* July 15, 1948: 4.
204 **"worst possible thing"** De Gasperi as quoted in "Italy: Blood on the Cobblestones," July 26, 1948.
204 **news of Togliatti's attack swept across the country** Jean D'Hospital, "Après l'attentat contre M. Togliatti," *Le Monde,* July 16, 1948: 1.
204 **Work in factories and many offices stopped** *BBC Radio ANSA* (Agenzia Nazionale Stampa Associata: Italian National Associated Press Agency) dispatches in Italian (Morse), translated and broadcast by BBC, July 14, 1948: 17, 20.
204 **"A wind of panic"; "the city wore the livid mask of fear"** Jean D'Hospital, "Après l'attentat contre M. Togliatti," *Le Monde,* July 16, 1948: 1.
204 **country teetered closer to the brink of revolution** In over two hundred hours of interviews, we discovered that an overwhelming number of common Italian citizens present during the protests and riots remembered being very fearful of a prolonged insurrection or revolution. Surviving Italian politicians of the era tended to have a more nuanced view, informed as much by information they had gathered in official and political meetings that wasn't shared publicly at first, as well as their own political biases. Our epilogue discusses historians' varying perspectives on this moment.
205 **Loud demonstrations in Ponte a Ema and Tullia Grifoni remarks** Author interview with Cesare and Tullia Grifoni, July 31, 2009.
205 **Stalin "outraged"** United Press, "Stalin is 'Outraged' by Togliatti Attack," *New York Times,* July 15, 1948.
205 **"I am a Communist"** "Bomb Threat Brings Police to Cathedral," *New York Times,* July 15, 1948.
206 **"Go! Go home!" and exchange with reporters** Gino Bartali with Romano Beghelli and Marcello Lazzerini, *La leggenda di Bartali* (Firenze: Ponte Alle Grazie Editori, 1992), 194–95.
206 **Gino and other cyclists' fear of country heading toward violent chaos** Bartali, *La leggenda,* 195; author interviews with Giovanni Corrieri (July 15, 2009) and Vittorio Seghezzi (August 13, 2009).
206 **"Bartali is no longer young enough"** "L'échec de Bartali n'a pas surpris Binda," *L'Équipe,* July 14, 1948: 4; "Bartali a mal couru," *Le Parisien Libéré,* July 14, 1948; Paul Guitard, "Leçon des Hommes et L'Ecole des Femmes," *L'Équipe,* July 18, 1948: 4.
207 **Gino beginning to feel old** A year after the Tour, Gino said that he first started really feeling his age on July 8, 1948, when he discovered that Bobet was a decade younger than he. Gino Bartali and André Costes, "Mes Memoires," *Bibliotheque France-Soir* (Paris: Serie Sport, 1949), 36.
207 **Announcement of general strike** Arnaldo Cortesi, "Riots Sweep Italy After an Assassin Wounds Togliatti," *New York Times,* July 15, 1948. Not all sources

agree that the telegraphs were shut down by the strike. *Il Tirreno* suggests that the telegraphs, along with the radios and telephone lines, continued to function after the shooting and the strike that followed it. "L'attentato," *Il Tirreno,* July 16, 1948: 1.

208 **Leading Communist deputies were dispatched** Author interview with Giulio Spallone, Communist deputy in 1948, August 10, 2009.

208 **"Indeed it is an ironic twist"** "A Madman's Act," *New York Times,* July 15, 1948.

208 **chaotic flurry of meetings** "Due ansiose giornate," *La Nazione,* July 16, 1948: 1.

208 **De Gasperi discussed the possibility of sending a telegram** Jean D'Hospital, "En Italie Bartali e Coppi font figure de heros nationaux," *Le Monde,* July 29, 1948: 5. According to D'Hospital, the Italian foreign minister told his French counterpart that De Gasperi was considering sending a telegram to Gino encouraging him to win. It appears that this telegram was never sent, likely because De Gasperi had already contacted Gino by phone in the intervening period since he had spoken with his foreign minister.

209 **Phone conversation between Gino and De Gasperi** The dialogue of the exchange between Gino and De Gasperi is from one of Gino's autobiographies (Bartali, *La leggenda,* 197). In separate interviews, Giovanni Corrieri (July 15, 2009) and Vittorio Seghezzi (August 13, 2009), the surviving members of the 1948 Italian Tour team, who were there when the prime minister called, have confirmed that the conversation with De Gasperi took place. Adriana and Andrea Bartali also said that Gino spoke about the call. Dr. Benjo Maso, a former sociology professor and cycling historian, interviewed Giovanni Corrieri, Giordano Cottur, Aldo Ronconi, Vittorio Seghezzi, and Vittorio Magni, all teammates of Bartali from the 1948 Tour (Cottur is deceased at our time of writing), while researching his book about the 1948 Tour, *Wij waren allemaal goden, De Tour van 1948*. They all also confirmed that the phone call took place.

Elsewhere, the conversation has been written about widely in the Italian press. Outside of Italy, Ian Buruma, a frequent contributor to the *New York Review of Books,* the *New Yorker,* and the *New York Times,* and a professor of democracy, human rights, and journalism, wrote about the phone call in an article that explored the relationship between nationalism and sport (Ian Buruma, "Clash of symbols," *Financial Times Weekend Magazine,* September 24, 2005: 22). In the cycling world, various books in Italian, French, and English have cited it, too.

Some have expressed skepticism about the call, either because it seems singularly dramatic or it appears foreign to a modern perspective in which the worlds of politics and sport are more strictly separated. In the final analysis, however, it must be considered within the wider background of the moment. Gino and De Gasperi were two of the most prominent Catholics in Italy in 1948, and they had been on friendly terms for years. As the 1948 Tour progressed, the two men exchanged telegrams. When Gino won, it is telling that he wasn't visited by fashion icons or movie stars, but by De Gasperi's Christian Democrat secretary, a future prime minister of Italy. In this context, the phone call between Gino and De Gapseri would have been much less unusual than it might now seem.

CHAPTER 13. A FROZEN HELL

211 **A Frozen Hell** photo caption from *L'Équipe,* July 16, 1948: 1.

212 **loudspeakers at four o'clock; 311 members of media** H. W. Heinsheimer, "Le Tour de France," *Holiday,* July 1949: 85 (although this article was published in 1949, it is exclusively about the author's experience attending the 1948 Tour).

213 **"the Dreadnought"** "Renault sur le Tour," *L'Équipe,* July 28, 1948: 2.

213 **"the Broom Wagon"** Bill and Carol McGann, *The Story of the Tour de France* (Indianapolis: Dog Ear Publishing, 2006), 28.

213 **"Car Number 1"** Heinsheimer, "Le Tour de France," 85.

213 **"Cannes has never awoken this early"** Henri Chapuis, "Les coureurs s'attaquent aux trois cols d'Allos, de Vars et d'Izoard," *L'Équipe,* July 16, 1948: 1.

214 **"Pushing: It's cheating"; "Those racers who struggle"** "Le Tour . . . à l'envers," *L'Équipe,* June 22, 1948: 3.

216 **"How is Togliatti?" exchange** Gino Bartali with Romano Beghelli and Marcello Lazzerini, *La leggenda di Bartali* (Firenze: Ponte Alle Grazie Editori, 1992), 200.

216 **"Bartali fights the final battle of his career"** Jacques Goddet, "Dans les Alpes, les grimpeurs resteront-ils des auxiliaires?" *L'Équipe,* July 15, 1948: 1.

217 **"Let's think about the race"** Bartali, *La leggenda,* 200.

217 **Bobet's decision to use hollow axle** Benjo Maso, *Wir Alle Waren Götter: Die berühmte Tour de France von 1948* (Bielefeld: Covadonga Verlag, 2006), 187.

217 **Belgian racer had died** "Le Tour . . . a l'envers," *L'Équipe,* June 18, 1948: 4.

217 **Gino's teammate injured by car** Maso, *Wir Alle Waren Götter,* 113.

217 **Press car accident and fatality** Ibid.

218 **"With the hope that the hours spent here"** J. Vidal-Lablache, "Vive Robic," *L'Équipe,* July 16, 1948.

218 **"The weather is unstable"** "Prévisions Meteorologiques" (July 14–15 forecast), *Le Monde,* July 14, 1948: 6.

218 **freak summer weather patterns** "Été 1948: Quel temps fera-t-il?" *Le Monde,* July 13, 1948: 6.

218 **over 100-degrees Fahrenheit** Maso, *Wir Alle Waren Götter,* 118.

218 **"menacing waves and white foam"** Jean Marchand, "À la Croisette des Chemins," *Ce Soir,* July 15, 1948: 4.

219 **"smiling eyes"** Chapuis, "Les coureurs s'attaquent aux trois cols d'Allos, de Vars et d'Izoard," 1.

219 **first over the Izoard mountain pass** Maso, *Wir Alle Waren Götter,* 178.

219 **"The three cols today"** Robic as quoted in ibid.

220 **"Gone were the gay crowds"** Heinsheimer, "Le Tour de France," 87.

220 **heart squeeze** Dante Gianello, "Bartali m'a dit: 'Je croyais mourir de faim,'" *L'Équipe,* July 16, 1948: 4.

220 **"I could hear the shouts of the Italians"** Gino Bartali, *Tutto sbagliato, tutto da rifare* (Milano: Mondadori, 1979), 144.

221 **Newspaper car sliding into ravine** "La Voiture de 'L'Intran' Verse Dans Un Ravin," *L'Équipe,* July 16, 1948: 4; J. Vidal-Lablache, "Le Tour de France est au lit," *L'Intransigeant,* July 18, 1948: 1.

221 **wet snow** *L'Équipe,* July 16, 1948: 1.

221 **noontime radio updates** "Le 'Tour' sur l'antenne," *L'Équipe,* July 15, 1948: 4.

222 **"My heart was going boom-boom"** Roger Dutilh, "Cueilli pour vous dans la presse épique et lyrique du Tour de France," *L'Intransigeant,* July 17, 1948: 4.

222 **Louis Bobet's axle breaking** Ibid.

223 **"Heavens"** Gianello, "Bartali m'a dit,"4.

223 **Gino felt his legs surge beneath him** Gino Bartali with Mario Pancera, *La mia storia* (Milano: Stampa Sportiva, 1958), 84.

223 **"The cold blocked"** Jacques Goddet, "Bartali avait rendez-vous avec L'Izoard," *L'Équipe,* July 16, 1948: 1.

224 **"The good Lord took a pair of wings"** "Gino le veut, Gino le veut," *L'Équipe,* July 19, 1948: 6.

224 ***I feel like a giant*** Bartali, *La mia storia,* 84.

224 **"Bartali! You're immortal!"** Chevalier as quoted in Leo Turrini, *Bartali: L'uomo che salvo l'Italia pedalando* (Milan: Arnaldo Mondadori Editore, 2004), 93.

224 **Radio signal in Italy** BBC Rome 19.00, 16.7.48. While the BBC reported that radio came back on at 1:00 p.m. on July 15, other Italian sources like the Italian newspaper *Il Tirreno* reported that "telephones, telegraphs, and radios worked continuously" through the shooting and afterward (*Il Tirreno,* July 16, 1948: 1). The different experiences may be attributable to reports being prepared in different parts of the country. In any event, we have used the more conservative reporting of the two.

224 **"*Attenzione!* Great news"** Crispino, "Sia lodato Bartali," *Giornale dell'Emilia,* July 24, 1948. Giulio Andreotti also describes this episode, and identifies the deputy as Matteo Tonengo. However, writing thirty-five years after the event, he erroneously gives the day of Bartali's victory as July 14 rather than July 15. Giulio Andreotti, *De Gasperi, visto da vicino* (Milan: RCS Rizzoli Libri,1986), 143–44. In a later filmed interview, he appears to have corrected his timing. "L'Attentato a Togliatti," in *Rai Storia* (documentary), directed by Gabriele Immirzi, Giulio Spadetta, and Francesco Roganato.

224 **Togliatti's health** Togliatti's doctors would update the press with regular bulletins about his health. Although he had a pneumonia scare for a brief period, he soon made a full recovery.

225 **Celebrations** Crispino, "Sia Lodato Bartali." Various interviewees shared happy memories of the celebrations that followed Gino's victory throughout Italy (Ivo Faltoni, July 18, 2009; Mario Bellini, August 19, 2009).

225 **Rietti's recollections** Author interview with Giorgina Rietti, August 5, 2009.

225 **"No event in the world"** Jean D'Hospital, "En Italie Bartali e Coppi font figure de heros nationaux," *Le Monde,* July 29, 1948: 5. D'Hospital's observations are reiterated in the writings of the correspondents for the *Giornale dell'Emilia* and *Il Tempo,* the latter who memorably wrote that Bartali's victory "was even able to ridicule the greatest revolutionary framework that was about to strike Italy." (Natale Bertocco, "Bartali vincitore del Tour acclamato trionfalmente a Parigi," *Il Tempo,* July 26, 1948: 1; Crispino, "Sia Lodato Bartali"). This theme was echoed in many of our interviews with Italians who witnessed this moment, and it has appeared in other interviews as well. Allessandro Portelli, who interviewed a factory worker from Terni named Valtèro Peppoloni, quotes his characterization of the moment: " 'Bartali's victory had a lot of influence,' says Peppoloni. 'I was a fan and all the fans, when the radio brought the news, felt some kind of a let-down. As I listened to the radio the anger for Togliatti's wounding simmered down.' " Allessandro Portelli, *The Death of Luigi Trastulli, and Other Stories: Form and Meaning in Oral History* (Albany: SUNY Press, 1991), 155.

225 **"I lived for art, I lived for love"** Maso, *Wir Alle Waren Götter,* 187.

226 **"I'm hungry"** " 'J'ai Faim,' s'écrie Bartali a l'arrivée," *Ce Soir,* July 16, 1948.

226 **furrows where tears had fallen** Dutilh, "Cueilli pour vous dans la presse épique et lyrique du Tour de France," *L'Équipe,* July 17, 1948: 4.

226 **Togliatti's hospital room** "Le giornate di Togliatti al Policlinico," *Il Tirreno,* July 18, 1948: 1.

227 **Togliatti's last memory** " 'Non vidi nulla,' ha dichiarato Togliatti," *La Nazione,* July 23, 1948: 1.

227 **"What happened at the Tour? How did Bartali do?"** Palmiro Togliatti as quoted by his secretary Massimo Caprara in Orio and Guido Vergani, *Caro Coppi* (Milano: Mondadori, 1995), 72. According to Caprara, Togliatti first urged: "Calm. Steady nerves," likely because he must have sensed that his shooting would have caused some unrest, even if he did not yet know the full scope of what had happened. He then asked these questions about the Tour and Bartali's progress. The Verganis offer a telling observation about the significance of these questions as they explain that if even Togliatti, who was recovering from an operation and who had a reputation as a cool-headed intellectual with a firm control of his emotions, "was anxious about the Tour, an anxiety ready to become enthusiasm, one can understand the 'Bartali effect' on the crowds, on the population of fans." Both Verganis wrote for the *Corriere della Sera,* Italy's newspaper of record.

CHAPTER 14. THE ROAD HOME

229 **"Bartali doesn't have *my* yellow jersey yet!"** Albert de Wetter, "Il n'y a pas de justice" s'écrie Bobet qui ajoute: Bartali ne tient pas encore mon maillot jaune!" *L'Équipe,* July 16, 1948: 1.

229 **"It was horribly cold"** Gino Bartali, *Tutto sbagliato, tutto da rifare* (Milano: Mondadori, 1979), 146.

229 **Gino got a few sips of a coffee . . . cognac** Ibid.

230 **"you lazy bum?"** "Sur les bords du lac . . . Bobet lit son courrier et Robic pleure," *L'Intransigeant,* July 18, 1948: 4.

231 **"Like all elderly people"** Orio Vergani, "Piange Bobet come un bambino nel passare a Bartali la maglia gialla," *Corriere della Sera,* July 17, 1948.

231 **"A world of difference . . . that had set his heart ablaze"** Jacques Goddet, "Le Maître," *L'Équipe,* July 17, 1948: 4.

231 ***I feel like a lion*** Bartali, *Tutto sbagliato,* 147.

231 **Bobet's dream of winning the Tour was over** Louison Bobet, "Mon Tour Heroique," *L'Équipe,* August 5, 1948: 2.

232 **a surprise visitor, a Christian Democrat deputy** Benjo Maso, *Wir Alle Waren Götter: Die berühmte Tour de France von 1948* (Bielefeld: Covadonga Verlag, 2006), 222.

232 **"defeated everyone and everything"** Vergani, "Piange Bobet come un bambino nel passare a Bartali la maglia gialla."

232 **"His Holiness wishes that you win"** "Gino le veut, Gino le veut," *L'Équipe,* July 19, 1948: 6.

232 **"My God, you nearly killed me" and dialogue between Binda and Gino** Paul Guitard, "Leçon des Hommes et L'Ecole des Femmes," *L'Équipe,* July 18, 1948: 4.

232 **"Your father is a champion again"** Ibid.

232 **"feeling of resurrection"** Author interview with Oscar Scalfaro, October 7, 2009.

232 **union meeting ended abruptly** Maso, *Wir Alle Waren Götter,* 222.

232 **young priest put a radio on the altar** "Au Courrier du Monde: 'Don Lino et Bartali'—Par Enrico Foresti par courrier electronique," *Le Monde,* May 15, 2000.

233 **"southern temperament"** Maso, *Wir Alle Waren Götter,* 275.

233 **"Their unbridled praise"** Felix Levitain, "Cueilli pour vous dans la presse épique et lyrique du Tour de France," *L'Intransigeant,* July 18, 1948: 4.

233 **"Bartali wrote in these last two days"** Vergani, "Piange Bobet come un bambino nel passare a Bartali la maglia gialla."

233 **"From snowstorm, water, ice"** Jacques Goddet, "Le Maître."

234 **"Calm and enthusiastic"** "Bartali ha telefonato ieri sera ai genitori," *La Nazione,* July 18, 1948: 3.

234 **fourteen people were killed** Domenico Tarantini, *La maniera forte. Elogio della polizia. Storia del potere politico in Italia, 1860–1975* (Verona: Bertani, 1975), 302–33, as cited by Mark Mazower, *The Policing of Politics in the 20th Century: Historical Perspectives* (Oxford, UK: Berghahn Books, 1997), 89.

234 **two hundred were seriously injured** "Italy: Blood on the Cobblestones," *Time,* July 26, 1948. This article says some twenty policemen and rioters were killed.

234 **Italy's GDP in 1948** Michael D. Bordo and Forest Capie, *Monetary Regimes in Transition* (Cambridge, UK: Cambridge University Press, 1994), 331.

234 **Togliatti's penicillin** Arnaldo Cortesi, "Italy Checks Most of Violence: Togliatti Takes Turn for Worse," *New York Times,* July 17, 1948: 1.

235 **Togliatti's son reads him the sports section** "Togliatti giubilante per la vittorie di Bartali," *Il Tirreno,* July 20, 1948: 1.

235 **"great national pride"** Author interview with Pallante, October 10, 2010.

235 **Fifteen million people in France** André Chassaignon, "Considerations Commerciales Sur le Tour de France," *Le Monde,* July 23, 1948: 6.

235 **Los Angeles Olympics attendance** Craig Glenday, *Guinness World Records 2008* (New York: Random House, 2008), 261.

236 **Gino would win a little over a million francs** All figures on earnings and appearance fees for Gino and the other racers come from the article in *L'Équipe,* one of the newspapers that organized the Tour ("Les Contrats sur piste de Bartali multiplieront par trois le million que lui rapporte le Tour de France," *L'Équipe,* July 30, 1948: 2). We consulted the French National Institute of Statistics and Economic Studies' online Euro conversion table and the U.S. Internal Revenue Service's yearly average currency exchange rate table to calculate the present-day USD values for all the racers' earnings.

237 **Gino boxes a police officer** "Gino boxe un gendarme et donne le maillot jaune à son soigneur," *L'Intransigeant,* July 26, 1948: 4.

237 **Final day of the Tour opened with a light drizzle** Luigi Chierici, "Oggi cala il siporio sul Giro di Francia," *La Nazione,* July 25, 1948: 3.

237 **anonymous death threat** Maso, *Wir Alle Waren Götter,* 282.

238 **"Gino Bartali, after having beaten his adversaries"** Gianni Granzotto, "Bartali vinse Marie," *L'Europeo,* August 2–8, 1948: 3.

238 **Tour is televised** "Roubaix-Paris: Apothéose," *Miroir du Monde: Le Tour de France 1948 Numéro Spécial,* 31; "Le Tour de France à l'écran," *L'Équipe,* July 31, 1948: 2; Christopher Thompson, *The Tour de France: A Cultural History* (Los Angeles: University of California Press, 2006), 45–46.

238 **"Bartali stood out in his yellow jersey"** Félix Lévitain, "Gino Bartali était imbattable dans le Tour 48. Mais l'épreuve par *le Parisien* et *L'Équipe* a revelé des talents nouveaux pour la formation tricolore," *Le Parisien Liberé,* July 27, 1948.

239 **Bartali's Tour record for longest span between victories** The list of all Tour winners can be viewed on the official Tour de France website, www.letour.fr .

239 **"The war ruined us old men"** Granzotto, "Bartali vinse Marie," 3.

239 **"Everyone in their life"** Gino Bartali, "La mia lotta contro la morte," *Tempo,* January 21, 1954: 14–16.

240 **"I have won the most beautiful race"** Jean Leulliot, "J'ai remporté la plus belle course du monde,' déclare le vainqueur du Tour," *L'Intransigeant,* July 27, 1948: 4.

EPILOGUE

We first spoke with Giorgio Goldenberg in November 2010, after hearing about his family's incredible story from an Italian Jewish friend of his late sister, Tea. We subsequently interviewed him four times (December 20, 2010; January 25, 2011; April 4, 2011; and November 14, 2011).

242 **Italian Jewish journalist found him as well** Adam Smulevich, "Sono vivo perché Bartali ci nascose in cantina," *Pagine Ebraiche,* January 2011: 39; Adam Smulevich, "Bartali nascose ebrei in cantina," *La Gazzetta dello Sport,* December 28, 2010.

242 **RAI filmed segment** Giorgio Goldenberg television segment about Bartali story, "La Vita in Diretta," *Rai Uno,* January 27, 2011.

243 **"There is no doubt"** Author interview with Giorgio Goldenberg.

243 **"In my opinion, he was a hero"** Ibid.

243 **Word about Gino's involvement** Various Italian Jews we interviewed confirmed that this information spread through the Jewish community in Florence in the months and years following the war, including Renzo Ventura (author interview July 27, 2009); Giorgina Rietti (author interviews August 5, 2009; November 6, 2009; and September 10, 2010); Cesare Sacerdoti (e-mail response to author, November 17, 2010). Enrico Maionica, who helped Niccacci prepare the false identity documents, describes in his testimony that he discovered Bartali's involvement in the network and transport of false documents in the frame of his bicycle after the war as well (USC Shoah Foundation interview with Enrico Maionica by Susanna Segrè, April 30, 1998).

243 **opted to willfully ignore the difficulties of the recent past** Philip Morgan, *The Fall of Mussolini: Italy, the Italians and the Second World War* (Oxford, UK: Oxford University Press, 2008), 5.

243 **Gino reacted to the coverage with anger** Andrea Bartali, foreword to Paolo Alberati, *Gino Bartali: Mille diavoli in corpo* (Firenze: Giunti, 2006), 4.

244 **"I don't want to appear to be a hero"** Archival filmed interview with Gino Bartali in *Coppi e Bartali: gli eterni rivali* (documentary), Instituto Luce, 2004.

244 **Ciampi posthumously awards Gino a gold medal** "25 Aprile: Ciampi a vedova Bartali, e'stato grande uomo,"*ANSA,* April 25, 2006; Cecilia Dalla Negra, "Adozioni e passaporti falsi in questo modo agiva la rete—Il pisano trovava i fondi, il campione nascondeva documenti nella bicicletta—Bartali—Nissim—la storia—i protagonisti," *La Repubblica,* April 25, 2006; "Da Ciampi medaglia a Gino Bartali," *Corriere della Sera,* April 25, 2006.

244 **two surviving members of this network in Lucca** Author interviews with Don Arturo Paoli and Don Renzo Tambellini, February 2007.

245 **Father Pier Damiano at the San Damiano monastery** Author interviews with Padre Pier Damiano, July 29, 2009; December 2, 2009; and December 4, 2010.

245 "If you're good at a sport" Andrea Bartali, foreword to Alberati, *Mille diavoli,* 4.

245 "an explosion of joy" Author interview with Oscar Scalfaro, October 7, 2009.

246 "Milan, Turin, and Genoa appeared on the brink of insurrection" Patrick McCarthy, *The Crisis of the Italian State: From the Origins of the Cold War to the Fall of Berlusconi* (New York: St. Martin's Press, 1997), 39.

246 "insurrection was feasible" Paul Ginsborg, *A History of Contemporary Italy: Society and Politics, 1943–1988* (New York: Palgrave Macmillan, 2003), 119.

246 "savior of the Fatherland" Benjo Maso, *Wir Alle Waren Götter: Die berühmte Tour de France von 1948* (Bielefeld: Covadonga Verlag, 2006), 290, 292, 296.

246 "To say that civil war was averted" Alessandra Stanley, "Gino Bartali, 85, A Hero in Italy for his cycling championships," *New York Times,* May 6, 2000.

247 two Italian historians The historians are Silvio Pons and Daniele Marchesini. Silvio Pons filmed interview in "L'Attentato a Togliatti" *Rai Storia* (documentary), directed by Gabriele Immirzi, Giulio Spadetta, and Francesco Roganato. In his book *Coppi e Bartali,* Marchesini concludes that Bartali's triumph "was a factor in the lessening of tensions at that time." Daniele Marchesini, *Coppi e Bartali* (Bologna: il Mulino, 1998), 92.

247 "I don't know if I saved the country" Marc Dewinter, "Gino the Pious," *Cycle Sport,* July 1999: 31.

247 Valkenburg disappointment Maso, *Wir Alle Waren Götter,* 292–96; Gino Bartali with Mario Pancera, *La mia storia* (Milano: Stampa Sportiva, 1958), 90–92.

247 "that one" William Fotheringham, *Fallen Angel: The Passion of Fausto Coppi* (London: Yellow Jersey Press, 2009), 104.

248 De Gasperi's insistence that Gino and Coppi race together Ibid., 116.

248 Togliatti agrees Ibid.

248 Binda engineered an alliance Ibid.

248 Enduring loyalties to Coppi and Bartali Our interviews with dozens of contemporary Italians revealed that the loyalties for Coppi and Bartali still run deep. Also see Juliet Macur, "Long-Ago Rivalry Still Stirs Passion at the Giro d'Italia," *New York Times,* May 18, 2009.

249 2009 cycling pilgrimage Aili McConnon attended the pilgrimage that traveled from Terontola to Assisi on September 13, 2009.

250 *Il Vecchiaccio* and Methuselah Gino Bartali, "La mia vita," *Tempo,* November 29, 1952: 13–15.

250 "and a beard so long it reached his navel" Ibid.

250 "We athletes are not like beautiful women" Ibid.

250 Account of car accident Gino Bartali, "La mia lotta contro la morte," *Tempo,* January 21, 1954: 14–16; Gino Bartali, *Tutto sbagliato, tutto da rifare* (Milano: Mondadori, 1979), 218; Alberati, *Mille diavoli,* 154–56.

250 "car was turning over and over" Bartali, "La mia lotta contro la morte," 14–16.

250 "Don't touch me" and dialogue with Adriana Ibid.

251 **Photograph of De Gasperi visiting Bartali** *Epoca*, October 25, 1953: 81.
251 **Gino retires** Gino Bartali, "Non correrò più," *Tempo*, February 17, 1955: 41.
251 **Bartali bike company** Bartali, *La mia storia*, 92; Bartali, *Tutto sbagliato*, 159.
252 **"It's one thing to ride"** Ibid.
252 **"If I had remained"** Ibid.
252 **Bartali razor blades** Paolo Costa, *Gino Bartali: la vita, le imprese, le polemiche* (Portogruaro: Ediciclo Editore, 2001), 114; author interview with Andrea Bartali.
252 **"eternal youth"** It was called "Chianti Bartali" and was made by Fattoria Casebasse of Siena.
252 **small department store** Author interview with Andrea Bartali; Alberati, *Mille diavoli*, 168–70.
252 **"It was the era of paying"** Alberati, *Mille diavoli*, 168–70.
252 **twenty million francs in contracts** Benjo Maso, *The Sweat of the Gods: Myths and Legends of Bicycle Racing* (Norwich, England: Mousehold Press, 2005), 79.
253 **$517,000** French National Institute of Statistics and Economic Studies' table for converting historic francs into 2010 Euros, and the U.S. Internal Revenue Service 2010 yearly average U.S. Dollar/Euro exchange rate table.
253 **Bicycle sales decline** Maso, *The Sweat of the Gods*, 81.
253 **"in order to tell us"** Maso, *Wir Alle Waren Götter*, 295.
254 **"A Mistake a Day"** Alberati, *Mille diavoli*, 168–70.
254 **"At my age, I think I know"** Ibid., 170.
254 **Adriana Bartali's recollections** Author interviews with Adriana Bartali, July 17, 2009; August 3, 2009.
255 **Conversation with Maria Callas** Bartali *La leggenda*, 285.
255 **Andrea Bartali's experience and details about Torello and Giulia** Author interviews with Andrea Bartali, July 17, 2009; August 3, 2009; and September 14, 2009.
256 **"For a quarter of a century"** Bartali, "Non correrò più," 41.
256 **370,000 miles of cycling** Gino estimated that he had cycled a total of 600,000 kilometers during his life (Bartali, *La leggenda*, 1). In official races alone, Gino cycled nearly 94,000 miles (150,739 kilometers) according to Tim Hilton, "Gino Bartali—Obituary," *Guardian*, May 9, 2000.
256 **Gino's physical decline** Dewinter, "Gino the Pious," 38–41.
256 **"Life is like a Giro D'Italia"** Gino Bartali interview with Marco Pastonesi in Costa, *Gino Bartali*, 173–80.
256 **Gino's funeral requests** Alberati, *Mille diavoli*, 182.
256 **praying that he would die peacefully at home** Ibid.
257 **Details of Gino's death** Pierangelo Di Sapegno, "Addio Bartali: Con lui l'Italia ha scalato il Dopoguerra," *La Stampa*, May 6, 2000; "Bartali, lacrime e assenti ingiustificati," *Corriere della Sera*, May 9, 2000.
257 **"great sportsman"** Archival video clip of John Paul II giving radio address, *Tour des Légendes*, a documentary about 1948 Tour de France, directed by Erik van Empel, Scarabee Films, 2003.

257 **"Good-bye, *Ginettaccio*"** "Addio Ginettaccio," *Corriere dello Sport,* May 6, 2000: 1.

257 **"When we were poor and weary"** Maso, *Wir Alle Waren Götter,* 291. Maso and director Erik van Empel interviewed fans outside of the church during Bartali's funeral for Empel's documentary *Tour des Légendes*.

257 **Description of the funeral** "Cycling—Hundreds bid farewell to 'eternal' Bartali," *Reuters,* May 8, 2000; Pierangelo Di Sapegno, "Addio Bartali: Con lui l'Italia ha scalato il Dopoguerra," *La Stampa,* May 6, 2000; "Bartali, lacrime e assenti ingiustificati," *Corriere della Sera,* May 9, 2000.

Acknowledgments

The idea for this book sprang from a conversation we had in 2002 shortly after Andres spent a memorable day watching the Tour de France and savoring the carnival atmosphere created by thousands of cheering, clapping, and, often, mildly inebriated cycling fans. The most lasting memory of that day was the brute strength and endurance of men who brave the elements and cycle thousands of miles over the course of three weeks. When we spoke soon after, we kept returning to the topic of the incredible physical toll of cycling, especially on those who race the Tour many times throughout their life. We started looking in to some of the historic Tour greats and became fascinated by the Italian cyclist Gino Bartali. In a sport that celebrates endurance, he endured longer than most others, winning the Tour at twenty-four and then again at thirty-four. When we delved deeper and learned about the ways he used his bicycle between those victories—to help save lives during World War II—we discovered how rich and multifaceted his life had been and realized that his story needed to be shared with a much wider audience.

Writing this book has been an endurance event of another sort. Over our multiyear journey, we owe a significant debt of gratitude to all the people who helped us see it to completion. Adriana and Andrea Bartali were profoundly generous with their time, speaking candidly and answering questions about Gino for hours during different interviews, and showing us key Florentine landmarks from Gino's life. They never tried to influence the angle of our work, wisely acknowledging in their first interview that readers would be best served if the book retained total journalistic independence. Gino's surviving teammates and training partners (with whom he said that he had spent almost as much time as his family) were similarly magnanimous, patiently guiding us through the minutiae of their experiences living and competing with Gino. We extend our thanks particularly to Giovanni Corrieri and his nephew Marco; Alfredo Martini; and Ivo Faltoni, who all went above and beyond to share their memories and photographs of their time with Gino.

Giorgio Goldenberg deserves a special note of gratitude for speaking at length about how Gino helped him and his family during the war. Eldad Doron, the husband of Giorgio's late sister, Tea, kindly recounted various memories Tea had shared with him of her life in hiding during World War II. In Assisi, Padre Pier Damiano and Suor Eleonora Bifarini shared their wartime memories of seeing and speaking with Gino respectively. Giulia Donati, an Italian Holocaust survivor, and Renzo Ventura, the son of survivors, generously answered questions about Gino's involvement in their families' wartime experiences. Other survivors including Giorgina Rietti, Cesare Sacerdoti, Graziella Viterbi, Gianna Maionica, Hella Kropf, Claudia Maria Amati, and Lya Haberman Quitt gracefully helped illuminate the diverse and evolving circumstances of the broader Jewish community in Italy throughout this difficult period.

Raffaele Marconi and Maria Pagnini, historians and librarians at the Bagno a Ripoli library, proved invaluable when it came to answering questions about the world of Ponte a Ema and Florence during Gino's youth. Dr. Iael Nidam-Orvieto, editor in chief of Yad Vashem publications, answered many contextual questions about the Holocaust in Italy. Harry Waldman shared his photos and memories of Trento Brizi when Trento received the Freedom of the Press Award organized by the Graphic Arts Association under the leadership of its president Walter Zerweck. At the Library of Congress, David Kelly, a reference specialist, helped us navigate the library's impressive collection of World War II–era Italian and French newspapers. Dr. Benjo Maso, a former sociology professor and cycling historian, who is a leading authority regarding the 1948 Tour de France, proved an unparalleled resource regarding all cycling topics.

Collectively, these individuals and all the other people we interviewed have helped us make *Road to Valor* a richer book. Any mistakes that remain, however, are our own.

Our research was aided by several gifted individuals. Journalist Gaia Pianigiani worked doggedly and deftly to help us interview dozens of Italians and investigate archives throughout Italy. In the United States, Ken Fockele, Ilan Shahar, and Lindsay Eufusia offered assistance translating materials from German, Hebrew, and Italian. Anne-Laure Bourquin, Corinna Lautenbach, Virginia Napoleone, and Marina Rytvin helped us carry out different research initiatives in France, Germany, Italy, and Israel.

In New York, our agent Peter McGuigan, a longtime cyclist, offered wise counsel (and good cycling tips) throughout the research and writing of this book. He answered questions at all hours of the day and guided this project with ease through a rapidly changing publishing environment. His associates at Foundry Literary + Media, particularly Stéphanie Abou, have also been tireless advocates of this book. At Crown Publishers, Charlie Conrad has been a model editor, offering equal measures of insightful criticism and comforting assurance. His sound judgment and deep understanding of Italian culture have enriched our work. His colleague Miriam Chotiner-Gardner skillfully shepherded the manuscript through production.

The assistance of friends, near and far, has been considerable. Karen Murphy reviewed our proposal and provided astute suggestions for improving it. In Paris, Bernard and Chantal Bourquin offered up the inimitable comforts of their home as a research base. In Buenos Aires, Carlos Layus tracked down two evocative photos of Gino. Lia Kaljurand used her design talents to help undo the ravages of time for photographs that survived World War II. Liz Appel, Mart Kaljurand, Kristi Laar, and

Sam McHugh read drafts and offered thoughtful critical feedback. Both a sounding board for research ideas and a source of excellent editorial commentary, Benjamin Eachus championed the project when it was just a nascent idea.

In Italy, Kiiri Sandy, a professional translator, proved herself to be a selfless friend and this project's most valued contributor. During the course of our work, she always found time to help with translations, revealing her impressive grasp of the linguistic nuances of military, cycling, and other technical terminology. She also helped us coordinate interviews, located many photographs, and edited countless drafts. Taken together, her efforts made our work easier and the book much stronger.

Lastly, we wish to acknowledge the immeasurable support of our family. Peter Adamson was an energetic advocate of this project. Our cousin, Bernadette Cousins, welcomed us with open arms into her home in England so we could get back and forth to France and Italy easily. Aili's husband, Geoff, an avid cyclist, offered sage editorial suggestions on several drafts, and became a proponent of this book long before it found a publisher. Our brothers, Peter, Thomas, and Paul, their wives Robyn, Lindsay, and Amanda, and their respective growing broods, have been unwavering in their enthusiasm. Our final thanks go to our mother, Mari-Ann, and late father, Joseph, who first nurtured our shared interest in history and literature.

Photo and Illustration Credits

Page ii: © STP/AFP/Getty Images; page 7: © Roman Sigaev/shutterstock.com; page 22: © ANSA under licence to Alinari Archives; page 31: Photo courtesy of Giovanni Corrieri; page 47: © Luce Institute/Alinari Archives Management; page 68: Random House; page 91: © PUBLIFOTO/OLYCOM; page 111: Photos courtesy of Giorgio Goldenberg; page 123: Photo courtesy of Aili and Andres McConnon; page 144: © Alinari Archives; page 165: © The Horton Collection; page 181: Courtesy of Biblioteca Panizzi; page 193: © Toscani Archive/Alinari Archives Management; page 211: Random House; page 228: © OLYCOM; page 241: © Photoservice Electa/Centro Documentazione Mondadori

INSERT

Page 1: Courtesy of Giorgio Goldenberg; page 2: © PUBLIFOTO/OLYCOM; page 3: (top) © Interfoto/Alinari Archives, (bottom) Courtesy of Biblioteca Panizzi; page 4: Courtesy of Giorgio Goldenberg; page 5: Reproduced under authorization of *El Gráfico* magazine, Argentina; page 6: (top) Courtesy of Aili and Andres McConnon, (bottom) Courtesy of the Graphic Arts Association; page 7: Reproduced under authorization of *El Gráfico* magazine, Argentina; page 8: © ANSA under licence to Alinari Archives

About the Authors

Aili McConnon is a Canadian journalist based in New York. She has written for *BusinessWeek*, the *New York Times*, the *Wall Street Journal*, and the *Guardian*. She has appeared on ABC, MSNBC, and CNN, and has earned degrees from Princeton University, the University of Cambridge, and Columbia University.

Andres McConnon graduated magna cum laude from Princeton University, where he majored in history. He previously worked as a historical researcher for several books. While researching and writing *Road to Valor*, he lived for a period in Paris and Florence, and on the Italian Riviera. Aili and Andres can be reached via the Internet at www.roadtovalorbook.com.